Conducting Elgar

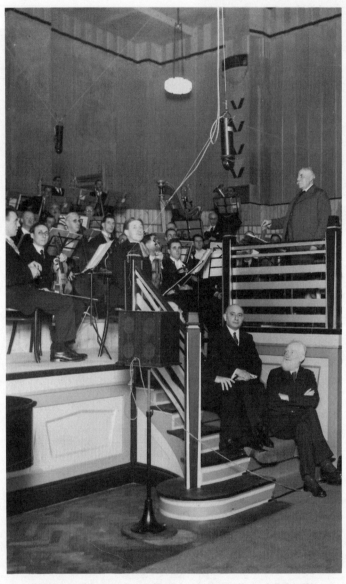

Elgar (standing on the podium) at the recording of *Falstaff* in
Studio 1, Abbey Road, St John's Wood, London, in 1931.
Photo: EMI Records.

Conducting Elgar

◀▶

NORMAN DEL MAR

Completed and edited by
JONATHAN DEL MAR

CLARENDON PRESS · OXFORD
1998

Oxford University Press, Great Clarendon Street, Oxford OX2 6DP

Oxford New York
Athens Auckland Bangkok Bogota Bombay
Buenos Aires Calcutta Cape Town Dar es Salaam
Delhi Florence Hong Kong Istanbul Karachi
Kuala Lumpur Madras Madrid Melbourne
Mexico City Nairobi Paris Singapore
Taipei Toyko Toronto Warsaw
and associated companies in
Berlin Ibadan

Oxford is a trade mark of Oxford University Press

Published in the United States by
Oxford University Press Inc., New York

British Library Cataloguing in Publication Data
Data available

Library of Congress Cataloging in Publication Data

Del Mar, Norman, 1919–
Conducting Elgar / Norman Del Mar; completed and edited by
Jonathan Del Mar.
p. cm.
Includes index.
1. Conducting. 2. Elgar, Edward, 1857–1934—Criticism and
interpretation. I. Del Mar, Jonathan. II. Title.
MT85.D338 1998 781.45'092—dc21 97–25755

ISBN 0–19–816551–X
ISBN 0–19–816557–9 (pbk.)

1 3 5 7 9 10 8 6 4 2

Typeset by Seton Music Graphics Ltd., Ireland

Printed in Great Britain
on acid-free paper by
Biddles Ltd.
Guildford & Kings Lynn

Preface

◀▶

THIS is the last of three books which my father wrote in his final years but did not live to see through the press. It therefore stands as a conclusion to his considerable output as an author, which he nevertheless always viewed as entirely subsidiary to his work as a conductor. Ironically, his books (especially the three-volume biography of Richard Strauss, and *Anatomy of the Orchestra*) may prove at least as enduring a legacy as his extensive activity on the rostrum.

Why Elgar? For many, the composer to whom my father would most naturally turn for his next *Conducting* book, and to whom he was often requested to turn, was of course Strauss; yet the prospect of opening once more that Pandora's box, so thoroughly closed and sealed many years earlier, was one which he frankly viewed with little enthusiasm. Closest of all to his heart had always been Wagner, but his chief ambition, to conduct *The Ring*, remained sadly unfulfilled. He will be remembered, however, as a great Elgar conductor; and I entertained the hope that he would live long enough to write *Conducting Delius* and *Conducting Mahler* too, for in these three composers, I have always believed, lay his greatest strengths and perceptions as an interpreter.

At his death, the manuscript of *Conducting Elgar* was by his bedside almost, but not quite, finished: the final chapter broke off towards the end of the Demons' Chorus. It seemed then a forlorn hope that I should be equipped to bring it to fruition, and the book might perhaps have remained in limbo had it not been for the exceptional generosity of my good friend Brian Brown, whose excellent and endlessly willing St Cecilia Choral Society gave me a memorable performance of

The Dream of Gerontius in the beautiful parish church of Coggeshall, in Essex. Without this invaluable and most happy experience, it would have been unthinkable even to attempt to complete the book, and my ever-grateful thanks extend to him and to them for having made this task possible.

I would like to thank my father's long-standing friend and colleague Barrie Iliffe for much help and encouragement, both to him and to me, in the preparation of this book. It is a pleasure also to thank László Heltay, Richard Hickox, Donald Hunt, and Sir Charles Mackerras very warmly for their generous and invaluable advice on some of the problems of mounting a performance of *Gerontius*; finally, a lifetime's gratitude is the least I can offer to my long-suffering mother, Pauline Del Mar, for typing (and, indeed, helping to edit) this and all my father's books.

An additional word, somewhat in the nature of a caveat, is at this point perhaps not entirely inappropriate. Metronome marks are the subject of so much heated debate and controversy, and yet they seem to bring us no nearer an understanding of the interpretation of music, whatever extravagant claims of precise intent may insistently be made for them by certain performers. Just as composers' own metronome markings, calculated in the quiet ambience of a work-desk, often prove quite unfeasible once an orchestra actually starts playing, so even authors, discussing the practicability of those very metronome marks, inevitably fall into the same traps. There are countless examples in this book, as similarly in those by other interpreters, where comparison of my father's recommended speeds with his own recording of the work under discussion reveals a discrepancy of anything up to 50 per cent; moreover, many passages are in practice subjected, largely instinctively or subconsciously, to so great an element of ebb and flow as to render any definition of a metronome mark almost meaningless. On such flexibility, after all, does the lifeblood of a spontaneous performance depend.

J.R.D.M.

September 1996

Contents

◀▶

Variations on an Original Theme, Op. 36

◀▶

THE Enigma Variations, as this work is always called, is without doubt the best known and most often played of all Elgar's compositions. Apart from its intrinsic qualities, which are certainly of the first rank, its popularity is to some extent due to the subtitle 'Enigma', which has given rise to so much speculation over the possible solution to the riddle of the theme, conjectures ranging foolishly enough from Mozart to 'Auld Lang Syne' played backwards.

The controversies, which have arisen quite recently all over again (as commentators continue to discover that the melody can be made to 'fit' with yet another motif from the inexhaustible repertoire), have fortunately not reached any conclusive solution. Elgar himself, who loved conundrums, merely said that with the melody 'goes' a well-known theme which is not alluded to in the variations themselves.

It would be safe to say that had Elgar had any intention that the mystery should one day be solved, he would have helped to bring about such an end to the arguments instead of further confusing the issue by implying that the 'theme' forming a counterpoint need not necessarily be musical at all. Moreover there would be considerable loss if the solution were to be found, much of the work's attraction lying in the impenetrability of the riddle itself.

Furthermore, an additional unifying thread lies in the portraiture, to be found within the variations, of close friends and associates, as well as the composer's wife (Variation I) and a self-portrait in the Finale. It could therefore be hazarded that one solution may well lie in the theme of love and friendship which holds the whole work together, and the puzzle, intriguing as it is, best allowed to rest there.

From the point of view of programming the Enigma Variations, one asset lies in its duration, somewhat under the half-hour, and another in its instrumentation, which is modest for so important a work. There is not even a harp, unusually for Elgar, and the organ, only used briefly in the Finale, is optional and can quite easily be omitted even if this does detract a little from the stature of the whole.

The work is played without a break, although a short pause is made after 'Nimrod'. There is only the one edition (Novello), but Elgar made a number of small revisions incorporated into later printings which have to be taken into account, for some are materially important but are nevertheless not in the parts. The metronome marks are generally pretty reliable except for Variation VIII, which is quite wrong.

In Elgar's autograph the theme carries the superscription 'Enigma' (not in the composer's handwriting, however) alongside the tempo marking, given as Andante $\quad$ = 63. It is a quiet 4 in a bar with some minor allowances for the tenutos in the second and sixth bars; while these will be observed, they need not be overdone. Such rubatos are particularly indigenous to English music and should be in the conductor's blood for a truly characterful performance, especially as not all are so clearly marked in the score. The **pp** at the fourth bar must also be featured, being subito, but without a hold-up of pulse.

The subsidiary section of the theme in the four bars before fig. 1 is very flexible, each bar with its tenuto on the fourth beat but with a pronounced forward movement at the beginnings of the phrases to compensate. The approach into 1 itself makes what is almost a little rit. after the greater flow of the previous bars, so as to arrive at the sostenuto of the theme's return. This threefold structure is retained as one of the main characteristics in all the variations, often with the same feeling of extra momentum in the middle section.

In the return of the theme's initial idea a new counter-point brings a surge of emotion on the lower strings. To this the horn can add a greater element of warmth than the restraining mark of piano might suggest, and similarly in the following bar the sharp accent in the violas and basses can almost amount to a sforzando.

The triplet has its own allargando which the stick can exaggerate, thereby also evoking the brief crescendo to forte. Elgar's scores are always full of additional details and there are several to be carefully observed in the bar of rit., such as the accented D on the 2nd violins and cellos, and the 'mesto' (mournful) in the *pp* diminuendo of the 1st violins' cadence. The last two quavers can be gently subdivided. In the final pause the bassoons and horn should be quietly released with the eyes while the stick controls the continuing diminuendo, linking the music into **Variation I**.

Fig. 2 is marked with the clearest of downbeats taking away all but the 1st violins, who continue in exactly the previous tempo until at the *f* diminuendo molto some relaxing of pulse is necessary.

The variation proper begins at the double bar and portrays Alice, the strong-minded wife without whose ceaseless encouragement and inspiration Elgar could hardly put pen to paper. Here, as mentioned earlier, the composer had a number of second thoughts which it is important to incorporate into the orchestral balance.* Since this variation traverses broadly the same terrain as the theme, if greatly ornamented, he brought forward into sharp perspective certain new counter-motifs while withdrawing the theme itself into the background during the bars before 3. The flute and clarinet are accordingly marked back to *pp*, while oboes and bassoons are increased to *f* espressivo, the original solo bassoon being in addition doubled by the 2nd player. The filigree string work remains *ppp* as before, as do the first three

---

* These revisions are most reprehensibly ignored in the recently published Collected Edition.

horns; but the solo 4th horn, with his accented syncopations on each half-bar, is all too rarely heard.

From 3 everything is as it was before, and it is worth noting the bass clef of the 3rd and 4th horns which is, most unusually for Elgar, in old notation, as contrasted with the bass clef entries in the Finale which are in new. There is a further such use of old notation in the Overture *Cockaigne* of much the same period.

The pictures we have of Alice Elgar suggest a homely, old-fashioned lady but the return to the main theme after the brief middle section reveals an unexpected degree of passion in their relationship which quickly and suddenly boils up 3 bars before 4. This brings, however, less change in tempo or rubato than in the theme itself, and when it subsides a meticulous beat is necessary for the syncopated ascending passage in the violins, as well as for the staccato figure in the violas which should be taken off the string.

In the ritardando before the end the violins repeat their ascending syncopation ***ppp***, but only in the fourth beat is subdivision necessary lest the pull-up be unduly exaggerated, distorting the theme on the clarinet. Nor should the fermata, with its diminuendo from ***ppp***, be too long or the violins may be unnerved before **Variation II**, the most difficult passage in the work for ensemble and bow control. There can be no exaggerating the lightness of their spiccato in this most treacherous of variations.

The tempo of ♩. = 72 is perhaps not quite as fast as one might expect and needs a very precise upbeat, though without click, before a clearly focused downbeat triggers the players into starting the variation. If the gap is not made too long after the dreamy end to Alice's movement is cleared, this should not be unduly hazardous, although it will always need time spent at rehearsal. There can be no question of marking the speed of the quavers, the beating being in a crisp 1 throughout.

The isolated answering 3-bar phrase on the 2nd violins can be a trap, and it is not unknown for conductors to try and minimize the potential dangers by writing extra overlapping notes into the parts. But this practice, analogous to a similar danger spot in Beethoven's Overture *Leonora No 1*, can always be heard with scrappy results.

Extreme punctuality in the wind entries is one of the conductor's main preoccupations. This is, of course, an exercise in very quick tonguing and can create a noteworthy problem most of all for the oboe, but it is of paramount importance that the pulse is maintained strictly, especially in the bars before 7 where any floundering has been known to have disastrous consequences.

By now, however, the movement should have acquired a positive momentum, and the stick can give a real swing to the treatment of the theme and the bar-by-bar emphases in 2nd violins and upper wind.

No fussiness of stick style can be allowed to disturb the players in the bars before 7, and the syncopated clarinet must be most careful to preserve the basic pulse. The delicacy of the instrumentation won the work and its composer especial critical acclaim in Europe when it appeared just at the turn of the century.

The 1st violins are markedly less ill at ease at 7 itself than at the outset, the tempo having now been long established, and the imitative to-ing and fro-ing with the 2nds being this time delayed for 4 bars. Here Elgar revised the dynamics for even greater clarity with the timpani brought up from *pp* to *p* ma marcato so that the thematic allusion will not be missed, while the woodwind are dropped to *pp*.

As the violins climb to top A eight bars before the end there is always a danger that they become too obtrusive, and the passage should be taken over the fingerboard. There must be not the slightest suggestion of rit., the end coming quite abruptly with the cello/bass pizzicato capping the motivic fragments on flute and clarinet.

Elgar seems to have thought of the contra as being still a rare bird, cueing it into the basses as he had done in the Overture *Froissart* some nine years earlier. But it is perhaps significant that he no longer marks it 'ad lib.'; for indeed the humour of **Variation III** depends on the rumbling tone breaking the silence, this being a movement of considerable whimsy conducted in a rapid 3 at ♪ = 144. The lightest stick movement is again called for, there being no traps of rubato or tempo changes from beginning to end.

The composer himself described the oboe as 'pert', and it should be projected stylishly. After fig. 9 (where the repeat, the only one in the work, is always observed, constituting the greater part of the movement) the successive 1st violin tenutos will be less pronounced than those in the theme; the crescendo with the three trumpets then leads to a considerable snap in the bar before 10, needing a sharp gesture of the left hand. A jocular theme follows in the bassoons and cellos which Elgar subsequently marked up to *sfp* on each plunge, and the triplet semiquavers must then flow but without hurrying as they accompany the return of the theme's scherzando variant.

The second-time bar leaves clarinets and horns holding an expectant chord which is then taken off before setting out exuberantly on **Variation IV**, a rumbustious piece and the first really noisy variation, conducted in a vigorous 1 in a bar at ♩. = 72. The main part of the theme is accentuated on every note while the *alternativo* (fig. 12) develops a great swing which the beat must bring out with enthusiasm on each successive sforzando barline.

Fig. 13 introduces a good deal of woodwind banter with the theme, but it is the string interpolations which need the most direct attention from the stick, and not least the violas who, piano as they are, should be played in a vivid spiccato.

At the *fff* of 14 Elgar brings back the use of tenutos which had featured so strongly in the theme. Here, however, they carry a problem: not only is there, at this speed, hardly time for them to make their effect (so that they are too often ignored entirely), but they are also unreliably given in both parts and score. It is apparent that they should apply to all instruments equally, and on just the specific crotchets, first

and second in alternate bars. The last note comes off brusque-
ly like the slam of the door it is indeed describing.

There is now a slightly longer gap before **Variation V**,
which is broadly lyrical with scherzando elements in its
central section. The metronome mark of ♩. = 63 is only very
approximate, being both too fast for the G-string rhapsodizing of the first few bars and too inflexible for the playfulness
of fig. 16. Yet it does caution the conductor against too self-
indulgent a view of what is marked not 'Andante' but
'Moderato'.

An imaginative use of the stick in the delineation of the
four dotted crotchet beats should guide the violins round the
contours of the melody, the theme itself transformed into no
more than a countersubject. The grace-notes and octave leaps
need plenty of time, as does the harmonic G two bars before
16, yet all without distorting the shape of the theme beneath.

It is fig. 16 that tends to give continental orchestras the
greatest trouble, this being a style of writing quite foreign
to their background and one whose freedom is in fact
peculiarly English. After the relaxation of the previous bar's
diminuendo the flute, oboe, and clarinet can be encouraged
to flow upwards, guided no more than is necessary to ensure
ensemble between the last semiquavers of each group and
the continuing semiquavers of the flute.

This gives quite a different feeling from the breadth of the
first bars and different again from the light patter of the next
with its gentle staccato in oboes and horns, only briefly supported by violins. There can be no corroboration with the
metronome which shows the tempo to be basically unaltered, and yet the pulse of the movement really does undergo
the most delicate changes. The bar before 17 is different
again, with the solo clarinet exercising considerable freedom
in each group of six notes; here the little pairs which accompany him on each fifth and sixth semiquaver can be nursed
in with a friendly left hand. The whole process is then
repeated from 17 itself with extra instruments picking out
the background shape of the theme while all the strings join

in the great largamente melody, now no longer purely on the G string. Fig. 18 corresponds with 16 except that the linking bar is omitted, so that the change of tempo, slight as it is, becomes more abrupt, with a new and springy beat portraying the suddenly contrasting idiom.

There is a short coda in the last four bars of the movement in which a final return is made to the broad melodic style. Here there is an important misprint in the timpani part which, having no points of reference in its whole-bar rolls, merely supplies the hairpins without specifying that they should occur only on the third and fourth beats in each bar.

It can be hard to obtain a soft and beautiful enough *pp* quality on the three solo trombones as the movement subsides, especially since the stick needs to concern itself with the rhythm in the cellos, who must play spiccato with measured accuracy. There is no vestige of ritardando during the lead-in to **Variation VI**.

It goes without saying that Ysobel was a viola player, and the emphasis is on that instrument throughout the movement, whether in tutti as at the beginning or solo as at fig. 21.

The tempo does not relate to the previous variation but is struck anew by tiny but evocative indications of the violas' and bassoons' figures within the minim beats. The metronome ♩ = 48 is on the steady side for Andantino, and there wants to be an element of the grazioso alongside Elgar's mark of espressivo.

Where the leaping theme passes to the horns a little broadening is justified in this gently cadential phrase. The solo bassoons then move off again in rising thirds, the instrumentation being once more of the utmost delicacy.

In the solo viola passage at 21 the little woodwind demisemiquaver flips are all marked up in the revised version and can be encouraged with twisting gestures of the left wrist. The horns again present a cadence leading into 22, after which the coda becomes more expansive, however briefly.

Overlapping groups from the leaping theme bring the mood back to its original restraint, during which the divided

1st violins' sequences can be kept very gentle. The last clarinet flip is once more brought up from *ppp* to *p* and the bassoons share with the solo viola the wistfulness of the closing bars, apart from a horn who has to continue sustaining together with the viola as softly as both can still add refinement to their tone. As their sound dies away to nothing the pause will have become quite extended and the atmosphere in the hall breathless.

Variation VII is the famous timpani movement of great virtuosity, marked with a giant '1' for its Presto ○ = 76. Pieces with such a bold tempo indication are few and far between, the Scherzo of Borodin's Second Symphony being the outstanding other example, and as there, so here the speed needs to be stunning.

Griffith's variation is graced with his unusual name—Troyte—instead of the initials of the earlier character studies, and the hilarity of the music masks real affection. The 1-in-a-bar beat has to keep the cellos and basses with the timpani (not the other way round) without any restraint in tempo, and the drummer has accordingly to play with marked clarity—perhaps with hard, but not wooden sticks—or in many resonant halls the clatter will degenerate into confusion, especially later in the movement. Hence the players look to the conductor for reassurance even if the actual size of the beating cannot be allowed to become extravagant in the pursuit of *élan*.

It should not be overlooked that the opening 4-bar crescendo to *ff* has to be judiciously gauged, keeping in mind the return of the same passage at 24 with its rise to *fff*. The rejoining of the timpani onto the continuing ostinato of cellos and basses 4 before 24 and again in the 9th of 24 must be synchronized with particular care.

At this crazy tempo the violin writing of 25 can raise difficulties which leaders have been known to try and solve with changes of the text, sharing between the 1sts and 2nds, but this must be resisted; the passages can be played at the full tempo as Elgar, himself a violinist, well knew. The wind chromatic lead into 26 should be dazzling, as also the sweeping scales in the strings which follow.

The pianos in the horns and wind before and after 27—as also those of the 1st violins, in between their moments of spectacular rushing up and down—are often neglected, but are of great importance in the balance and phrasing. The sudden forte in the bar before 28 then becomes a new dramatic stroke to be brought out with a lunge.

After the brass chorale the coda gives another string flurry, spreading a cross-rhythm over the second and third last bars not easy to effect clearly in all the hurly-burly. Here is another gentleman who slams the door when he goes out of the room.

After orchestra and audience have recovered their equilibrium, the Allegretto $\frac{6}{8}$ of **Variation VIII** quietly begins, beaten in 6 at ♪= 104, as later authenticated by Elgar himself although it is not in any score*. How he ever thought it could go at ♩. = 52 is a mystery, but there is no question of misprint: the manuscript is clear enough.

It is again patently a lady we are concerned with here, and one of high breeding. The atmosphere of taking tea in an English country house is extraordinarily well caught and must be interpreted with the lightest possible touch and flexibility. The refrain-like pairs of bars (the third and fourth, and the two before 31) cannot be over-precise in tempo, or the movement will seem wooden.

A new sentence is clearly started, needing a little more elbow-room for its staccato and trills, with a warmth of contrast for the tenutos in the third bar. The repeat of the phrase introduces a gracious cello solo which contains a tricky little trill often dodged by converting it into a simple 5-note turn. There are so many short trills on the oboe that there should be no excuse for so hurrying the pace that this subterfuge is necessary, but it is surprising how many cellists fall back on it.

---

* Except a recent (1985) new edition published by Eulenburg. (J.R.D.M.)

In the 2nd of **31** the score lacks the harmonic in the violins (see four bars later), but it is present in the parts and very characteristic of Elgar's style. There will be many similar instances as the work progresses, and a decision may have to be made lest it becomes a mannerism.

If the movement is mainly kept within the realm of chamber music, the few effusive moments of forte towards the end will not seem out of place. These can even be given corresponding breadth so long as the tempo picks up immediately afterwards, as at the 1st and 5th bars of **32**; the latter is of particular importance so that the largamente of the third last bar is not anticipated.

The 2-note phrasings of the 2nd violins and violas should be marked with the stick, and the last two 1st violin semiquavers leading to the fermata can be very gently subdivided with the fingers of the left hand. The pause itself is composite, the clarinet being nodded away, followed after a moment or two by the strings, leaving the infinitely soft 1st violins to make the bridge into the magical start of 'Nimrod' in the distant and velvety key of E flat.

Elgar's autograph of **Variation IX** gives 'Moderato $\bullet$= 66', but this only survives in an early set of string parts. It was altered by the composer in 1903 to the Adagio $\bullet$= 52 which is the reading we all know; but this has led to the movement acquiring an elegiac quality and it has come to be played at the funerals of important personages, which was not at all Elgar's intention. It has even earned a kind of national anthem status whereas it should, on the contrary, reflect an affectionate glow of deep friendship. The name 'Nimrod' derives from Genesis, where he is said to have been a 'mighty hunter'; the German for 'hunter' is *Jäger*, and A. J. Jaeger was a distinguished figure at Novello, the music publishing firm which handled the greater part of Elgar's output. Jaeger gave Elgar constant encouragement at the time he most needed it and became a staunch and very dear colleague.

Elgar wrote to Jaeger: 'I have omitted your outside manner and have only seen the good, lovable, honest SOUL in the

middle of you.'* The first eight bars move off quite steadily
and without rubato, but when the wind join in at 34 the
tempo can flow a little and no longer wants to be quite so
serious. He later wrote enthusiastically: 'What a jolly fine
tune your Variation is: I'd forgotten it & have been playing
it thro'—it's just like you—you solemn, wholesome, hearty
old dear.'ᵦ

In the four bars before 35 the upper cello line joins the
violas in an evocative melody with rising sevenths which of
necessity pull the tempo back again, so that 35 starts once
more quite peaceably for the middle section. The stick has a
real function in describing the phrase shapes both for the
sevenths as they continuously rise and fall, and for the details
of phrasing at 35. The quaver rest in the middle of the legato
2-bar horn line is a most attractive idea as are the touches of
colour on the timpani, all to be picked out in the conducting.

When the tune proper resumes at 36 it is to be observed
that the largamente occurs only at the third bar, so that the
legatissimo first two bars should have enough forward movement to take this into account. Nor should the broadening
overstay its welcome, or the build-up to 37 will become very
heavy-handed.

The next largamente 2 before 37 contains the inescapable
feature that the strings and brass do not come together and
cannot be made to do so. Indeed, the marcato in the trumpets will assist in ensuring this, for if they play in strict
rhythm the strings, with their delayed semiquaver within the
triplet, will automatically come later, and not until immediately before the second beat. This looks more complex
than it is, and—given clear direction to the strings—will
generally play itself. Where there is a problem it is that these
largamentes are never contradicted, and the tempo should
have moved forward conspicuously in the 5th of 36 and now
again, however briefly, in the molto crescendo before 37.

---

* Letter, 13 Mar. 1899, quoted in *Letters to Nimrod*, ed. Percy M. Young
(Dennis Dobson, London, 1965), 41–2.
    ß Letter, 4 Nov. 1900, in *Letters to Nimrod*, 113.

The *ff* of fig. 37 naturally needs a Mahlerian *Ausholen*, after which careful pacing for the diminuendo allows the movement to subside peacefully. The 1st violins' last quaver is naturally controlled with the left hand and the 2nd horn is, as so often before, nodded away. The fermata is long and the silence which follows is still longer; for this is the half-way point of the work.

The choice of so featherweight a movement as **Variation X** to follow the solid stuff of 'Nimrod' was inspired. The two silent beats of the first bar are conducted out, and the given tempo of ♩ = 80 is admirable. The very smallest and lightest of beats are essential throughout, as befits the 'Intermezzo' subheading.

By far the hardest element in the opening bars is the lengthening of each first semiquaver as shown by the line over these notes in the oboes and clarinets. This rubato persists until just before the very end and can upset the ensemble unless the players are well acquainted with the work. It represents an attractive stammer which afflicted Dorabella, the subject of the variation, when young, and is maintained continuously without ever becoming tiresome. The whole movement should appear to come from far, far away.

The viola solo at 39 can sound tentative and in revision Elgar marked it up to a single *p* for its entry, but retaining the *pp* with that of the accompanying instruments four bars later. Before 40 the momentary rise to *mf* must melt away to nothing with a kind of *frisson*, given by a total withdrawal from the conductor.

Fig. 40 provides the one real crescendo, the chromatic ascent extending over nearly four bars to arrive at the *sf* third beat with its timpani and cello/bass hops at the half beat, all incorporated into the stick gestures after the legato style of the rising phrase. The third beats of the first three bars of 40 also need stressing, however, the forte phrases on the low flutes being in particular evidence.

Suddenly the mood returns to far-away colours, even the little third-beat hops now continuing in piano, but nevertheless having to be pointed even as they fade, bringing a total withdrawal at 41 for the return of the theme. Here a little yield in the pulse is legitimate, though nothing is marked, so that the restatement is made even more distant than before. The flutes have dropped out in preparation for their unison low entry, and this can be made a colourful feature. The ending prior to the central episode is also entirely in character, having a tiny crescendo followed by a subito *pp* which should be barely audible.

Much more animation suffuses the contrasting section, with its composite string textures. These apparently, however, ran the risk of becoming somewhat too extrovert, for in the revised score the melodic top and bottom lines (1st violins and cellos) are marked back to piano 4 bars and 1 bar before 43, while the middle voices retain their crescendos to forte as before, the rushing semiquavers hardly obtruding. Again touches of colour add to the picture with woodwind interpolations, the bassoons being most attractive. The tempo is quick enough to allow the upward rushes of viola demisemiquavers to be splendidly brilliant though still soft, another effect which clever use of the stick can portray elegantly.

The timpanist expects to be cued for his little spaced-out entries before and at 43, after which one more rise and fall leads with exquisite subtlety back to the main section, now even softer, and with the bassoons *ppp* in octaves like miniature horns. The *pp* 2nd horn and flute at 44 also expect to be noticed as they have not played for a long time; in fact this one bar is the horn's single appearance in the movement.

A truncated whispering return of the middle section maintains the *pp* throughout and includes a charming bar of bassoon solo emulating the string figure with the viola demisemiquavers in *ppp*. If the tempo has continued to be maintained scrupulously this solo is not difficult to play and comes across with magical effect like the fairies in Elgar's own *Wand of Youth*. The *ppp* coda (now without the element of rubato that had characterized the opening) is still handled with the smallest beats until just before the very last one, where the sudden *mf* is subdivided for the upper strings. The cello/bass ultimate *pp* pizzicato can be a trifle delayed, the conductor turning across the orchestra with a touch of whimsy.

Variation XI is a famous piece of illustrative writing, guaranteed to wake up any audience. There can be no mistaking the plunge of Dr Sinclair's bulldog into the river, his frenzied paddling to find a landing-place, and his triumphant return.

The prescribed tempo of ♩= 100 is searching, especially for the tuba at 50, but will give the bassoons no trouble in the earlier scrambles, now marked up to *mf*. The beating can also be graphically pictorial, with a tremendous sweep to break the spell. The dog's barking in the fifth bar warrants a ferocious side-slash, after which the process repeats in miniature, the rush down the bank being *pp*, but leading to a veritable paean for the brass, all flags flying, at 48, which is kept at full tilt.

The high spot of the piece is naturally fig. 50 as punctuated by the riveting timpani *ff*, but it is noteworthy that Elgar stepped up the dynamics which lead to this splendid climax. The coda begins at 51 and drives forward with rows of descending sevenths on the horns and cellos doubled by clarinets and bassoons. The final flourish and thud can be conveyed for all they are worth with the brilliant semiquavers rushing headlong in the 1st violins, then with 2nds and violas added in turn, the pace having been maintained right to the end.

Variation XII is a melancholy movement featuring the cello, and the first and last phrases are a solo for the principal player, representing the subject of the variation who, one will not be surprised to learn, was the amateur cellist of the ensemble with whom Elgar played chamber music.

The tempo ♩= 58 does not apply to the opening bars which are free, the cellist taking the entry in his own time while the stick brings in the background lower strings on the third beat.

When the movement gathers a little momentum violas are added to the cellos, all of whom have joined the leader at the third bar. The violas, nevertheless, only provide an enrichment of the cello quality which should continue to dominate even for the impassioned climax of the song at 53 where the violas and oboe supply a note which might have proved awkward.

The echoing 1st violins should be almost feathery in quality despite their mark of only one *p*, and since the conductor is turned towards the right-hand sections of the strings there is drama to be derived from giving the violins their entry and phrasing over his shoulder, thus accentuating their quality of restraint.

In the central section the 1st violins continue to play no part, leaving a few extra wind to be added very softly to the texture. Only the bassoons and horns give real strength to the colour, and then only in a single bar. But in the return to the main theme at 54 the 1st violins, now playing sul G, are given their due attention just as the cellos momentarily move off from the great unison.

The basses have been silent and now can be a little emphasized in this fuller restatement which climbs to a truly impassioned *ff* before subsiding to the return of the solo cello. As at the beginning, he starts in his own time, the conductor taking the tutti off as he begins. The 'lunga' fermata should not be over-long, nevertheless, and this little *envoi* is more of a link to the next variation than a substantial closing passage in its own right. Most cellists observe the printed harmonic here, having ignored it at the beginning; one may regret the earlier omission, but it must remain the soloist's prerogative.

The extra fermata bar to be 'omitted except when Var. XII is played separately' is inexplicable; Variation XII has never been played as a separate item, any more than the other variations which connect in this way, and must simply merge into fig. 55 as unobtrusively as possible.

Variation XIII: Romanza provides an enigma within the Enigma, and again numerous solutions continue to pile up.

The Novello booklet 'My Friends Pictured within' supplies a photograph of a distinguished society lady, and Michael Kennedy's *Portrait of Elgar* accepts the proposition of Lady Mary Lygon with hardly a reservation,* as does Dora Penny in her book.ß Yet Elgar held his peace as to whom the three asterisks might represent, saying merely that she was on a sea journey at the time of composition, hence the quotation from Mendelssohn's *Calm Sea and Prosperous Voyage*. But as Kennedy is obliged to concede after giving lengthy biographical details of this lady, she was not in fact on such a voyage at the time, and the mystery continues to be unsolved.

A particularly interesting conjectural novel was published recently, detailing a journey Elgar himself is known to have made up the Amazon in 1923.† His purpose was to refresh his tired and disillusioned soul, and the book makes a profound psychological study of his state of mind at the time. On his arrival at the furthest point on the river, the city of Manaos, he is sought out by, and has a short encounter with, a lady who was emotionally involved with him in his earlier life but whom, because of Alice, he had been obliged to hide from the world. It may well have been a disturbing incident leaving a scar in his life; she married a German and did indeed make a sea journey over the Atlantic to take up residence in South America at precisely the time when Elgar was at work on the Variations.

Needless to say the story cannot be substantiated, but it is by no means improbable, and in the novel it is skilfully and very movingly worked out. At the least it offers an alternative, and even perhaps a more likely, thesis to solve the problem of the asterisks than the somewhat far-fetched suggestion of Lady Mary Lygon.

There are two strongly contrasted elements in the movement, whose title 'Romanza' is also a key. The first main

* (OUP, London, 1968), 67–8.

ß Mrs Richard Powell, *Memories of a Variation* (OUP, London, 1937), 114–15.

† James Hamilton-Paterson, *Gerontius* (Macmillan, London, 1989).

section is light and buoyant, the metronome mark of ♩ = 76 being altogether too heavy-handed. A much more suitable speed, and one still in keeping with the mark of Moderato, would be ♩ = 96, which is the tempo Elgar himself recorded late in the 1920s.

The second section, corresponding with the *alternativo* of other variations, is the nostalgic suggestion of the sea voyage with swaying violas supporting the quotation from Mendelssohn's overture, the whole under a whispering drum roll. The score marks this to be played with side-drum sticks, but every timpanist in Britain knows that this is a mere euphemism for the two pennies which Elgar always insisted upon at his performances and which give a quite individual hollow, almost clattery quality in the prescribed **ppp**. It is particularly unfortunate therefore that our 'old' pennies, in their day the largest coins for their value, have been super-seded owing to the introduction of decimal coinage. But two such coins, skilfully secreted into the timpanist's hand so that they can be interchanged with the sticks at fig. **58** in a split second, are without doubt the proper agents for this passage.

An absolute hush pervades, or else the pennies, which sound incredibly soft, cannot be heard at all, and the tempo will have dropped for the tranquillo to as slow as ♩ = 56. Where the clarinet is quoting he should practically 'ghost' (the Germans use the word *Echoton*), but he can come up a very little for the remainder of his solo, as can the violas in the two bars before **57** where a solo bass also briefly replaces the timpani roll. Extreme stillness must reign in conductor and orchestra alike.

The timpani, now played with the usual sticks, accompa-nies the brass and full strings at **58**, in a passage which Elgar himself said was intended to suggest the distant throb of a liner's engines. There is a short rise and fall, but conductor and orchestra only return to life, quite suddenly, at **59**.

After a full repeat of the process, the movement returns to the slow tempo, this time even more tranquillo than before, for a still softer evocation of the sea voyage, with its swaying violas (now with cellos), the clarinet quotation, and the timpanist, once more using pennies. The total stillness has resumed, and, like the lady herself, the whole vision recedes to the farthermost distance. The clarinets, both the grace-note of the 1st player and the entry on C♯ of the 2nd, are controlled by the forefinger of the left hand after the same finger has secured direct communication with the players during the long 'dim. e rit.'. There should be no need to take the orchestra off, as it will simply fade to silence over the long pause, the Finale following without a break.

This creeps in almost surreptitiously since **Variation XIV** is a self-portrayal, 'Edu' being a family nickname for Edward. The introductory bars, which also recur later, are given the completely satisfactory tempo of Allegro ♩ = 84. The wide-spanned descending figure is bandied about through the orchestra against a constant syncopation in the lower strings, brass and timpani which always requires a sharp beat, whether extremely small as at the start or gradually wider at the approach of the *ff* largamente.

The bar of **62**, as again **64** a little later, is beaten in 4 for just the one bar, the hold-up in each case being considerable. Only the first and third crotchets, however, are fully marked with strong gestures, the second and fourth being predomi-nantly cut-offs, a feature not always understood by those to whom the work and Elgar's style as a whole are still unfamiliar territory. Every time the return to the a tempo is instantaneous and carries the movement forward with the utmost fervour.

The theme in the brass acquires a new and swashbuckling character which must not be restrained by the second-beat tenutos, important though these are, and the side drum in the 4th of **62** should be extremely arresting after the inten-sely vigorous beats of the a tempo. Before **63** the trombone and tuba *ff* scales have an undeniably brash quality which does not find favour everywhere, but which cannot be underplayed on that account, as it too is in keeping with Elgar's style and English music of the Edwardian era.

Animato is often an ambiguous marking, and here at **63**, as in the 'Pomp and Circumstance' March No. 1, it signifies not so much più mosso as an emphatic animando, corresponding to Mahler's 'nicht schleppen'. The piano swishes of the cymbals in alternate bars lead to the largamente's return, held up exactly as before, after which the a tempo is extremely brilliant (the offbeat cymbal stroke at the fifth bar deserves a dramatic left-arm sweep) and builds to the bar before **65**, which has to subside quickly in both speed (although nothing is actually marked) and dynamic, the controlling instruments being the timpani and middle strings, who need a clearly rhythmic beat.

The movement now takes on its basic flow at ♩ = 72 in a long melodic stretch during which the fourth beat pairs of quavers are of particular interest, doubled first on horns at **66** and then, as the momentum increases, on upper woodwind a few bars later. The horns have extra tenuto marks which add greatly to their expressiveness, while the 3rd and 4th players join the woodwind and 1st violins in their long descending scale passages. These are later inverted, the horns again joining with a 2-bar scale in thirds in which they will revel, if encouraged to make the most of the imaginative writing.

It is too often assumed that the Grandioso at **68** slows the tempo, whereas on the contrary the forward plunge carries on right through to the stringendo of **69**, the Grandioso referring only to the stature of the music which can lift up its head and throw its shoulders back without having to go more slowly. The impetus must lead headlong to the mighty timpani triplet in the bar before **69**, which can be hammered with the left fist.

It should be apparent that fig. **68** is a new portrayal of Nimrod, but so altered that he is scarcely recognizable in this proud and majestic guise. The reference is, however, primarily for musical reasons, and there should be no attempt to relate to the gentle friend of Variation IX. Moreover the triple pulse of that variation is outlined in the score across the duple barring of the present movement, but there is, needless to say, no question of the beat changing in any sense from the same purposeful 2 in a bar.

At **69** the pace quickens enormously, the text being simplified to a row of stark minims which race forward to the cut-off at **70**. This is accomplished by a strong upbeat leaving the stick suspended in the air, to come down again for the tempo primo, the delay being as minimal as acoustics will allow.

The horns are the instruments to watch with their *pp* F#'s, after which the conductor turns to the *ppp* trumpets. More quickly than before the build-up takes us to *fff*, the largamente at **71** being beaten as previously. The a tempo is even more brilliant than that in the bars before **65**, and breaks off into a rhythm on lower strings which is marked with the stick by means of half-pulses.

At **73** the music of Alice's variation returns, the theme suppressed to *pp* in the same way as before although the countersubject, which had been so strongly brought out at fig. **2**, is now left unchanged, perhaps because it has been so prominently identified already from the four bars before **73**. The percussion, who, as softly as they can, refer to the rhythm of the Finale theme, should be given leads with the left hand, the stick being reserved for Alice's music at **73** which during the preceding bars has been prepared for a tempo that will exactly match its earlier $\quarternote = 63$, though it is written out here in double notation.

For the sake of unity in this elaborately constructed finale there is no mark for such a tempo change, but the animando at **74** will confirm that some relaxation has indeed been assumed. As at fig. **2**, the strings are kept as a remote background, but the Finale's figure, now on trumpets and percussion, needs pinpointing for its two entries, soft as they are. In the second of them, the trumpets have humorous anticipations which can be coaxed in with the left hand.

After a maximum diminuendo, fig. **74** initiates a reprise of **65** but with a new degree of momentum which continues into 75, its rushing scales carrying the music up to the peroration of 76 where the organ makes its first entry and which originally led directly to the ending. Jaeger was not the only commentator who wisely advised Elgar to extend the culmination of the work and it is indeed hard now to imagine the movement without these 66 extra bars.

The long accelerando has to be very finely graded to arrive at the Presto. The bar before 79 is conducted with 2 sharp and swift beats for the pair of sforzandos and 79 itself is then in 1 to the end, Elgar's mark of $\mathbf{o} = 84$ being perfectly judged.

Here too the triple phrasing of the 'Nimrod' theme is indicated in the score, but again there is no justification for any inference that a beat of 3 should be adopted. At the 10th bar of 80 it is attractive to cue the alternate rising melodic strands of 1st violins with violas and 2nds with cellos, leading to the return of 4-bar phrases at 81 and culminating in the great climax of the finale theme at 82.

Elgar instructs that the cymbal here be struck with a metal beater, but it is not every percussionist who will risk complying with this, the danger of damage to the cymbal being considerable. But if the stroke is made across the cymbal and not just at the edge it can be done safely.

The end comes with a series of heavy chords indicated together with their two-quaver upbeats. The closing rit. should not be too extravagant but can be used to regulate the brief down-and-up which precedes the final bar. The last G major *ff* is a broad minim and has to be conducted as such with the kind of beat which signifies precise duration before the final take-off.

Symphony No. 1 in A flat, Op. 55

◄►

ELGAR's two symphonies are very large affairs. Indeed the Second is even more so than the First, though both last just under the hour and are scored equally for full-size orchestra. It might be said that the First especially represents the essence of the Edwardian era, with its processional opening and motto theme, but it too has its areas of deep poetry on the one hand and brilliance on the other.

Written in 1908 and hailed as a masterpiece almost before it appeared, the work gave the impression that Elgar was exerting himself to the full in showing the world that England too could produce a great symphony. Its reception at the first performance, conducted by its dedicatee Hans Richter, was nothing short of rapturous, both from the point of view of critical acclaim and from that of the audience. The orchestration is for triple wind, the standard brass group with timpani, three percussion (though these are only added in the second and last movements), and two harps, the second of which is to a considerable extent a doubling part but essential none the less.

I

Beginning with two drum rolls, the introduction is virtually a complete movement in itself, consisting of a double statement of the march which establishes the stature of the work as a whole. Marked with Elgar's favourite 'Nobilmente e semplice' at ♩ = 72, it progresses firmly but not languorously, so becoming dignified rather than pompous. The staccato cello/bass line is taken with short strokes on the string at the upper half, as are the 2nd violins and violas in the crescendo molto before fig. 3 though the bows will naturally become longer.

The colours are generally mixed, in what is primarily a tutti symphony, but this should not prevent echo effects such as the *ppp* at fig. 1 from making their proper impact. The mark of 'molto sostenuto' at 3 is not intended to slow the tempo, which must continue absolutely without variation until the procession dies away at the poco rit. before 5. In conducting this enlarged repeat of the motto it is a mistake to become too extrovert; even the interesting brass dynamics can be left to the players, and a simple undemonstrative style prevents the statement from itself becoming over-inflated. The harp parts make their mark against the massive wind and brass by being in double octaves, the first player an octave higher than the second.

The wider spanning of the crotchets at the rit. into 5 has to be very consciously measured and ends with a feeling of expectancy without beating through the long cello/bass Ab, however strictly it should be counted out within the conductor's awareness. The astonishingly distant key of the Allegro then starts up with a vigorous minim preparatory beat, the quaver which initiates the first subject naturally corresponding exactly with the crotchet of the new tempo, ♩ = 104.

This is certainly a very fast choice of speed to match the impassioned and agitated mood Elgar was invoking. He himself was prone to begin a little steadier and increase the pace even as early as the third bar (compare the opening bars of the Violin Concerto). Here the forward drive aims at the 4th bar of 6, the climax being emphasized by a sharp snap on the brass *ff* which can be communicated with the flat of the left hand.

The subsequent rubato indicated by Elgar's personal shorthand notation 'L......, A......' (Largamente, Accelerando) is an overstatement and not one that he himself succeeded in bringing off, but it does nevertheless give some guidelines over the shaping of the phrase-end leading to 7, where a new and almost frenetic agitation begins.

A mounting excitement carries through this third and *ff* working of the main theme, the approach to 9 being the immediate goal. The astonishing virtuosity of the cellos' upper line, which takes them to their top G above the stave, is worthy of good-humoured encouragement. The harps, though not marked 'glissando', are often taken so, as the speed has now made fingered-out demisemiquavers hardly a viable concern in *ff*.

At the $\frac{6}{4}$ of fig. 9 the mark of $\downarrow. = \downarrow$ is largely wishful thinking in the tempo we have reached, and again Elgar made no attempt to observe the marking in his own reading. At the same time there must undoubtedly be an urgency as the beat presses through the rising crescendo to each new minim sforzando.

The agitation, which persists at first through the 3 against 2 of fig. 10, dies down as the diminuendo leads to 11 with its calmer transitional material. This is an altogether more peaceable, even lyrical, area, and although the flow continues to have a swiftness not to be lost as the shaping of the phrases at 11 is introduced, or at the quasi $\frac{9}{8}$ across the bars at the 5th of 11, a gradual drop in tempo to $\downarrow. = 88$ can be recognized to have taken place. Similarly the second subject at fig. 12 is too affecting and full of exquisite detail to be spoilt by a ruthless adherence to the agitation of the earlier material; yet Elgar was right to consider that no mark was necessary to that effect, just as the wonderful hush of the *ppp* needs no cautionary rit. to ensure sensitive handling of the turning point into the poetic second subject.

Here the mood is entirely different and the beat should be mobile yet very gentle. The harps want placing in the first two bars of 12, after which it is the 2nd violins and flute whose $\frac{6}{4}$ passage-work requires primary attention, even though their line is subsidiary to the ₵ melody of the 1st violins.

At **13** the textures are simplified as the whole orchestra goes into alla breve, and accordingly the pace increases slightly for the rising octave of the second subject's opening, now rearing up in full instrumentation including the horn in its best and most expressive register.

Such enthusiasm subsides again after a *Lohengrin*-like turn, and the flutes control the pace with offbeat crotchets, at first in triple and then in duple rhythm, giving an elegant touch for the *pp* ending of the section. The tempo also sags slightly in the approach to **14**, where the new period begins overtly with a return of the 3-against-2 pattern and a resumption of uneasiness leading, after eight bars, to a reappearance of the first subject at its original tempo and vigour. It is particularly important that by this $\frac{2}{2}$ the beat should have regained its firm forcefulness, in order to press into a new fervour the remaining $\frac{6}{4}$ passages (lower strings and wind with energetic horns) and the brilliant figurations on the violins.

Three bars before **15** a tutti syncopated figure is set in motion with such impetus that Elgar thought it as well to mark its powerful continuation at **15** 'giusto' for fear that it might be allowed to run away too soon, a real danger only held in control by the *ff* brass snaps. Nevertheless the forward thrust of the music cannot be restrained to any extent, as the excitement is building through the upward sweeps and the salvo of brass quavers to fig. **16**. Here a true precipitation develops through the descending strings, bringing the movement back to the original ♩ = 104 by 3 before **17**.

This is, however, another turning-point, with a new theme in $\frac{3}{2}$ marking a climax to the whole exposition so far. The upward careering of the first subject links into this new motif with such vehemence that for the minim to remain the same would be too tame, and it is no surprise to find the bar is prescribed to equal the previous bar. Yet in practice this is not really a viable proposition, nor did Elgar achieve it himself. In the first place **17** has to be conducted in an extremely vigorous 3, and if the bar were to remain at 52 (equalling

♩ = 104) the new minims would have to be driven at 156, which is unrealistically hectic. The impression, therefore, has to be given of a fresh urgency without in actual fact going any faster, despite the quicker beat which will send the upward rush of quavers into a flurry at the 4th bar.

At the allargando we reach the true culmination of the exposition, and the tuba's deep sforzando dotted semibreves must be given the utmost weight. The ultimate *sf* is, however, 2 before **18**, after which the sound subsides into the little interlude which forms the bridge before the development.

Like all the formal hinges of the movement this consists of a recollection of the opening motto theme, still with a processional character in the staccato minims of the cellos and basses. The four muted horns carrying the tune will easily give the requisite remote quality, and the Poco meno mosso should enable the opening tempo to be recalled as well, although after all the excitement of the exposition a too exact and scrupulous return to ♩ = 72 could allow it to become static.

This is a matter of fine judgement, for after the horns have faded away there should be an impression of the development picking up, even though there is in reality very little difference in actual tempo between the printed meno and più mosso. Even so, **19** should give a clear new initiation for the development with its abundance of new themes. The whole section from **19** to **21**, two sentences of eight bars each, is very quiet in mood though swiftly flowing, and is guided in its duality of $\frac{2}{2}$ and $\frac{6}{4}$ with a wide, gentle beat.

There follows a working-out of the 3-against-2 figure from **14** now, however, in calmer guise and descending peacefully to a new and subtle undulating motif. Here the shorthand 'R......' for ritardando suggests something altogether too slight for what will in fact be a significant hold-up, as again four bars later. Each time, the delicate spread of the harps is a primary colour, and these bars are conducted with a tenuto downbeat addressed to them, followed by a flourish of an upbeat restoring the tempo.

In the first instance this leads back to the swaying 3 against 2, but the second, shortly before 22, presses on to a series of flurries which the stick should urge ahead with excitable sweeps. The once characteristically ritardando bar is now played at full speed, supporting a new set of themes all marked 'piano' but no less agitated on that account.

The broader phrase introduced by the upper woodwind at 23, and reiterated on each occasion by the horns, has a particular urgency with its surging quaver accompaniment carrying the intensity of the flow forward. The printed poco accel. is both belated and overcautious, for it must begin already at 23 itself and only subsides during the three bars before 24.

It has been a considerable span since 22, and now a new and powerful idea is presented, consisting of huge swells across two bars. However, in revision the muted 1st and 3rd horns were marked up to sustained *ff*'s, and with their angular tone they should penetrate the swells of the whole tutti. The violence of these bars is such that the tempo will inevitably be somewhat expansive, and therefore the last *pp* bar before 24 will be one of preparation, with a slight lead-in.

A *pp* ma sonore development of the figure in the cellos and basses at the tempo primo creates a vigorous agitato and should sound hasty. The syncopated 2nd violins start down-bow at the upper half using short strokes, the accents in the alternate bars coming up-bow in the second bar, down-bow in the fourth, and so on. (It is as well to fix this bowing in rehearsal, as it can be confusing.) The passage finishes up-bow for the *pp* subito at 25, where the string section is inverted so that the roles are reversed.

The top of the crescendo gives another pair of violent swells, but this time no hold-up is warranted as the main tension is kept for 26, where the beat changes again to one of sharp rhythm for the cumulative syncopations.

Elgar states in his prefatory Note that 'the stringendo 26 to 28 should be very animated', and indeed this increases right through the poco animato of 27 until the sudden pull-back in the bar before **28**. The metronome marks cannot, however, be taken literally; in the handling of so large an orchestra the powerful instrumentation makes some of the idealistic tempos largely illusory, even though they certainly give an indication of the relationships of speed.

The height of the development is reached at **28** after a considerable widening of the beat. Even here tempo I $\; \downarrow$ = 104 is incompatible with the passionate violin arpeggios, and it would be unrealistic to aim at more than **92**.

This section is built on another new theme which rushes up to a *sf* on its second bar, at first synchronizing with a three-trombone *ff* snap so that the top of the violins' passage, the snap, and the entry of the horns conveniently come together for a single gesture. As its repetition, however, the top of the violins' swoop coincides with an important entry for the trumpets, and the snaps become more isolated, all having to be strongly indicated with the flat of the left hand. The rising motif continually overlaps with itself until it begins to fall exhausted into the 2-bar swelling theme which interposes at **29**, now presented in double augmentation and exaggerated to a maximum of *pp* to *fff* and back.

This is clearly a dramatic gesture, and as such it is preceded by a single-bar rit., followed by a meno mosso marked at $\downarrow$ = 72, which is really uncommonly steady. The issue here is the next, especially delicate, section featuring the harps and solo violin, which certainly must not be too fast, even though it should seem to float past in what Elgar directs to be a 'veiled and remote manner'.

Little splashes of colour in the 5th to 8th bars of **29**, such as a staccato oboe and pizzicato cellos and basses, help to restrain the tempo, swift as they must sound. The trombone and bassoon chords extend the phrase to five bars with a moment of complete quiet before the upward floating passage leads to a return of the 'R......' bar from after **21**. This time, however, there is an additional feature in that the harps' arpeggio comes not on the first beat, but just before the second; accordingly they now need an extra signal, which must not mislead the quavers on alternately the wind and strings into moving too soon. But the rubato does work in the same way as previously, so that the first beats are in effect exaggerated tenutos which are made up in the second halves of each bar, restoring the tempo with little flurries of the left hand to indicate the flow of the quaver figures.

One quiet reminiscence of the swell bars in resumed tempo brings back the isolated still bar, though it is entirely differently set in high strings and flutes, the violins having a swell of their own which has to be most carefully monitored, again with the left hand despite the extreme calm.

The 4th bar of 30 stands alone, graphically described by the stick, before the whole routine of the four bars before 30 is repeated, conducted exactly as before, but passing this time into the 3-against-2 motif which concludes the development by descending into the ritualistic linking return of the opening processional, this time hardly more than a distant memory. It would be an easy matter to let the tempo drop with the temperature of the music, but Elgar is careful to give no excuse for this, and even in the link it should get no slower than the $\lesseqgtr = 72$ of the meno mosso which gave fig. 29 its more spacious possibilities of instrumental elaboration and colour.

The return to the reprise is highly ingenious: fig. 31 corresponds closely to the poco più mosso of 19 which began the development, but by means of a poco accelerando and a whittling-down of the orchestration until only a bass clarinet is left, followed by cellos and basses, the principal subject is superimposed on the latter and the return is accomplished smoothly. It is important in conducting this most subtle transition that the accelerando back to the original $\lesseqgtr = 104$ be carefully judged. Furthermore the cellos and basses continue at 32 to be primary voices, strongly doubled as they are by lower woodwind, in their efforts to continue the $\frac{6}{4}$ material against the ultimately victorious first subject of the upper instruments who would normally expect the conductor's exclusive attention.

A boradly regular reprise follows until fig. 40. However, whereas at 14 the exposition began urging forward, this is now reversed into a subsidence, with even a drop in tempo for the diminuendo and *ppp*, although there is no mark in the score.

Four bars before 41 is the next corner-stone marking a new section, and this wants a clear fresh start; abruptly the beat becomes vigorous, stressing the harps' punctuations and the syncopated wind, while a smooth left hand nurses the *ppp* trombones. A violent crescendo to *ff* at 41 is interrupted and sets out on another build-up, this time of nine bars, during which the sharply staccato cellos should be prominently featured by the stick.

This pile-up is both longer and more ferocious than the corresponding passage in the exposition (the bars prior to fig. 16), and it is important to give ample accentuation to the trombone chords before 42, as well as to the upward rush on the strings, so that 43 has no difficulty in recalling fig. 16. The low G isolated staccato crotchet on the bass trombone and tuba is also a splendid extra point at the 4th of 43, to be emphasized by a thrust of the left arm.

If this brilliant piece of orchestration has been shrewdly handled, the change to 3 rapid minim beats at 44 should relate exactly to the quasi bar = bar of fig. 17, and, as there, can in the event only be a compromise. The sentence from 45 to 47 is a considerable extension of the original idea and must not hang fire; yet on the other hand if the speed of minims is too hasty, the cello/bass staccato scales linking the 4-bar phrases can hardly be pounded in with sufficiently intense second beats after the preparatory hiatuses.

But in the bars before 46, where the deep tuba notes come in a descending sequence, the tempo can edge ahead, adding maximum brilliance to the mighty *coup de théâtre* of timpani, strings, and horns at 46 itself. Moreover the three trumpets should be able to make a tremendous sustained crescendo to *fff* in their unison upper A♭ over all of six bars, without being distressed for breath. Here they cannot be allowed to cover for each other, and if the tempo is urging ahead they can fulfil the design spectacularly in what is, after all, marked 'cresc. molto e vibrato'.

This time the poco rit. comes after the climax, and the rearing semiquavers in the cellos and basses as well as the spectacular bottom G♯ of the tuba are all in full tempo. This climax self-evidently comes at the 5th of 47 and takes all of four bars to subside into the coda.

Appropriately after so extensive a movement, this coda too is on a generous scale, beginning with the last of the formal links with the opening processional melody, but marked to be played at a slightly faster tempo. Other motifs from later in the movement are combined with it, and the instrumentation, which it is the conductor's province to appreciate and to portray, is particularly imaginative and immensely complex.

The first feature to be observed is Elgar's use of just the back desks of the string groups to carry the theme, these being instructed to be as far apart from each other as possible. Whether or not the idea came from earlier instances such as Strauss's *Zarathustra* or the imaginary idealized evocation of Dulcinea in *Don Quixote*, Elgar's use of the device is not so much an imitation as an incorporation into his own work of an ingenious innovation of an earlier master; it must unquestionably be carried out to the letter, as it gives an almost spectral quality, which shortly after 50 becomes absorbed into the strong, positive tutti colour with the grand return of the melody.

The quicker tempo must not detract from the stateliness which begins the coda, and an overlay of dreamlike memories, such as the $\frac{6}{4}$ motif or the harp quaver runs, contributes to the subtlety of the invention.

Elgar's natural love of pomp takes over gradually so that by the 4th of 50 the massive background of horns and trombones gives this last full statement of the motto theme (before its significant returns in the Finale) a typically pageant-like splendour. Though this would necessarily become over-inflated in a slower tempo, it can indeed be portrayed in a magisterial manner by the conductor.

The bombast fades away eight bars after 51, and a bell-like figure on the flutes and oboes, clearly delineated with the stick, restores the magic of Elgar's more sensitive style as one theme after another is reviewed, all at the slightly quicker pace. At 52 the 2-bar swells are also recalled, now in a remote *pp*, after which a mysterious passage gives just the hint of an accelerando; this is conveyed entirely without emphasis by a beat which simply carries the almost feature-less structures along.

Restatements of the passage-work from the development suddenly appear with the ritenuto bars, still characterized by the familiar rubato, the harps' arpeggiandos now always delayed to the crotchet before the second beats. These are carefully spread by the left hand to avoid propelling first the strings, then the wind, too soon onto their quicker quavers, exactly as at 30.

This is a deeply poetic section, and although the più lento is interrupted after only two bars, it returns even more meaningfully 4 before 54, leading to two more bars of real allargando which are the only bars actually beaten out in 6.

The a tempo (poco tranquillo) of 54 restores peace of mind and the gentle quavers form a quiet ornamentation to the motto theme as they float by with equanimity until turning into staccato crotchets on the bassoons. Another ghostly reference to the introduction (more the processional rhythm in cellos and basses than the melody itself) again creates the misguided temptation to become slower until this too fades. Fig. 55 is a beautifully poetic interpolation in distant A minor, a most delicate *pp* which is indeed often conducted in 6, but wrongly perhaps, for the immensely quiet last $\frac{6}{4}$ bars need no such spelling-out as they simply dissolve back into A flat for the final cadence and the held clarinets, who persist even a little after the final pizzicato.

II

The Scherzo follows, introducing for the first time the three percussion: side drum, bass drum, and cymbals, who reappear in the Finale but, like the trumpets, are silent in the Adagio. For these reasons, with routiné orchestras already well acquainted with the symphony, it may often be convenient to rehearse the Scherzo and Finale first, followed by the first movement and taking the Adagio last.

Marked 'allegro molto' at ♩ = 69, the $\frac{1}{2}$ time signature differentiates to a small but significant degree from the straight 1 of 'Troyte' in the Enigma Variations. The present movement is not quite as fast, and is mostly beaten in 2, although there is a considerable element of precipitation.

A single weighty downbeat starts the movement and is followed (without any second beat) by a sharply syncopated lead to the lower strings for bar 2, the pattern being repeated in bars 3 and 4, in which self-evidently bar 3 is less forceful than the opening bar. These pounded first beats must reflect the depth of the colouring with bass drum and growling violas, cellos, and even low basses on their E string.

The scurrying semiquavers which constitute the main idea enter on the 1st violins in bar 5, but here too the stick has no need to mark crotchets vigorously, which would merely obstruct the players. It continues rather to be the succession of downbeats which are the conductor's concern, even though technically this is positively not in 1, preparations always being of crotchets, however small. Rapid as they are, the semiquavers are significantly thematic, and the ear should have no difficulty in recognizing their pattern when this is spelt out in extremely slow motion for the melody of the Adagio.

The afterphrase before 56, and again when it is slightly extended before 57, is entirely in quaver movement and might suggest an easing of pulse, but this is erroneous, the essential ♩ = 138 being maintained inexorably until just before 64 and then similarly with the merging into the Trio at 66.

Nevertheless a major change of beat occurs at 57, where the furious interchange between string groups requires a true and violent crotchet direction with, for the first time, equally strong first and second beats. Before 58 and 59 the connecting bars need no more than single indications, the one portraying the upward harps' sweep, the other the descent into the very quick march-like second theme. Here is another passage requiring crotchet beating, this time with small, but still intensely energetic, pulsations.

With the theme relegated to the bass instruments, including the galumphing tuba, there could again be the danger of the tempo being pulled back, but this needs to be guarded against; instead, the incessant upward sweep in the violins and flutes is given passionate encouragement in the beating until, at the *fff* tutti statement of the march at 61 with all the percussion going hammer and tongs, the suggestion is on the contrary of pressing ahead.

At 63 there is a differentiation between the phrasings of wind and upper strings which Elgar endorses with the bow strokes, the quavers being taken as separate up-bows. Only the first bar is so designated in the score (the first two bars in the parts), but the bowing is obviously intended to continue for the duration of the passage. The alternating lower instruments are supported by all the heavy brass, who need to be forced ahead with pronounced syncopated downbeats until the formidable entry of all the percussion.

Only a single ritardando bar ('R......') leads to the big *ff* statement of the semiquaver primary theme, but the beating must once more be restrained despite all the frenzy, concentrating on the upbeat tuba and basses followed by the trombones' and horns' crash chords, which recur four times. Immediately, however, a fifth culmination within a single compressed bar brings the final whip-crack on the second beat, reinforced by full brass and percussion.

While the strings continue their semiquavers, still taken off the string even in fortissimo, the beat now attacks the horns' and cello/bass line, which is emphasized by timpani in the bar before **65**. Three more crash chords in decreasing order of intensity start the descent into the Trio. That there is a loss of pace here is inevitable, but it should be minimal, even the staccato cellos and basses in the last bars before the double bar retaining much of the impetus.

The Trio is another of Elgar's most imaginative ideas. It has to be a shade steadier, but as Elgar says in his Note, this must not 'absolutely break the flow of the tempo', so that a drop to ♩ = 120 might be suggested. This contrasting section is still very swift but is conducted in a real 2 to control so much detail. There have been those who take it in 1, but this could be thought unsuitable for the filigree work of the flutes and harp (note the intricacy of the 2nd flute line), as well as too unrelenting for so poetic a passage.

At the 7th of **67** there is a greater feeling of expansiveness in the string writing which can be attained with a wider beat, but one should return abruptly to a rhythmic stick movement for the elegance of **68** with its alternate staccato and legato triplets, which should suddenly be a trifle faster once again. This continues into the duet for the two clarinets with its repeat on the violins at **69**, the latter needing a little breadth.

The phrase ends with a cadence which on its echo in the oboes can even wilt slightly, thus giving the triplet passage a feeling of renewed agitation as at **68**. The harps then restore the lyrical Trio theme with a strong forte chord, and while the theme itself remains very soft, the beat's attention will be occupied by the marcato harps and, above all, the cellos' climb up to top B♭ and subsequent octave drop. The tempo must then be edging forward (except briefly in the bar before **71**), so that with the return of the Scherzo semi-quavers at **71** the original pace and manner of beating will resume smoothly even while the Trio theme is superimposed for a few bars. The cellos will here divide front and back so that the upper line is clearly playing with the violas, the lower with the basses.

The Scherzo maintains its regular return until **75**, where the excitement builds with the combining of the march theme

and the semiquavers, the trombones taking over the former
with great flamboyance. By 76 the tempo should have
mounted so that the trumpets' triplets carry the music, as if on
the crest of a wave, into 77, the peak of the whole movement.

The rumbustious return of the Trio is, if anything, somewhat quicker than it had been on its first appearance, the
triumphant counter-passage on the trombones ascending
jubilantly to their high B♭, which the conductor can portray
with a briefly upheld left arm. Then quite suddenly, after no
more than four bars, the panache evaporates, leaving only
the increased pace in which the original delicacy of the Trio
has to scurry along until 78.

By the 7th of 78 the temperature has noticeably cooled,
and the descending tritones on the bass clarinet benefit from
being pointed with a left-hand index finger. The offbeat
lower string chords and the overlapped 3-bar phrase at 79 all
ease the flow until by 80 there is a real breadth of lyricism in
the writing for the strings and harps, intensified in the rise to
ff ma dolce.

The four bars before 81 move quietly forward once more,
but in the approach to 82 the harps' triplets and solo violin
need some extra time. Although at 82 itself the violas and
clarinets are clearly the leading part, the violins inevitably
depend on a rhythmic beat in what is in fact a return to
tempo, even though it is not marked so. The quicker speed
carries through the crotchets of the augmented after-phrase
and into the triplets from fig. 68, now, however, entirely
staccato whether on oboes or violins.

Fig. 84 is conducted with marked emphasis for the *fpp*'s
in alternate bars, but taking care not to disturb the 1st
violins' triplets. These can give trouble unless bowed as
shown in Ex. 1, and it may be worth spending a few minutes

Ex. 1

establishing this style of bowing in all the violin parts, after which the passage will play itself.

There is a feeling of aftermath and regretfulness from **85**, the solo violin and upper wind outlining the Trio theme in **pp** against an atmospheric background of harps and 2nd violin tremolo. The crotchet beating is smooth once again until 4 before **87**, and at regular intervals the pulsating pattern returns on cellos and basses as at the beginning of the movement, marked by strokes on timpani and bass drum as before, but now very subdued.

It is a long coda, and great care has to be exercised to prevent the increasingly relaxed mood from becoming steadily slower. Only in the four bars before **89** will time be allowed for the staccato flutes to be pointedly placed. At last, however, at **90** the beat goes into 1 for the outline of the march theme, still in pianissimo.

At **91** the five bars of offbeat wind chords need to be given sharply with the left hand immediately after each barline. In the remaining bars the beating marks the pulse infinitely quietly with mere guidances to the strings in their 2-bar, and then at last 4-bar, phrases in an almost religious calm as they merge into the Adagio.

III

Beautiful as it is, the long melody which begins the slow movement turns out to be none other than the notes of the quick semiquaver opening theme of the Scherzo spelt out. Accordingly it needs an alert imagination to conduct the row of notes so that it emerges as a freshly inspired spread of melody in constantly varied metre and harmonization.

The tempo at $\flat$ = 50 is slower than the previous $\downarrow$ = 69, but not so much that the mutation of the one into the other is improbable. Moreover, in typical Elgarian manner, the actual pace should not appear to drag, but on the other hand events have always to be given plenty of time and shaping with the

stick, such as the semiquaver triplets in bar 3 and at fig. **93** as
well as the extremely tender dissolution from the forte in bar
6 to the whispered **pp** in the following bar. After each of
these the tempo is constantly resumed so that the fifteen-
and-a-half-bar sentence does not lack cohesion.

Only at the melody's closing cadence marked 'molto rit.'
is the music subdivided with 8 real semiquaver beats, 4 in the
second half of the one bar and 4 in the first half of the other.
The consequence is that with the return to quaver beating
the new section is displaced by half a bar, which sounds so
positive that it often misleads the 1st harp who needs a warning finger against entering too soon before **94**.

The first transition theme has to be continually kept in
check, both for the figure shown in Ex. 2, in which the long
note is held with the stick before the descent of the little
notes running downhill, and for the triplets whose octaves
are, on the contrary, broad in style. Two bars before **95** the
figure quoted in Ex. 2 comes in sequential repetition on the
wind, but it is always played with the same rubato.

Ex. 2

A somewhat sombre passage follows at **95**, but with much
less detail, so that it can move forward. A more natural style
of beating will thus be adopted in which the alternate horns
and **ppp** trombones are not too slow to be recognizable as a
truly thematic idea.

One brief upsurge in the 5th of **95** can be activated by the
conductor but is soon deflated, and the harps' pronounced
spread chord provides a striking link. From here the timpani
pp syncopated taps bridge the somewhat awesome brass
chords into the glowingly melodic second subject, to be
characterized by a new flowing beat.

The tempo is, however, continually restrained both by the
complexity of the textures and by the tenutos in the melody

with their attendant piano subitos. The flutes' semiquaver triplets may have to be stressed if they are to be heard, and in any case disappear well before the big emotional rise to forte with its drop to *pp* in the very next bar. A prominently featured horn solo echoes the descending phrase 1 before 97, after which the melody is repeated in violas and cellos enriched with horns, the beat encouraging the violins, who now carry the elaborate embroidery together with harps. After only four bars of this luscious repeat in double counterpoint comes a sudden return to the fragmented transition material, conducted once more in a rubato style as before except for the virtuoso bars for clarinet and solo violin, whose runs must be allowed fluency.

The use of a single harp forte at 99, and again at the 3rd bar, is like a clutch at the heart, followed in the 2nd bar by a relaxation where two harps answer in *pp*. The burst of emotion at the 5th of 99 relates to the 5th of 95 and is activated by the conductor in a similar way but to a greater degree, so that the consequent pressure on the tempo takes all of five bars to calm down; but this time in subsiding it returns to the same quiet mood as at the beginning of the movement.

In the following complete restatement of the long first melody several differences from the original exposition will, however, be brought out, such as the change in the fifth bar from the continuing legato to a quite jumpy staccato in the lower strings positively reflected in the beat, or the cor anglais, who takes over the *pp* subito in the 7th of 100. But by far the most pronounced variation in this return is the passionate burst of intensity at the 3rd of 101, interchanging the lines of the 1st and 2nd violins in such a way that the final cadence, once again conducted in a real 8, comes now in a single bar instead of being stretched across two half-bars.

Accordingly the end of the melody arrives at the downbeat of 102 for the *pp* return of the second subject, which, by means of a short cut, comes back straightaway in place of the transition material. Hence this, having been lingered over previously at such length, is now omitted except for a brief but very thoughtful few bars at 103 which take the music into the coda. The two bars of 'R......' come after a passage in semiquaver triplets which, spread across the orchestra, need a degree of nursing even while remaining in tempo, whereas the rit. bars are only beaten for the demi-semiquaver little notes of the transition motif. The last group of these broadens significantly into the melodic triplet figure before leading into the chords of brass and harps. The final beats before the coda of 104 are pointedly stressed, still very softly, however, by the basses' pizzicatos.

The coda is deeply affecting and must be conducted with a rapt style in a slightly slower tempo of ♪ = 46. The fermata in the fifth bar is not altogether easy to manipulate, as the moment for the 2nd violins to move must be indicated while still holding the 1sts on a crescendo. It must nevertheless be organized as simply as possible with no more than the stick, the left hand being kept in reserve for the timpani **ppp** and the harps.

There is a close parallel here with the nostalgic expression in the Larghetto of the Serenade for Strings, and both represent a particularly endearing side of Elgar's expressive writing. The clarinet flourish from the transition, reminiscent of Brahms's Clarinet Quintet, is heard in the background, answered by a well-featured upward corresponding flourish in the 2nd violins. The primary subject-matter is built on the figure quoted in Ex. 2, but this can no longer be held on a tenuto with a subsequent release, as it has to be consciously fitted with the continuing triplets on the two harps. This needs great awareness of ensemble, as does the cadential triplet which, first heard at the 5th of 105, is to become more and more in evidence as it acquires the tenuto and dotted feature of the earlier motif.

Gradually all dies away, with harps, timpani, and cellos continuing the pulsation and ending in total calm for one last **ppp** recall of the coda subject. Most important, however, is that there should be no reduction in tempo except for the considerable allowance which has to be made for the two wistful triplets on muted trombones, timpani, and harps, these being purposefully beaten out. The hushed string chord between them is back to tempo but can never be soft enough after the rise to *mf*, especially as pulse must not be lost in such a subito collapse, and still avoiding any extravagance in the abrupt gesture of withdrawal. Finally the clarinet solo in the second last bar is controlled by the fingers of the left hand, much as at the end of the '* * *' variation of the Enigma.

IV

A substantial pause should intervene before the start of the Finale, whose introductory section recalls much material from the first movement as well as using effects such as the recurrent use of the back desks of the strings.

The extremely sinister beginning should not mislead the conductor into believing the tempo to be inordinately slow; in fact the prescribed ♩ = 56 is markedly less slow than the Adagio. After the opening bar of bass drum solo the bass clarinet and bassoon are heard crawling around with the swell-bars theme from the first movement (the swells themselves now only minimal), and the passage is extended to three bars, at the end of which the chord on the two harps should sound quite arresting even though it is only marked 'piano'. A vigorous cue with the left hand will ensure this, in the midst of so much serpentine movement with the stick.

Basses and timpani are also cued by a left-hand judder, after which regular beating inaugurates one of the prime motifs of the Finale on bassoons and cellos, albeit in the slow tempo. Elgar himself initiated the custom of a hold-up before the quavers at the end of the third bar, and this is to be observed here, as well as later, with a tenuto on the third crotchet; the bar is thus virtually elongated to $\frac{5}{4}$.

The two harps always enjoy their solo bar of triplets at 108 and appreciate a look from the conductor before he brings in the far-flung string desks with the motto theme of the symphony. No sooner is this under way, however, than a flurry on wind and harp disturbs the calm, actually hurrying the demisemiquaver groups so that they do not sound measured and the next bar arrives a fraction early. After that momentary spasm peace returns, and when the swell theme re-enters, overlapping the motto at 109, the latter may well become imperceptible if Elgar's mark of 'sonore' in the lower strings is given too free a rein.

The horns again have their accented note in the 3rd of 109 as at the beginning, but the harp stress is absent, being delayed to mark instead the entry of the trombones, who take over the finale motif, playing it as before with a pronounced rubato before the quavers. Here too there is no sign of this in parts or score, and the trombones, with their back-up of divided cellos, have to be well tutored in Elgar's own treatment of the phrase. This repeat of the motif features a most striking *ppp*, which should be prepared by placing the beat well forward for the harps and bass drum on the tenuto third beat and then suddenly withdrawing dramatically for the fourth.

In the following bar the flutes' entry is combined with trumpets, and since these have not played since the Scherzo they need to be alerted. The swell theme returns in more extrovert manner, to be conducted after the preparatory crescendo chord with more signs of strength and presence than the shadowy introduction has evinced so far. The timpani *ff* at the top of the swell can be indicated with a left arm held aloft before being dropped to an exaggerated *ppp*.

The back desks once again hint at the motto melody but, enhanced by the rising triplets of the clarinets, lead to an elaborate effect on divided strings. Although *pp*, this can be conducted with an element of almost graphic portrayal, as again the flutes' and clarinets' wisp of colour two bars later, contrasting with the extreme asceticism of the beating style controlling the motto melody elsewhere.

Fig. III starts to suggest one of the Finale's most evocative phrases from the transition, but before it can fulfil itself there is a violent change and the introduction plunges to a silent fermata. This can be quite hard for the conductor to negotiate due to the 'L......' and 'A......' in the 2nd of III, which have to be controlled at the moment of a change to 2 in a bar, the accelerando then continuing precipitately until the cut-off at the double bar. Moreover the largamente, having abruptly risen to forte, equally suddenly drops to piano within the space of a single extended minim, and as a result the subsequent beats have to force the orchestra along even while portraying the triplet crotchets. These are made to career forward to the cliff-edge, lemming-like, with a brusque sforzando on the last upbeat, but taking care to give the trombones their cue, which must be sharply in evidence even though they, uniquely, are only marked 'piano'.

A silence, not too long, precedes the sharp downbeat which fires the strings into their violent semiquavers (a subdivided beat for the beginning of the bar is a woeful complication not to be adopted on any account), indicating with a twist of the stick the two-semiquaver advance moment of their upbeat entry. The violas take their cue from the 1st violins rather than from any precise half-bar extra cue from the conductor, who on the contrary must simplify his direction to the utmost.

The metronome mark of $\downharpoonleft$ = 84 for this Allegro will be found to be quick but in keeping with the overflowing energy this risoluto first subject demands. Each minim beat has to spark not only the Brahmsian offbeats of the cellos and basses but the excessively awkward bowing style Elgar imposed on the theme itself. Players are often disposed to dodge this, and it is true that in due course Elgar himself drops the marking, but here it is mandatory, as is shown by the fact that it was a well-thought addition to the revised printing of the score. The short, inevitably accented, up-bows seem to contradict the half-bar slurs, but the sense of effort and struggle, especially at the tearing tempo, is all fundamental to the character of the music. It is further important that this unnatural bowing persists through the *ff* of 112 until replaced by the slurs of the four bars before 113, where a more flowing beat can also be adopted.

A bar of panic is the 5th of 113, where the upper strings seem to demand time if only to get the notes in. But this concession cannot be granted, and the beat must have the energy to force them through the elaborate passage-work to arrive at the *ff* in strict tempo.

There is a slight calming before 114 so that the cantabile transition theme can seem to reanimate the movement with its pounding crotchets in the basses and back-desk cellos. (Some analogy may be detected between this theme and the second subject of Brahms's Third Symphony finale, which is even stronger in the reprise when it is doubled by horns.)

The lyrical phrase at 116 is curiously held back to strict tempo by forte pizzicato basses, which are to be conducted to the exclusion of all else, and a long rising section ensues in which half-bar ascending groups are pitted against syncopated phrases falling in contrary motion. The conflict between these has to be fought in building this passage resolutely towards a complete break in idiom for the second subject at 118.

This, which we have already met in the introduction, is appreciably faster (even as much as $\downarrow = 92$) and is repeated sequentially with brass fanfares at the third statement, followed by rising horn gestures which can be graphically portrayed with the left hand. The percussion also deserves attention, the combined cymbal and bass drum stroke at the 8th of 118 being particularly telling, *pp* as it is. The last climactic *ff* is prepared with an 'R......', the three crotchets after the downbeat being weightily indicated but not actually subdivided.

The cut-off before the quavers discussed earlier is at first withheld but returns vehemently in the final fortissimo statement, where it is conducted with an elongated upbeat, the orchestra having been forewarned as there is still no sign in score or parts. In the bar after the cut-off a timpani figure maintains the *ff* while the rest of the orchestra makes a brief diminuendo, only to resume again at 120 with the principal subject at full energetic tempo and with, as before, the violins' strenuous bow strokes. The beating is again passionate and forceful, driving ahead the continuous syncopations in the lower strings.

At 121 a new motif appears on the horns, to be featured with a sustaining left arm and leading to two violent chords on the trombones, which are also marked by left hand gestures. This is all now part of the development, and from the brass chord in the 4th of 120 the back desks are combined with woodwind to smooth the jagged edges of the phrases in the other strings with half-bar slurs. These are only interrupted at the new horns' motif where the beating can be so sharp as to be positively bouncy, the slurs resuming immediately in the phrases descending to the development proper, which begins 2 bars before 122.

With so much urgency infusing the build-up, a considerable momentum has developed, and the next section, largely formed out of imitative brass entries of the second subject in an intensely vigorous working-out, is quite furioso in style at ♩ = 100. The violins' triplet bars will scurry at breakneck speed and there must be a violence about the cello/bass quaver passages as well as the hectic descent of triplets in cellos and then violas at 127, given with quite vicious slashes from the stick.

In between, the returns of the syncopations at 124 and the 5th of 125 have also become frenzied, with the sustaining brass swells pealing out in alternation and always urged on with the left arm. But the character changes at 127, where the Brahmsian transition melody sweeps over the texture, eventually coming, after so long a turmoil of precipitation, to a quite sudden and surprising halt.

Now at last the tempo moderates considerably as the lower instruments mark gentle separated crotchets to prepare for a long-delayed reminiscence of the motto theme on the back desks, who as always need careful cohesion from the stick, especially in so different a pulse. The speed should naturally have reduced sufficiently to relate to the motto's veiled reference in the introduction, but without needing to be quite so steady.

More important is its ability to melt into the totally unexpected lyrical episode of the development which follows and which will float along at about $\downarrow$ = 60. An almost unrecognizable metamorphosis of the second subject, this is an extremely beautiful interlude featuring the harps and strings, in which the arpeggiando work in the 2nd cellos should be particularly nursed and encouraged while the violins soar along with their ecstatic melodizing, the harps having almost concertante parts. At 132 it is noteworthy that they have individual lines to a greater extent than elsewhere in the symphony.

The interlude leads directly to the reprise, there being only the least *einleitend* before 134 sets forth once more, sustaining horns included, at the original energetic tempo, though now with bracketed bowing replacing the earlier down-and-up strokes of the violins. The tutti *ff* of 135 is more detached and springy than ever before, and this will be reflected in the beat before it careers ahead again at the fifth bar, the reprise now covering familiar ground.

As on the earlier occasion the transition theme (136) is clothed in a mass of complicated string lines, for which no allowance should be made in the tempo, although it is equally important not to hurry to the point where the fifth bar becomes a mere scramble. Here the timpani part has a note not in the score which derives from an earlier version and should be erased.

From here to 143 the music closely corresponds with 114–120 and is conducted in the same way; but where 114 pressed forward into the development, 143 inaugurates the peroration and coda. Of necessity therefore it broadens perceptibly as the four horns peal out in *ff* unison an inflated version of the transition theme punctuated by the harps (it is again

apparent that two are an essential requirement) and capped
by brilliant triplets and scales in the upper strings. It is,
however, to the horns and brass that the stick is directed.

The 4th bar of 144 develops into a kind of pendulum with
the beat swinging from side to side over the four bars to 145,
from which point an eight-bar repetition of *fff* C's on the
horns in three octaves is placed with emphatic downbeats.
But this is the least of the conductor's problems: the *ff sf*
violin figure in $^6_4$ just preceding the second beat of each bar
depends on a punctuated stick gesture, joined canonically
from the third bar by similar overlapping figures in the 2nd
violins and violas, these also needing sharp entries with the
stick, while the half-bar beats are also to be placed emphatically for the lower instruments of all wind, brass, and strings
with the climactic addition of bass drum in the eighth bar.
The cumulative effect of these bars can hardly be exaggerated and is further enhanced by a long crescendo to *fff* on
sustaining trumpets, which can only be indicated by the
conductor's eyes, all available limbs being fully occupied.

One extra bar before 146, with downward harp glissandos
and formidable string quavers in groups of threes, brings
in the motto theme in its ultimate statement of purest
pageantry. Marked 'Grandioso', the tempo has to broaden
still more to ♩. = 60 to accommodate the elaboration, much
of which is of the variety just discussed, with elbowed leads
and stick gestures for the bursts of tutti on third and sixth
crotchets.

The motto itself is to a large extent rather more implicit in
the harmony than stated overtly amid so much overlying
detail, and it would be idle as well as confusing to try to
isolate and emphasize it. The tutti sforzando explosions and
skyward rockets occupy the beating until the bar before 147,
when all the parts come together and a straightforward last
grand statement of the motto appears in all its glory and
with a simplified beat at long last.

Not that Elgar can resist touches of extra sonorities, such
as horns at the 7th of 147 or rising octaves on the strings. At

148 a great counterpoint with added brass contributes to the building of the final climax, and pounding downbeats with elbowed sforzandos as at 145 are brought back into service. The last four bars of this tumultuous peroration before 150 are given over primarily to the trombones, and if the 2s against 3s can be skilfully manœuvred they should aim at an accelerando rather than the ponderous sostenuto which is too often the case.

The coda proper flies off like the wind at 150, and its stringendo at first concentrates more on speed than power despite the *ff* of the strings and lower wind. The timpani triplets are solo at 151 and must only use the initial piano as a starting-point for the huge crescendo with which the closing quaver group ends. There is no ritardando for the final half-reference to the motto on *fff* brass, and the trombones' motif with its 2 against 3 plunges forward as before.

The A♭ on the timpani might seem curious, and players sometimes take it on themselves to change it to B♭; but A♭ is the tonic note of the symphony, and Elgar is likely to have meant it. The final sustained crescendo brass chord is held a little beyond its strict length, and the trumpets can never resist the '8va ad lib.' to end so mighty a work.

Symphony No. 2 in E flat, Op. 63

◄►

ELGAR's Second Symphony is on an even larger scale than its predecessor, and the orchestra itself is also more generously laid out, with an E flat clarinet added to the woodwind department and no fewer than four percussion in addition to timpani. It lasts a full 55 minutes, which, although only a little more than No. 1, does just make the difference when planning the programme, while the profound thoughtfulness with which it ends, militating against a rousing reception, also has to be taken into account. The composer was less than perceptive in his disappointment at the end of the first performance, which he had conducted himself: 'What's the matter with them?' he growled to his friend Willie Reed, the leader of the London Symphony Orchestra, 'they're sitting on their hands'.

It could hardly have been otherwise, for unlike the tumultuous close of the spectacularly successful First Symphony, the later work involves the listener in a much more introvert experience, taking time and repeated hearings to absorb. Today, in the light of familiarity, this is generally considered the finer of the two with a deeper message, epitomized by the quotation from Shelley on the title page, which comes from a 'Song' published by his widow, Mary Shelley, amongst the posthumous poems.

The difference in emphasis is apparent from the very beginning, for whereas the First Symphony opens with an air of pageantry, the Second plunges in immediately with the lengthy and impassioned Allegro primary subject. It is often hazarded that the Shelley quotation relates to the descending phrase in the third bar, partly because of its nostalgic returns at the end of both the slow movement and of the whole symphony, but this is not an open and shut case. On the contrary, there seems something essentially heroic about this opening sentence, which, from the very first forte, rising at once to fortissimo, must be characteristically arresting despite the prescribed up-bow of the first note which starts with the bows actually touching the string to achieve the requisite thrust.

After a mere preparation the first beat is a powerful 2, given sideways with stick and left hand together, followed by a syncopated 3 with crescendo molto, and a fully subdivided 4 in real quavers, to observe Elgar's 'L......', his shorthand for Largamente. Two bars of violent accelerando ('A......') follow, the full tempo being set to arrive only at the fourth bar.

Yet even here the overflowing energy which pulsates through this $\frac{12}{8}$ does not settle at the marked $\downarrow$. = 92, pressing forward through the even stronger *ff* of bar 6. The urgency of this restlessness of tempo is greatly enhanced by the accompanying figure with its quaver anticipations (trombones and harps, then passing to violins and flutes).

The horns rear up in unison with a trumpet, the semiquavers a little hurried, incited by a forceful left arm for two bars, and the first immediate climax is reached at fig. 1, where already a new metronome mark of $\downarrow$. = 104 is given. With sforzandos coming on the second beat of each bar, a huge impetus is created as if the symphony were running headlong downhill.

At the 2nd bar before 2, however, the bottom of the slope is reached and a heavy uphill naturally ensues, as in any cycle ride, needing immense energy and strength to build towards the tenuto marks on every third beat in a broader stick-style. The crest of the hill arrives at the con anima of 3 with the four horns pealing out the principal subject and benefiting from a clearly directed beat to ensure strict timing. Fig. 4 develops the theme of the upward semiquavers, initiated as before by the horns but carried on an extra octave, so that the 'poco più sostenuto' marking implies a restraint that would be unwarranted. The first beats of the third and fourth bars, moreover, each have great lifts to a staccato sforzando which need to be exaggeratedly short and pointed with the left hand. The cellos now divide front and back, allied as the two halves are to 2nd violins and basses respectively.

The adoption of a very steady metronome mark at the a tempo of 5 is actually a resuscitation after a minor lead-in during the bar before, starting a new and lengthy pile-up of no fewer than thirteen bars in which the excitement and the tempo are continuously driven forward, especially at 6, and forcing the countermelody on horns and lower strings four bars later not to fall behind with their prodigality of notes and detail.

It is integral to the interpretation of this whole first para-graph, as indeed of other passages in the symphony, that the conductor thinks in enormously long sentences so that the back and forth of subsidiary rubato never disturbs the 38-bar-long structure from bar 2 to fig. 7, which is the first true point of arrival.

Here the 'tempo primo' mark is misleading, and many conductors put the brake on so fundamentally that they seriously defuse the climax. Elgar himself used to drive straight on, and very exciting this reading is. To slow to any great extent also anticipates the descent into the second subject of 8 after what should have been a huge eruption of orchestral detail. The semiquavers must just have time to sound clearly, and the brass snaps at the 2nd and 3rd of 7 with their quaver upbeats have to be quite violent; the style of conducting then changes totally 3 before 8, calming down to the point where the staccato quavers at the end of each beat are given with bounces of the stick and left elbow. It is also important here that the strings do not use bracketed bowing but give little staccato up-bows.

The melody of the second subject stabilizes the tempo for a time in the new, gentle atmosphere of repose. The orchestration has some points of interest: the two harp parts so much at variance with each other show that, even more than in the First Symphony, Elgar is positively thinking in terms of two instruments; and his antiphonal treatment of the 1st and 2nd violins suggests that he had in mind that they be seated to left and right of the conductor, a formation which, so ardently championed by conductors of the old school such as Sir Adrian Boult, is rarely adopted at the present time.

At fig. 10 the violins combine in a countermelody of great nobility and generosity, rising in both tempo and dynamics with an upsurge of intensity before falling to an introspective middle section devoted to the cellos, who need plenty of time with which to negotiate their octave leaps. The violins' diminuendo hairpin in the 2nd of 10 is lacking (cf. 48), as is also the 2nd violin pizzicato 3 before 10 (cf. 2 before 9), though this is also the case in the return.

The cellos need no fussing in their drawn-out, dolce e delicato melody, and the conducting is directed more to the very soft background on second and fourth beats rebounding off the pizzicato basses. When the principal second-subject melody returns, it is again treated as subsidiary to new counterpoints on oboe and clarinet (fig. 13), then cellos and clarinets (14), which should be featured more prominently by the conductor than the melody itself.

The poco animato of 14 is very slight, and after the rise and fall to forte, in which the cellos are once more the primary voice, the whole episode of the second subject falls away, fig. 15 initiating a new paragraph with restored energy for the repeated mark of 'animato', which this time has positive significance. It should be as if, after a period of listlessness, the conductor has suddenly found once more his sense of power and vigour, the beat having a real drive, especially towards the 2nd and 4th bars of 15 whose accented anticipations beat after beat create an intense feeling of impatience. At 16 the Impetuoso gives the stick a kind of cut and thrust, much as in fencing and with similar athletic power in the style of direction.

In the bar before 17 the beat changes, the three sforzandos being indicated with heavy rising stresses and giving way to semi-subdivisions for the largamente *ff* duplets in the second half of the bar. This leads up to a most elaborate passage which obviously requires time, as the semiquavers in the violins cannot be hurried unduly and the trumpets' triplets in duple rhythm have, for clarity, also to be given their leeway. (The 1st trumpet's F♯'s in the bar of 17 should, it must be stressed, be F✕, being wrong in all scores and parts.)

This outburst gives way to a further build-up of energy at 18, the tempo driving forward in a veritable eruption. Places to watch, however, are the dovetailing brass figures at 19 and the surging violins at the end of the second bar. Against the trumpets and woodwind the 1st violins' sforzando entries on alternate beats have to be emphasized leading to the high A♭, which, especially being another duplet effect, needs to be graphically directed.

So extended and cumulative an approach to 20 has precipitated the music to such a point that the ultimate arrival bar must not be too exaggeratedly pulled back, for all the 'Largamente' indication. Care has even to be taken, in all the exultation of the huge orchestral forces, that fig. 20 does not become too slow. This inflation of the cellos' meditative theme from the second subject group is admittedly marked 'maestoso' with repeated trumpet heraldings and passionately high violin and upper wind exhortations, but the peak of the exposition does not come until the 2nd of 21, where, with the upsurge to *fff*, one has to imagine the giant figure of the composer rising from his seat to cap the whole of this mighty edifice with all the strength at his command.

In the bar of 21 itself the duplet on the fourth beat is worthy of an indication within the beat, as also (during the allargando) in the 3rd of 21, although the climax is by now past. Moreover the sforzandos in the 2nd and 4th bars need extra power, coinciding with *fff* trumpets and backed by octave leaps on the basses.

Each repetition of the culminating phrase is less strong than the last in the gradual subsiding of this monster climax, and the exposition dwindles to a funereal concluding passage which, from 2 before **22**, should no longer be allargando until the new poco a poco rallentando 2 before **23**. In the whole of this declining section the harps are the solo instruments, especially after the timpani have ceased to mark the measured tread. Their regular bell-like tolling harmonics are to be picked out with the left hand at **23** followed by the not-too-final dominant–tonic resolution on the timpani.

Fig. **24** announces the beginning of the development, a haunting new 2-bar idea on the violins falling, rising, and falling again through whole octaves. The poco meno mosso has for the first time no metronome mark, although a new pulse has undoubtedly to be set, which must not be slower than ♩. = 88; moreover, there is a further rallentando to come after **26**, and it is all too easy to reach a slow tempo too soon in such an extended calando.

The ebb and flow of the new theme requires very smooth direction, alternating with various colourful gestures portraying the spread arpeggiandos of the harps at the 3rd of **24** or of a single harp four bars later. Then the *fpp* snaps in the 2nd violins' tremolos must be very sharp, and the alternations of memories from an earlier $\frac{12}{8}$ motif can be portrayed by a swaggering style in the beat. The unexpected splash of the two flutes 1 before **27** should be allowed to rush upwards through the scales, but with a slight hold-up in the quavers at the end of the bar where they are joined most delicately by the 1st violins. Meanwhile the mock drum 'drags' on the 2nds, taken ricochet, have to be positively directed because of the flutes' rubato.

The bar before **28** is a lead-in to another quite new and significant section in an even slower tempo, whose setting calls for great authority and nobility from the conductor. In principle this consists quite simply of an expansive line of 11 bars for the cello department, but the background is one of extraordinary complexity. The tempo is perfectly steady throughout, so that the first responsibility of the beat is to stay reliably with the bass drum semiquaver pattern, *ppp* as this is, and with the 1st basses who pick up the rhythm of their pizzicato ostinato from the 2nd violins' single bar before 27; but because of the slower speed it can be closed in a little here, after slightly elongated quaver rests.

Against these unremitting rhythmic figures, which should be audible (but only just so), come the motivic references on the upper strings, which have to be unobtrusive, important though they seem to be. They are derived partly from the swaying octave idea and partly from the opening bars of the symphony, which should now have a dreamlike quality, emphasized by the embroidery on the two harps and the florid scales on flutes and violas.

It is evident that there is too much for the conductor to attend to, and he must keep an air of detachment through the mass of detail over which the cello melody rides effortlessly. Two bars before 30 the rhythm eases, and as an oboe solo pierces the texture, the opening bars of the symphony become of primary importance in their now trancelike state.

The rallentando and largamente around 30 are to be interpreted lingeringly, the last beat of 2 before 31 being subdivided for the strings, who pick up the thread from the oboe. There has to be a great flexibility about this passage, the bar before 31 moving forward quietly, only to be held in the tranquillo and still more so in the following bar with its infinitely remote third beat.

The 3rd of 31 suddenly moves forward again, but still only for a single bar, the lead into 32 corresponding exactly with 31. The danger in all this is allowing the overall structure to become lost in so much lingering; a very firm hold has therefore to be kept on the wider sense of the phrasing, preventing the relaxed moments from acquiring too much importance in themselves.

In the bar before 33 a change occurs, with only half a bar each of accelerando and ritardando in order to arrive at a complete restatement of the great cello melody but in a new key and slightly slower still. The a tempo merely denotes that the pulse is once again stable, and this time the drum taps are quavers (as opposed to semiquavers), with the addition of side drum and bass drum marked exaggeratedly softly at *pppp*. Joined by the 1st harp, their rhythm accordingly takes first priority in the conducting. The background detail is also less elaborate, and the *Innigkeit* of the cellos' melody should therefore be even more affecting than at 28, although it is now a full third lower in pitch.

The melody is recapitulated, all eleven bars, subsiding as before into an atmosphere of profound tranquillity, marked by a most arresting *pp* spread C major chord over the span of the two harps which the conductor's left hand and wrist can splendidly evoke. One further bar of stillness (though without a fermata, it should be noted), and another cornerstone is reached, the dream vanishing as if on awakening suddenly from a deep sleep.

The return to real life comes with a pronounced bump in the lower strings. We are not yet at the reprise, but in order to get there, at once embark on a succession of Elgar's long-limbed sentences whose extent has to be foreseen and planned by the conductor. The eight bars before 37 call for a smooth beat after the initial thud, and though marked 'a tempo', they are not in fact at the full tempo of the opening, as the metronome marks make plain. From here the pace steadily gathers momentum, the energy growing by leaps and bounds with the change of beat-style at 37, corresponding to fig. 2, though allowing for an even more powerful *élan* than before.

Phrases and motifs derived from the opening bars of the symphony are passed to and fro across the orchestra at 38, the accented notes on the violins in alternate bars requiring new retaken down-bows to obtain sufficient attack and separation, even though this entails three successive down-bows in the bar before 39 and more such retakes two bars later.

The tempo is now headlong and punctuated by the trumpets every two bars. The urgent anticipations familiar from

16 are reintroduced with rising chromatic scales in what has become a strepitoso, the three trumpets being especially brilliant.

Fig. **41**, with its repeated emphases, naturally pulls the tempo back. Although nothing is stipulated in the score, the constant down-bows and wind sforzandos inevitably turn the strepitoso into a very pesante ♩ = 84, in which the bass drum and timpani on the second and third beats of each alternate bar will want stressing even though their actual marking is surprisingly reserved.

The climactic *fff* is carried by the horns and 1st trombone, who have to be firmly conducted with their reiterations on insistent B♭'s. The six bars from **41** to **42** are three pairs, the third considerably broader than the first two as the apex of the movement approaches; the last two crotchets before **42** must be extremely powerful and well separated, using both stick and left hand.

The bar of **42** itself is conducted in 12 steady quavers, the six semiquavers of the trombones and timpani being positively indicated even within this subdivision. The last two quavers are again vehemently enunciated with directive force to the brass tenutos, the second of these containing in addition a total take-off gesture. Though the pulse is certainly interrupted, the caesura should, nevertheless, be only momentary.

Tempo is gradually recovered in the 2nd bar of **42** with an almighty crash on the second beat. The reprise is now under way, and a further *ff* bass drum and cymbal stroke three bars later confirms the impetus with which it is being launched.

Even now the excitement is to be maintained: the horns twice rear up as at the beginning of the symphony, the wind and 2nd violins continue skywards, and the strings give a tremendous sweep, which is portrayed with the left arm. The effervescent energy boils over into **43**, where Elgar's long sequential phrases plunge precipitantly downhill again. As in the exposition this leads, at the bottom of the slope, to an effortful ascent marked 'con anima' but in actual fact more heavily pulsed for the consequent uphill part of the journey; this time, however, it is fully scored in high octave writing and therefore requires less of a feeling of laborious pedalling.

The tempo primo brilliance of fig. 7 is interpreted as before, with the addition of a very positive lead for the violins' sextuplet semiquavers at the second beat of the 2nd and 3rd bars.

From here the progress of the reprise follows in general outline that of the exposition and introduces no new responsibilities for the conductor except possibly at 52, where the lead-in ritardando is treated more heavily than before, because the return to the primary melody of the second subject is excised. The 2nd violins embark on a new and abortive subsidiary idea, which is worth bringing through before it dies in its tracks. The solo bars for the two harps at the 5th of 52 are another colouristic feature to be enjoyed by the players.

The coda begins at 63 after a long linking section corresponding with the funereal passage which ended the exposition at 22 and with the same concentration on the harps. It is tempting to linger at 63 on account of the languorous $\frac{6}{4}$ melody, but the continuing $\frac{12}{8}$ pulsations, which must just be heard on the violas and clarinet, will prevent the tension from leaving the music altogether despite the increasingly relaxed atmosphere.

The energy picks up again at 64 after two bars of premonition five and six bars earlier in which the basses' rhythmic pizzicatos, recalling their role at 28 in the development, are all too rarely heard.

An interesting feature in the horns should be accentuated as the movement regains momentum. The 3rd and 4th players, taking over the subsidiary motif from the 1st and 2nd, give it a stronger and more emphatic rhythm of duplet quavers, which adds enormously to the strength of the passage.

The second bar of **65** is a tricky one, for the principal motif, pealing out on the 1st and 3rd trombones against the syncopated figures of the tutti, holds on for a moment after all the others have stopped. This has to be made particularly clear with the stick directed at these two players, the left hand banishing the remainder who come off exaggeratedly short. A syncopated fourth beat then triggers the *fff* continuation of this closing section.

The secondary portion of the initial theme of the symphony, so often taken to identify with the Shelley quotation, is thundered out first in its natural $\frac{12}{8}$, then expanded into $\frac{4}{4}$ with a massive surge in the brass before the percussion are brought to prominence with their four hammered semiquavers in the allargando. These are steady enough to be pulsated within the conductor's first beat, after which a dramatic drop to *pp* has to be prepared over the whole orchestra.

Fig. 66 is a conundrum, for however clear it may be what Elgar meant—he described it as a flash of lightning—it is far from evident how to obtain the detail from the strings (apart from the fact that the *fp* snap of the wind which sets it in motion is unfortunately missing from the parts). In Elgar's own recording the effect is entirely successful, even if all the notes are not actually played, but for present-day conductors a desire to emulate the composer's reading is in practice to risk antagonism from the musicians and the comment that the passage is unplayable. Yet to tone down the accelerando is to sacrifice the whole concept, which should be dazzling. As so often the skill is in finding the best compromise which can still secure the co-operation of the orchestra.

II

The Larghetto which follows (so that the middle movements are in reverse order to those of the First Symphony) is one of the great funeral marches in all music, analogous with the slow movement of Beethoven's 'Eroica', where, as here, the mourning is on a national rather than a personal level. Elgar wrote in his dedication that the symphony had been intended as an expression of loyal tribute to Edward VII; that monarch died before it could be finished, and the work still stands to his memory.

Throughout the slow movement the mood is grave but not too slow, as indicated by the use of the term 'Larghetto' as well as the metronome mark ♩ = 60. Whether in long sustained notes, as in the 1st and 4th bars, or in moving quavers, the tempo is constant through the seven introductory bars with the exception of the last, which prepares the funeral theme itself.

There are, however, some features about this introductory section worth commenting upon, beginning at once with the opening low C in the 2nd bassoon, which dare not be too soft or it can fail to speak. The basses' first pizzicato initiates the strings' entry, whereas the next one comes on the beat after the strings start their second phrase and needs therefore to be placed with a positive click.

The strings themselves are by no means uninteresting in the distribution of their divided lines, as the melody is not in the 1st violins but in the upper strand of the 2nds and violas, the 1sts only taking over in the middle of bar 6. This unorthodox colouring must nevertheless be allowed to speak for itself, without artificial emphasis of this or that upper line. The conductor's beat preserves an impassive demeanour, with the sole exception of clear leads to the bassoons, basses, and 1st harp. The latter in particular not only answers the basses, with its spread chords placed irregularly one or two beats later, but motivates the strings' quaver movement in bar 2 without additional urging.

The only swell to forte is in the strings and muted horns in bars 6–7, even though it is the bassoon whose line carries the interest most of all. The violins have a tenuto accent during their diminuendo in the Largamente bar, and this must be well stressed as they hand the melodic line over to the horns, the latter becoming unmuted for the purpose.

Fig. **67** initiates the processional, the emphasis being constantly placed on the weighty second and fourth beats in preference to the melody itself, which is interpreted unemotionally. The small nuances of dynamics need no overt coaxing, though the crescendo to *pp* subito, in the background 3 bars before **68**, does on the contrary warrant some exaggeration in the placing of the appropriate crotchets, especially as it does not correspond with the dynamics of the melody itself.

The end of the theme is scored most imaginatively for the trombones, a change of colour which the conductor will emphasize before turning to the violins for their warmest G-string quality, which transforms the music at the central section of the long principal subject. This is in Elgar's familiar nobilmente style and is conducted with all due dignity, especially at the *ff* with its tenutos on the fourth beats, which are indeed held beyond their true value. Only in the 4th bar before **69** is the pattern changed so that the beat lifts the whole orchestra off, leaving, for an instant, only the 2nd and 3rd trumpets to be heard holding a unison semibreve with a rise and fall through to the end of the bar.

The horns and trombones then resume the last bars of the processional. Straightaway it seems most probable that they should diminuendo like the rest of the orchestra; Elgar himself did not insist on the printed text, though just possibly it was what he originally intended. This time the final semiquaver comes within a largamente, accordingly needing a little bounce to the beat, but the two bars briefly recalling the introduction end in a ritardando with the last crotchet subdivided. A codetta-like phrase in thirds then dominates the succeeding bars with so characteristic a style that the triplets at the end of each bar might presuppose an Elgarian rubato; but here the temptation should be avoided, the 1st harp still punctuating the funereal rhythm with spread chords on the second and fourth beats. The bar before **70** should reflect an interruption of mood rather than pace, the *sfp* on the second beat having a positive dramatic quality.

A ritardando bar, again ending with a subdivided beat, leads into the extremely *innig* section at 71, which is somewhat reminiscent of Bruckner, especially the violas' turn 4 before 72. This must on no account be hurried, the conductor shaping the phrase with them before turning to the 1st violins to encourage their richest tone.

Such growth in intensity carries with it a sharp gain in tempo; the più mosso at 73 is considerable, the 'sostenuto' referring more to the style of the simple crotchets after the elaborate figurations of the stringendo. The players should use the extreme lengths of their bows for the full three bars including the ritenuto, which is to be as pronounced as possible so that the *ppp* has a real element of surprise.

After such a long period of straightforward textures the complexity of fig. 74 is as strong a contrast as can be imagined, and the conductor's attention will be fully occupied in many directions simultaneously. The string divisions are taken at the desk, and all the filigree work including harps and trombones require maximum attention to detail, in order that the mass of varied dynamic marks and colouring may be clearly heard and differentiated.

This 6-bar passage of brilliant orchestration is then restated with the colours redistributed, so that the conducting is no less rewarding. The harps' triplets become semiquavers, and the 1st player's descending arpeggios are reversed and now ascend in order to penetrate the opaque mass of detail. The upper lines of violas and cellos are particularly interesting, the 1st violins having relegated their part in this affair to the lower instruments. The primary line set at 74 in the background then takes a forward place at 75 and can easily be featured without upsetting the balance. In the 3rd bar before 76 the trombones are often thought to have an error, their note being printed a quaver later than two bars previously, but there is no corresponding analogy after 84, which suggests that Elgar could have intended the slight variant.

The bar before 75 had merely turned the corner into the restatement, but this second time round it becomes a tremendous lead-in and has to be beaten in 8 real quavers. The swoop in violins and harps boils over into a huge new melodic outpouring scored most opulently, so that it is a temptation for the conductor to use over-extravagant gesturing; in the 2nd of 76, however, the half-bar must certainly be beaten out again in quavers for the strings' quick notes, which are taken off the string with strident articulation. The timpani semiquavers two bars later are also emphasized appropriately with the left fist, though this time a true subdivision does not arise.

With these exceptions the beating is in unproblematic crotchets, so that the Nobilmente e semplice will have no need to pull the tempo back, despite either the *ff* espressivo of the four horns, the sostenuto of the strings at the fourth bar, or the weighty counterpoint of the lower instruments reinforced by bass trombone and tuba in addition to all the bassoons and bass clarinet. It is a long climactic sentence and should be allowed on the contrary to move a little forward, so that the peaking return of the opening phrase at 77 can broaden once more for its swell to *ffz* in the second bar; for on its return during the reprise this will be the absolute high point of the entire movement, a structural element to be borne in mind even at this lesser apex.

The music now subsides totally to a return of the codetta-like motif passing through the orchestra with only a brief burst of emotion, as reserved in its handling as before at 70. From this nadir of expression a sequence builds up once more by means of *pp* pizzicato semiquavers in the lower strings offsetting the oboe triplets over two bars; there is no development section, and the course of the movement runs directly into a full-scale replay of the material from 67 onwards, although with considerable variation of textures. There should be no attempt to create a feeling of arrival at 79, which instead simply emerges from the quiet flow of the central bars without any further rubato.

The initial 8-bar stretch of the reprise corresponds very closely with its equivalent at 67, if on a more elaborate scale and with one major exception. The elaborations concern the persistence of the semiquaver pizzicato figures in the basses, reinforced only by the bassoons, together with a heavy pattern of slurred semiquavers on the second and fourth beats of each bar. As on the earlier occasion these are the main features to be stressed in conducting the impassive evocation of the processional.

On the other hand, the major exception lies in the extraordinary and freely meandering oboe solo which dominates the entire texture over all eight bars and ends on a prolonged high B♭, sustaining a poignant crescendo until 3 before 80, where it rises to B♮. This quite unusual idea has to be pinpointed not only in the orchestral balance but in the conductor's projection of mind and beat towards the oboist, whose voice is the only one stronger than *p*. The famous Dutch conductor Mengelberg used to make a habit of extending a pointed arm or finger at each wind player and for every solo, a somewhat disconcerting mannerism; but here such a directing of attention to a single instrument is not inappropriate.

The trombones take over the melodic line so firmly that the subito *ff* entry of the 1st violins and cellos doubled by upper woodwind at 80 needs an unusually powerful syncopated third beat. Through this inflated restatement of the central section of the principal subject, sight must not be lost of the basses, who are still pursuing their semiquaver pizzicato figure, although in the 3rd of 80, and again two bars later, there are moments where they miss their step, so to speak. As a result they need to be given particular (if half-whimsical) attention to prevent them from continuing the ostinato through the missing beats. The basses always enjoy such an *entretien* with the conductor here, and then make a splendid extra effort at the second re-entry which is arco as well as *ff*.

A short cut to the Brucknerian *ppp* transition music is effected by a sudden drawn-out 'R......' bar on the horns, showing that the composer means more by his use of these abbreviated symbols than the mere rubato they signified when he first introduced them; for this isolated bar is conducted in 8 with particular alertness to the sudden change in the accompanying figures, whose crotchet rest now becomes extended to two full quaver beats, with a real danger of accident. The semiquavers of the 2nd violins and violas are also unexpectedly steady and have to be pointedly controlled.

The section from 81 to 85 is virtually a direct reprise of 71 to 76, but this time the demisemiquavers in the bar of 85 itself immediately necessitate another half-bar of subdivision. Moreover, whereas the strings were previously spiccato, they now have tenuto lines, while the quaver beats have an additional function in marking out the chords of the two harps.

A further and highly dramatic change now occurs, for the long and powerful exposé of this mighty theme is greatly curtailed so that the massive Nobilmente turns instead into a considerable accelerando build-up, the timpani joining the lower voices in their counter-theme while the solo group of semiquavers is delayed for maximum emphasis until 86.

This is patently the climax of the movement, and there is a most moving suggestion of universal grief in the violins' melodic outpouring, with its marks of 'vibrato' and 'glissez' for the descending intervals in the *fff* molto espressivo. This style of evoking emotion by means of sliding with one finger between intervals is regarded today as sentimental and outdated, so that it is hard to persuade string players to observe the marks as positively as Elgar prescribed them. The sobbing effect is in fact a legitimate exaggeration and, though very much one of its time, should still be carried out with no fear of overstepping the level of permissible taste even with today's audiences.

The accelerando ceases to take further effect once 86 is reached, and the beauty of the climax is intensified by the semiquaver thickening of the background in the lower strings and the two harps. Little by little the intensity passes, and from the *pp* ritardando the passionate grief is over and with it the main body of the movement. Fig. 87 begins the coda in which a faint recall of the symphony's motto theme can just be heard on the clarinet if the *pppp* of the strings is faithfully observed. The two bars of Lento can be genuinely slow but without recourse to subdivision, perhaps ♩= 40.

Two bars before 88 the Quasi in tempo restores a brief memory of the codetta-like phrase with its woodwind triplets in thirds. Though naturally somewhat quicker than the Lento immediately preceding, the speed should suggest a distinct loss of momentum when compared with earlier appearances of this theme, and at 88 the 1st violins play a last descending version of the motto figure, now so de-energized that the group of triplets has to be measured out in a subdivided beat.

The sounds fade away to nothing. Suddenly the awesome hiatus is interrupted with a sforzando, initiating the increasingly soft string background figure to this last entry of the processional theme. The original basic tempo is resumed so that no further subdivision is needed, although the on-the-string semiquavers do need some demarcation within the beat. Where a breakdown of beating is unavoidable, however, is in the bar before 89, as well as the 2nd of 89, but only in these two bars.

The strings need a cautionary gesture in the bar before 89 exactly as in the similar change to quaver beats before 81; return has been made to the material of the movement's opening bars, but it is now greatly drawn out, with each quaver dwelt upon in the 2nd of 89.

The final steps of the funeral are not as slow as the term 'Lento' suggests, and the return to crotchet beats is an indication of this. The timpani mark the procession while the stick concentrates on the group entries: harps and bassoons, then harps and upper wind, followed by heavy brass and contra, the latter swelling to the new bar.

As they reach their *mf* the violins creep in; the second beat is a *fp* for the violas and cellos; the third is the top of the violins' swell, though a pale shadow of that of the trombones. The fourth beat takes the violins and brass off together while placing a last deep C on the harp and pizzicato basses. The final bar leaves a dying chord on a fermata in the violas and cellos even after the horns have been released with a third beat.

It is a complicated close to a complex movement, but one in which the sequence of gestures has to be clearly organized, or disaster can occur even at this eleventh hour when, on the contrary, a particularly moving effect is sought for so extremely solemn an occasion at the passing of an era.

III

The scherzo, or Rondo as the superscription on the score terms it, is one of Elgar's most successful quick movements and wants to be conducted with lightning speed and alertness, the periodic irregularities of the bar-phrasings adding to the fluid elusiveness of the structure. The mark of $\bullet$. = 108 is amply fast enough for Elgar's Presto, and yet gives the conductor time to shape the different phrase-lengths convincingly. This is relevant even from the very beginning of the movement, where the principal Rondo theme is in 4-bar phrases, because the theme itself is full of cross-stresses and syncopations, soft and shadowy as it has to be. All the downbeats will be springy therefore, and only 3 and 1 before 90 are strong bars, punctuated by the two harps, as again before 91; the second eight bars of the movement are then clearly conducted identically.

At 91 a running sequence follows in 7-bar phrases (3 + 4) as the little fragments chase up and down with a well-pointed subito *p* diminuendo on the descent. Here again the passage is repeated with intensified dynamics, more urgent string articulation, and additional colouring on harps and woodwind. The repeat sign back to the beginning is then mandatory, the brass entry on the second time needing a clear signal.

Regular 4-bar phrases return at **92**, the beat again being very springy for the continuous syncopated accompanying pattern, whether on strings for the return of the Rondo theme in the woodwind or on the trombones and bassoons for that in the upper strings. The four bars before **93**, however, lead into the subsidiary idea and are instead conducted with strong and incisive downbeats for the trombones' now punctual sforzandos and an especially powerful thrust in the last bar for the *ff* descent in the lower strings and woodwind into the change of key.

The strings' sonoramente at **93** must not be taken to allow for a broadening of tempo, but on the contrary should plunge ahead with the utmost energy. The ponderous tuba on the downbeat of each bar introduces another danger in this respect, and the syncopated horns and brass at **94** yet another. The trombones are especially liable to be late, to some extent on account of the trumpets, who, with upper woodwind, follow their syncopated chords a quaver later. It must be emphasized that these snaps have all to be short as well as punctual, controlled by beating of the utmost clarity and precision. The sforzando 3 before **95** then pulls the whole orchestra together, and the outburst collapses into an extended piano version of the motif, still however with offbeat short quavers in the middle strings and bassoons.

Piano retreats to pianissimo as the ostinato-like motif becomes the background to melodic ideas on the oboe, which must still preserve the momentum, while the bar-shapings now have to be followed with great alertness. Fig. **97** is a 6-bar phrase, and the lead into **98** a 3-bar extension of the continuing diminuendo, whose seven bars almost surreptitiously reintroduce fragments of the Rondo subject, whether on the wind or the middle strings. The wind, however, take this over canonically at **98**, and this should give a clear impression of the start of a new section, the phrases overlapping first in woodwind alone, then in strings and wind together before continuing with the elaboration of rising chromatic scales on the wind while a figure derived from the rondo motif is passed to and fro in the strings. It is extremely easy to lose count of these bars and find that the climax of 100 comes upon one sooner than expected; for this reason it is wise to pinpoint the 2nd bar of 99 as beginning a 3-bar crescendo, followed by four in forte, so that three diminuendo bars remain plus a sudden fourth bar surge into 100, the 2nd of 100 starting the new *ff* period.

Here the wide-spanned melodic line of the violins can be left to fend for itself while the beat concentrates on the cello/bass figures reinforced with lower wind, sparking them off in each alternate bar. In between, every second bar of the 8-bar period features a trombone lead which is thrown to them across the whole orchestra like a wizard hurling his spells.

The all-pervasive figure shown in Ex. 3 continues to dominate the beating, though keeping strict time through the climaxes and relaxations. The violas' and cellos' pizzicatos need to be emphasized; they are followed by the strings' sweep into 101 which brings another *ff* surge of lyricism. Even here the offbeat figure persists in the basses, bassoons, and tuba to whom a syncopated beat should always be addressed.

Ex. 3

A rising phrase on the violas marks a climax, after which the fervour subsides though not the tempo. Fig. 102 toys with the Rondo theme ever more forcefully until, after a 6-bar extended phrase corresponding with the highly charged *ff* lead-in at 93, the theme is restated in full orchestral colouring, the second syncopated bar of the phrase needing a strong offbeat thrust for the brass and harps.

The silent quaver rests at the 5th and 9th of 104 have to be very sharply indicated for the especially vivid tutti outbursts to which the descending chromatic semiquavers give brilliance in this textual variant. The 2nd trumpet, whose run is uniquely marked staccato, has to use double-tonguing at this tempo, but the trombones (marked with lines) should be able to avoid this.

The bar of 105 must be particularly dazzling with its rising arpeggio on 2nd violins (played on the string, starting and ending up-bow), woodwind, and harps, and is indicated with a cheerful flourish. This time the rising and falling sequences of little figures keep the 4-bar pattern, unlike their 3 + 4 at 91, which returns, however, before 106 when the idea is repeated with extreme rumbustiousness, acrobatic trombones and tuba reinforcing the cello/bass line.

This formal return of the Rondo subsides, by means of an introduction in the wind, to the central episode theme with its new and characteristic group of four semiquavers; it is accompanied by a ricochet pattern on the strings, which the beat has to control, as well as by the staccato quaver arpeggiandos, which are taken very lightly off the string. A word of caution is worth adding in respect of this motif: on account of the precipitate tempo, the note preceding the 4-semiquaver group often degenerates into a duplet quaver throughout. This weakens the phrase, as the first suggestion of a change of rhythm against the continuing triple pulse should come only with the spread-out semiquavers.

By 107 we are fully into the nub of the Rondo, having seemed to arrive there almost incidentally. This somewhat restrained central section consists primarily of long paragraphs, in slightly easier tempo, of sequences punctuated by pairs of ritardando or largamente bars, which for the first time in the movement interrupt the headlong flow. Here the 'R......' bars may be understood as amounting to gentle rubatos, whereas those of the 'L......' make substantial hold-ups.

After the episode motif has returned, 112 turns into the softest moment of all, though care must be taken that the tempo is kept at full pace so that after 113 the semiquaver runs up and down in woodwind and harps can scamper gaily across the string sequences. The surge to forte must still maintain the speed fully before another ritardando, this time three bars in length, returns to *pp* as the strings echo the clarinet. Then the last of the hold-ups is again of three bars, a largamente with a further sudden expressive rise to a full forte.

The rubatos past, two 6-bar periods send the central vignette receding into the far distance, giving way to the reprise of the Rondo with a violin figure recalling the lead-in to the second subject of the first movement (cf. 8 and 46), except that here it has no rallentando. All seems set fair now for a conventional restatement as the wind pick up the Rondo theme.

At first the fragments of wispy melody which drift along on the 2nd violins seem insignificant beneath the sharply articulated principal subject in the upper woodwind and then 1st violins; but gradually the repetitions of the 4-bar phrases become, on the contrary, pre-eminent. One in particular is curiously backed by three horns, whose independent rhythm in the fourth bar must be carefully identified without, as usual, holding the tempo in any way.

There are no fewer than six repetitions of this idea between 117 and 119, becoming stronger and more pulsated until the last group, which descends in intensity. Pizzicato chords on violas and cellos mark the pulses for a time with emphatic spread chords in the harps; then at 118 the arpeggiando cellos, now arco, add to the restlessness while wind and timpani start up a figure of triplet quavers.

In all this it should become apparent that there is a distinct relationship with the broad cello melody from the development of the first movement. The resemblance grows until at 119 it does indeed turn into that very melody, now sung out with long sustained bows by all the violins and cellos in octaves; the music has conveniently become transformed into $\frac{4}{4}$, four of the Rondo bars being joined together so that the conductor now beats in 4.

At first the throbbing background is *pp*, and the melody, for all its intensity, still only *p* espressivo, but this soon changes. Percussion is added to the quaver ostinato: first bass drum, then side drum and tambourine. The repetition of the theme is in a spectacular *ff* and is transferred to the united brass, trumpets ostentatiously joining trombones and tuba at 121. Elements of the Rondo join in, forming the elaborate background together with periodic references on the strings to the rising and falling octave theme (again from the first movement); and this is the one accompanying feature needing to be strenuously brought out in the conducting, which is otherwise wholly occupied by the now menacing quality of the massive tune, with the single exception of the mighty cymbal crash.

This must stand out as the absolute high point of drama of the work; indeed, an extra large 24-inch pair of cymbals is often brought in for just this one great clash. The effect as the player holds them outstretched should be nothing short of riveting.

As the terror passes and even the pulsating quavers fade out, the rising and falling octaves are gradually left, still clearly outlined in the beating, as the last remaining *pp* background sounds, before they too disappear leaving only sustaining horns, timpani, and basses. Here above all lies the temptation, yet again strenuously to be avoided, to relax the tempo, for the return has been most skilfully engineered without the need for any artificial manœuvring. The conductor's 4 in a bar becomes ever smaller until at the universal $\frac{3}{8}$ the same beats become whole bars as if nothing had happened, and without the slightest hint of their shaping into groups of four.

Tovey wrote highly imaginatively of this corner: 'It is always an interesting problem in aesthetics how, when a lively moment has mounted on to a sublime pedestal, it can come off it again. Elgar's solution of this dangerous problem is Schumannesque and classical. Without any preaching or tub-thumping the music resumes the first episode quietly, as Schumann's Florestan, or any other nice young undergraduate, might relight his pipe after he had allowed it to go out during an outburst of enthusiasm.'*

* *Essays in Musical Analysis*, ii (OUP, London, 1935), 119. There is an analogous place in the finale of Brahms's First Symphony, and a shortened reference to Tovey's happy description was made in my *Conducting Brahms* (Clarendon Press, Oxford, 1993). But this is undoubtedly the *locus classicus*.

The movement now resumes much as before, if with a few extra flashes of colour, such as the hilarious tuba solo at 123 and the sweeping upward woodwind scale, which certainly asks for a corresponding delineation in the conductor's gesturing.

Fig. 124 then corresponds closely with 95 until 6 before 126, when the bar-structure has to be carefully noted: this time there is a second 6-bar phrase leading to the change of key signature at the double bar, where previously there had been seven bars (4 + 3). The intrusive overlapping of the Rondo material is also more elaborate and confusing than the first time, and there are further structural elements which have to be kept firmly in the forefront of the mind. From 127 the dovetailed sequences form a 6-bar period, after which a rising 3-bar link carries the pattern to the now descending sequences over a further six bars in which, against the hurly-burly of fortissimo passage-work, the horn must be most carefully cued, even though his descending notes are only marked *mf*. This is a danger spot as his entry, coming at the upbeat to the second bar of the sentence, can feel misleadingly irregular.

At 128 the arrival point corresponding to 100 is extended by an entire phrase of eight bars in which the trombone snaps in every second bar need sharp left-hand indications, the stick emphasizing the cross-accented sforzandos of the strings and wind. The bar before 129 then restores both the unanimity in the orchestra and the relationship to the earlier context at 100; as at 123, the difference again lies in the increased intensity of the orchestral layout. The culminating passage for soaring trumpets at the 5th of 129 must be pinpointed in the conducting, as also the virtuoso cello writing over the whole twelve bars, in the last two of which the conductor turns to them for their slurred semiquavers with a suitably swaying gesture.

A major new idea is presented at 130, however, the whole orchestra dropping to pianissimo although the scoring remains full. The tempo eases at the brief return to *fff*, the cellos' arpeggiando semiquavers being the other way about.

A long quiet section follows this 3-bar 'L......', which is hard to restore to tempo. Nor is there any very positive injunction to do so: the piano dolce string interlude preceding the coda is meditative in character, and should only avoid falling too markedly below speed, especially at the solo passage for the cellos with brass background at 131. If the largamente is taken as no more than an *Ausholen*, continuity can easily be recovered without any impression of impatience.

The cellos too will have no need to be hurried, but can spread the phrase a little to the brief *mf* and back. This moment of poetic repose before the spectacular coda wants very sensitive and delicate treatment.

The movement springs back to life at 132 with most ingenious phrase-lengths which have to be shaped clearly, three 2-bar explosions of the Rondo opening answered by a 6-bar return of the previously 7-bar sequential row of short figures, but now three bars up and three down, followed by a repeat of the whole process.

Although there is no mark, a degree of animando is warrantable from here to the end. The cymbals are clashed in the little strokes before 134, after which a series of dramatic effects must follow hard upon each other's heels: tambourine (struck, not shaken); *fff* side drum, and whoops upon the horns; the con fuoco strings are also reinforced with a glissando on the two harps. The beat must press hard in delineating these effects, which pile up ever more vigorously with the four repeated crescendo bars before 135 (not five, it needs to be observed; the first is an upbeat bar).

At 135 the percussion notation in the score is misleading with its tails up and down (though the new Complete Edition score has been corrected). The downbeat is the cymbal stroke followed immediately by the bass drum on the second quaver, tutta forza. This must be clear in the direction, the brilliant woodwind descending chromatic scale coming after a syncopated lead at the second bar.

The concluding eight bars are not obvious, although they are in fact made up of two regular 4-bar phrases. The percussion enters at the second bar together with the hammered string and brass chords and ends on the ultimate quaver of the period after a crescendo. The last four bars begin deceptively with a powerfully syncopated beat giving the illusion of an upbeat, and the movement ends with a scrunch, again on the final bar of the phrase (not on the third as the passage is made to sound), an unusual and splendid subtlety to one of the most highly original and dazzlingly colourful movements ever written.

IV

After the hilarity and energy of the Rondo a pause is necessary before embarking on the serious Finale, whose grave, sombre mood is in the strongest possible contrast to that of the First Symphony. The structure is in regular 4-bar phrases, of which the first seven bars are repetitions of the opening motif, smoothly delivered by bassoons, horns, and cellos at an unhurried ♩ = 72. The linking eighth bar is hardly different from the others but makes capital of the syncopated accompaniment, so that a more springy beat-style is appropriate before the restatement of the quiet theme at 136 in its previous legato, now reinforced by *ppp* trombones and basses. The linking bar returns more briskly than before and enlivens the tempo a little so that the repetitious nature of the material is never allowed to become monotonous.

Fig. 137 places considerable emphasis on the third beats, the 2nd violins having the leading voice. After two bars trombones and trumpets emerge briefly from the background, and then the period is extended, the 4th of 137 being purely concerned with the four horns and the link passage, this time in yet another variant, occurring in the fifth bar. Here the harps need a very precise beat, as their phrases interlock with the upper wind.

The tempo continues to edge forward at 138, stimulated by the prancing staccato quavers in the cello/bass line, and the phrases derived from the opening plunge downwards full tilt into the second subject of 139. Here it is important to have increased the pace to at least ♩ = 88, lest this highly dignified music should tend towards pomposity, a danger not to be underestimated.

The continually rising intervals build upwards through the strings and woodwind in rich colourings so that the momentum grows ever more strongly until, after the big statement at 140, the martellato strings emphasized by accented quavers of the different horns are made as prominent as possible during the descending phrases. In the 8th of 140 the universal rest, whether quaver or semiquaver, is the sign to bring the orchestral tutti right off to prepare for the *ff* entry which follows.

Even this is not to be mistaken for a point of arrival, despite the weighty fortissimo triplet figures in the horns and trumpets. Unless positively contradicted, as at the Grandioso before 142, these sequentially repeating phrases of a single bar, much like the opening subject, must always be kept on the move, being one of Elgar's most characteristic constructional procedures. Here they are given natural impetus by the majestically ascending trombone crotchets and by the upward rushing string demisemiquavers leading into 141, where the pattern repeats.

The four bars before the Grandioso Largamente are the most strikingly cumulative and justify a forward thrust of tempo, as bar by bar the 1st and 2nd violins pile up their phrases with octave acciaccaturas to emphasize the insistence with which they step on each other's shoulders; the beats, freed from the emphatic 3-in-a-bar accents of the heavy brass, now stress only the first beats until the Grandioso itself, which, apart from being suddenly slower, lays the emphasis on the tenuto third beats once more.

The Nobilmente of 142 brings in the mightiest theme of the exposition. Reminiscent of *The Kingdom*, composed only a few years earlier, it has equally a dangerous air of the sanctimonious which is only avoided by not allowing it to become too slow and self-important, grandiloquent though it undoubtedly is.

A rescue operation in this respect must be perceived 5 bars before 143, where, instead of being ponderous, the expression should become fluid and flexible until the crest of the passage is reached 3 to 6 bars after 143, the climax being extended by way of the triplets in the horns and trombones followed by trumpets, and then the general *ff*, through to the sforzando. During this ultimate bar of ascent the tempo is broadened, and only with the third crotchet of the 6th of 143 is it allowed once again to flow forwards in the 8-bar descent to 144.

The upper cello line can be marvellously evocative as it leaps up with an acciaccatura before joining in the falling phrases. It is evident that all the front cello desks take part in this extra show of self-indulgence, the back desks' phrases being marked by the pizzicato basses.

At 144 the violins arrive up-bow for the quiet and reflective last exposition statement of the Nobilmente theme, and they play this with upside-down bowing for the G-string passage. This suits the third beat accent in the bar of 144 as well as the shape of the melody after the 1st violins have re-entered, starting again up-bow, and thus coming into line with the others. The lower strings and bassoons have an expressive bulge in the 3rd and 4th of 144 which, if made quite pronounced, will add to the general relaxation of tempo arriving at the più tranquillo, in which the cellos recall both speed and mood of the movement's opening theme while the violins and violas float upwards dreamily. Their crescendo should at first be only slight, becoming molto in just the single bar before 145.

The Poco animato initiates the development with an abrupt change of speed, the crotchet being at least 104 even though this will involve a good deal of highly virtuoso playing. The actual conducting is relatively uncomplicated, although the thematic elements to be controlled and juxtaposed are elaborate: in the first place comes the second subject, its energetically rising intervals turning into string figurations whose triplet semiquavers follow the sforzando attack and end with an ascending demisemiquaver swoop, always in 3-bar phrasings. This has to be portrayed in the beating, even while other elements are fighting for supremacy, such as the horn and trumpet quaver triplets, which are to be strongly accented in *ff* and require dramatic thrusts from the left hand in their 2-beat phrases. The cello/bass line is highly imaginative and so organized to keep the textures transparent, while the cello pizzicato 3 before **146** is also especially exciting if brought out vividly.

From **146** the different ideas are passed around the orchestra, and the beat-style has to emphasize the effect of this as the tension grows constantly with the brilliance of the writing. The trombones at **147**, the horns before **148**, and the brass snaps which highlight the exceptional vigour of the upper strings build up past the three-trumpet *fff* flash before **149** (given with a wave of the left hand) to the climax of the whole affair at **149**, where the tempo has even increased with the Con fuoco.

At this point Elgar made a dazzling revision, which he documented in his 1927 electrical gramophone recording, though it is not found in any edition of the printed score. The solo 1st trumpet at **149** holds his top C for a whole extra bar, continuing the crescendo throughout. The beat has to be much sharper and more militant here for the *ff* staccato return of the opening motif with its hammered brass and timpani.

From this high point the development gradually subsides, the beat also little by little losing its angularity after **150** as the theme becomes increasingly legato. By **152** the tempo will have calmed from the $\goodbreak$ = 104 of the development's beginning at **145** to the original $\goodbreak$ = 72, though here with a processional character. The two harps are integral to this, and within a few bars soft percussion, in the form of side drum, cymbals, and bass drum, are added for the first time in the movement.

Here, at 153, the original subject re-enters and combines with the procession, its legato character restored and at first always stronger than the new motif, although the latter grows imperceptibly until both are equally forte or, indeed, fortissimo at 154. The subsidiary part of the development section has now reached its peak, and pizzicato cellos with bassoons add a semiquaver ostinato figure, greatly reminiscent of the 'Marche au supplice' from Berlioz's *Symphonie fantastique*, which can be brought to the foreground. After 155 this dies out, and with it any necessity for such severe control over tempo.

A stepwise ascending cor anglais solo can be allowed to move forward, and the cello/bass references are once again jagged, so that 156 is actually, as so often in this symphony, a little faster for the last fading memory of the procession, percussion, harps and all, reaching perhaps $\bullet = 84$.

The poco a poco rit. then takes nine bars to return most subtly to the tempo primo of 157, where the reprise creeps in surreptitiously, only the cello/bass swell and the cessation of the timpani in the bar before 157 revealing what is about to happen. Indeed, so gradual has been the transition that there is nothing incongruous in the 3-bar intrusion of the procession, still with harps and percussion, always in combination with the first subject and both rising momentarily to forte; but by 158 it has gone, never to return.

The reprise is regular and brings few surprises. The downhill run into the second subject at 160 moves foward even more perceptibly than at 139, a further difference being in the highly arresting syncopated chords in the first three bars of 160, which completely take over the interest in the beating in lieu of the second subject on fortissimo horns and lower strings.

Subsequent variants in the reprise's treatment of the second subject material may be minor but are amply worth noticing. The accented quavers as at 140 are again martellato but this time both in strings and in the four alternating horns. At 162 the agitated 1st violin semiquavers do not correspond with the bars after 141, and the *ff* climax lacks the 'L...... Grandioso' indication. Important as it is, with the omission of the 'Nobilmente' of 142 on its return at 163, the pounding brass, harps, and timpani are actually the more significant in this rewriting of the section. In addition, the upward surging from a reduced dynamic at 164 makes a greater effect than in the brief rise to 143.

There is an *Ausholen* into 165 for the horns' evocative triplet, but as before this is not the objective, as is manifested by the tutta forza semiquavers of the 2nd violins and violas, which are to be played with the full length of their bows. The *Ausholen* is often taken a bar later by analogy with 143, but the two passages do not precisely correspond, and here this disturbs the impetus of the already established semiquavers.

The brass then have two more such climaxes at the 6th and 8th bars of 165, and care should be taken to honour principally the 2nd, where the cellos leap into unison for the *ff* sostenuto. By this time the semiquavers have double strokes as well as being joined by the 2nd harp, and are less obstructed by the pull-back into this ultimate upheaval, which has to acquire a tremendous breadth for the ringing trumpets.

This is all a vastly inflated version of the exposition high point of 143–4 and is therefore given a much longer period of unwinding than had been necessary in the earlier context. The final statement of the second subject is elaborated at 166, the 2nd harp needing sharply syncopated third beats in each of the three bars and the antiphonal phrases of the 1st and 2nd violins being dwelt upon with great tenderness, especially the tenuto on the lower strings during the ritenuto.

At 167 the drama is essentially over and the linking tranquillo, in which the pianissimo return of the opening subject is again set against upward floating violins, now leads to the deeply poetic epilogue. Here the two harps are particularly in evidence, decorating the wistful memory of the melodic fragment from the very first bars of the symphony. This comes twice with varied but always elaborate orchestral trellis-work in which the divided strings play a prominent part together with the harps, who are virtually concertante. The tempo remains unvaried, and the conductor's primary responsibility lies in sensitive handling of the exceptionally beautiful colouring, which stands out among all Elgar's orchestral work. In this respect the crescendo of the oboes and clarinets in the bar before **169** is not to be joined by the horns, although they are playing the same line. Dynamically these must follow the flutes and heavy brass if the strings are not to be totally covered.

In the 5th of **169** particular attention should be drawn to the semiquavers of the 1st harp and 2nd violins, after which the ascending passage in flute and clarinet leads to one further reminiscence of the yearning melody, still with soft but important touches of the harps, which the conductor's left hand can continue to pick out. Now the tempo has at last slackened, and it continues to do so even more as the più lento gives way to molto lento.

The second subject is recalled once more, followed at **171** by the opening motif on the cellos, for which tempo is momentarily resumed yet again with the upward floating violins, all in pianissimo and guided more by delicate hand movements than by conventional beating. This subject in particular has a new and final twist, arriving at the series of thought-provoking chords which close the symphony. The *fp* at the 5th of **171** has a poignance which should be conveyed by a heavy stress in the downbeat followed by a general drop preparing for the entry of the trombones, who then lead the orchestra towards the ultimate fortissimo. Except in the last bar of all, there is no fermata sign, but nevertheless the chords are held strictly counted but unbeaten. Elgar made another minor revision in the very last bars which never reached the score: the cellos divide as they change to up-bow, with the insertion of a B♭ below their E♭ in line with the 1st bassoon.

The upbeat semiquaver four bars from the end has to be bounced in with a distinct gesture, after which the long diminuendo is measured by the two chords of the harps as well as by the release of different instruments on each beat of the final bar. Thus the actual lunga fermata comes on the second as well as the third beat, in which only the strings, flutes, bassoons, and horns remain for the ultimate die-away, making a most affecting and well-constructed close to an exceptionally large-scale work that can well be regarded as one of Elgar's greatest and most profound scores.

Violin Concerto in B minor, Op. 61

◆▶

OF Elgar's two concertos the first is a large-scale work for violin, composed in 1909–10, when he was at the height of his powers. The second, for cello, was written at the end of his creative career, and though more intimate and in some ways less substantial, it has in latter years far outstripped the Violin Concerto in popularity.

Written for Fritz Kreisler, who gave the first performance and often played it thereafter (though he sadly never recorded it), the Violin Concerto lasts a full 50 minutes, so that its stature rivals the Beethoven and the Brahms. The orchestration is surprisingly modest, using only double wind plus contra, and full brass but no percussion other than timpani.

The outstanding feature of the work is the lengthy 'Cadenza (accompagnata)' which occurs towards the end of the last movement and is far from easy to negotiate. Ample time has therefore to be allowed for this final portion of the work just when one seems to be approaching the end of the rehearsal; nevertheless it is not the custom to start with the last movement on that account.

Though the dedication is indeed to Kreisler, there stands at the head of the score one of Elgar's enigmas in the form of an inscription, curiously enough in Spanish: 'Aquí está encerrada el alma de . . .' (Herein is enshrined the soul of . . .), a transcription of a passage from *Gil Blas* by the eighteenth-century French novelist Lesage where, however, the enshrined soul is that of one Pedro Garcias. In leaving the ownership of the soul blank Elgar once again presents a conundrum; none of his works is so personal as this, and in the cantata *The Music Makers*, composed soon after, there is a most wistful and touching recollection of the slow movement, implying that it may well have been his own soul which is here portrayed, had he thought it proper to be so explicit.

The work opens with a full-scale ritornello announcing the principal theme. The score marks it Allegro ♩ = 100, but, as so often with Elgar, the beating is not quite straightforward, the tempo being extremely flexible and the expression fluid. It begins broadly but moves forward already at the third bar to a vivacious tempo of not less than ♩ = 112, which remains the basic speed of much of the movement except in particular the areas around the second subject.

The energy generated at fig. 1 develops into an outright stringendo leading to an abrupt return at 2 of the original Allegro ♩ = 100 for the subsidiary principal subject, whose warm lyricism is offset by the rhythmic figure on the horns. That the pace must not be faster is confirmed by the triplet quavers at 3, which need to be delivered in cantabile style so that the little trills contribute without being hurried.

Three bars of urgent expression are counteracted by the allargando into 4, where the second subject is introduced in the lower strings, still within the original tempo. However, the withdrawal into the meditative repeat, more in its natural vein, produces a relaxed tempo of ♩ = 80 which also works well for the elaborate after-phrases of 5 with their demisemiquaver turns.

The stringendo before 6 restores energy with pronounced sforzandos at the beginning of each bar but subsides into 6 itself, where the secondary principal subject is used to stir up an affrettando capped by imperious descending crotchets in the brass. The last section of the ritornello should be driven with considerable energy, partly for the strings' counterphrase but especially for the swooping horns, who anticipate the tutti style of the Second Symphony. At fig. 8, in a majestic *ff*, the beat can encourage the alternating figures of the lower voices which, with a palpable sense of effort, bring the whole orchestral introduction to a triumphant climax.

The exhilaration of fig. 8 has of course increased the pace yet again, so that the ultimate return of the opening subject justifies the Come prima, followed by the molto largamente for the noble enunciation, long awaited, of the solo violin, the orchestra receding into a background trough of complete stillness. The clarinet has to be nursed round the 2nd of 9 in sympathy with the ending of the soloist's first phrase, which is then crowned with a chord on trombones, timpani, and tremolo cellos, all *ppp* with a meaningful swell. When this swell has died away the soloist is at last ready to start his rhapsodizing.

The conductor has throughout had to show the utmost flexibility with the constant changes of tempo, but this has been as nothing to the continual variations in flow which abound henceforward. The solo line is marked 'quasi Recit.', and soloists indulge this to the full, calling for alertness from the stick whether in holding up the strings' note-changes or in moving suddenly forward for a single bar, as when the violas insert a thematic reference marked, perhaps misleadingly, 'a tempo più lento'.

The two bars before 10 accelerate dramatically up to the *mf* staccato quaver and the entry of the horns, but equally suddenly the cello/bass crotchets are to be held back, as again two bars later, and still more in the poco largamente. The a tempo should still not be too slow, even though the soloist is singing out the subsidiary principal theme; he will not wish to be held up by the pianissimo violas and cellos, who merely float along.

With the bassoons' entry at the upbeat to 11 the roles are reversed and the same melody is now on the tutti, though kept very discreet and always subordinate to the commanding rhetoric of the soloist. But the orchestra takes the lead at 12, and a to-and-fro is set in motion in alternate bars. The accompaniment develops into a syncopated pattern which will be reflected in the beating, but this is interrupted for the downward swoops, first by the soloist, then in a show of brilliance by the clarinet leading to a short-lived, thoughtful solo reminiscent of the First Symphony, composed barely a year earlier.

A rapid passage, apt to catch the conductor unawares, brings the procedure round a second time, until the soloist takes a more extrovert part at **15**, with long-running scales having to be caught both on the half-beats at the bottom as well as in each new bar at the top. The pulse continues to change in every bar, the conductor aiming to restore movement whenever possible, such as 4 before **16**, where the quaver passage-work in the lower strings needs an element of vitality.

At last the second subject is reached at **16** and overall calm prevails. Only strings are involved from here to **19**, making the conductor's task less complicated in following the continuing waywardness of the solo line. Twice the illusion is given that a true resumption of steady tempo is about to be restored: the first time at the quaver pulsing of **17**, and again at the poco più mosso 4 before **18**, but in the end it is only with the appearance of the first subject at **19** that a suggestion of flow can be re-established, though still not without interruptions. The colla parte 5 before **20** is the most considerable of these, with a fermata over the first beat which concerns the 1st violins together with the soloist. The stick sets both in motion with the second beat, although the remainder of the bar still needs careful negotiation, especially in the free shaping of the last two semiquavers.

With the horns as genial companions, the solo violin strides forward at a steady, flowing pace which builds with a degree of momentum, though in the two bars before **20** the florid solo part may need a little extra time. The animato then carries the music through to the Tempo primo of 2 before **21**, which starts the long and exciting closing section of the exposition. Here there are no further hold-ups or rubatos, the soloist forging ahead in brilliant style until only the last bar before **23**, where each beat has to be emphatically placed for the closing exposition chords.

There follows a strong orchestral ritornello in classical manner, the conductor taking full control. Although starting in the original Allegro, this should press forward dramatically already in the fourth bar, justified by the 'con passione' in the tempo marking. This section constitutes the single extensive orchestral passage in the concerto, and much should be made of it. As so often in Elgar, the energy is transmitted by a series of sforzando second and fourth beats culminating in a heroic development of the originally gentle and lyrical second subject.

From the 5th of 24 as far as 26 the strepitoso uses all Elgar's most vivid devices to pile on the excitement with only a 4-bar interruption at 25, where the theme of the second subject pulls back the feverish intensity for a brief largamente brought into effect with long wide beats. At the animato, however, the beating is both rhythmic and intensely vivacious.

The addition of trumpets and timpani to the vehement syncopations heralds the ending of the ritornello, and the utmost weight can be given to the sledgehammer second and fourth beats at 26 which announce the opening subject's return, to be accomplished in the next two bars during the ritardando to Tempo primo.

This time, the long-awaited appearance of the soloist combines the principal theme with the subsidiary motif on four muted horns, settling on a fermata at the 5th of 27. Here the first beat is composite, with two pauses for the strings, one on their quaver (controlled by the conductor) and another after they have been taken off, so that the clarinet must still not enter until the soloist has begun to move very slowly onto his triplet quavers. This is quite a complicated manœuvre and may need explanation to an orchestra unfamiliar with the work.

Similarly, at the rit. into 2 before 28 the 2nd violins and clarinet must be prepared to linger for the soloist, while at the downbeat the stick will actually come to rest, the new phrase beginning once again on the triplet quaver. The rit.

then has the effect of another fermata before it subsides into the *ppp* at 28.

Against the soloist's triplet-quaver figurations, the cellos are encouraged in their highly expressive counter-melody and need to be guided round their demisemiquaver turn before the horn (unmuted, though the indication is lacking) is given his cue. A sharp third beat brings in the staccato clarinets, and the sequence of events is repeated; this time the horn solo continues for an extra bar into the lento, during which the strings are left alone once more in *ppp* for the soloist's great outburst of passion, the conductor merely placing the half-bar chord-changes.

The rubato merges into the secondary main melody, again marked 'Lento' but also 'in tempo', the actual speed being monitored by the quietly flowing triplet quavers in the 1st violins and lower strings. This is a meditative section, and when, at 30, the roles are reversed it takes eight bars for the animato and the restless semiquavers to bring back the surging intensity of the earlier part of the movement, 31 transpiring to be directly analogous with fig. 12 of the exposition; the development, so short and ruminative, is already over.

Until just before 34 the reprise broadly follows the earlier course of events, but then Elgar interposes an agitated build-up unlike the quietly romantic bars before 16. In fact the treatment of the second subject at this reprise is at a high-pitched level of intensity during which it is possible to overload the soloist, especially during his double-octaves passage before 36.

The fermata at the 2nd of 36 should not be over-long, the cellos' resolution to D in the lento bar being the signal for the soloist to round off this last recall of the melody and reintroduce the first subject, followed by its subsidiary, in another quick build-up of passion; the restoration of energy is markedly more violent and continuous than had been the case in the bars around 20. Indeed, the passage starting at fig. 38, with its use of trombones and horns, is highly dramatic and should be kept at a vigorous pulse until **39**, where a 2-bar broadening for the soloist's appassionato forms a bridge into the resumption of the reprise, now directly analogous with 2 before **21**.

This was, and is again, the closing section of the movement's main exposition. Here it is repeated virtually unaltered until **41**, where the second subject's opening bar is used to build up a huge edifice culminating in a fermata on the fourth beat, the strings being instructed to use two bows so that they will inevitably overwhelm the soloist, even though he continues into the climax.

The two bars of *ff* tutti want a tempo of at least ♩ = 112, with a bouncing beat for the violas when the soloist interrupts. At the 3rd of **42** the half-bars are pointed with extravagantly sharp emphases for the strings' *f* pizzicatos as well as for the horns' and woodwind figures, which, though starting piano, have to be very striking. The soloist needs no attention as he drives on at full tilt in double-stoppings, semiquaver passage-work, arpeggios rising to the top of his compass, and so on, all demanding no more than sharp half-bar emphases.

Three bars before **44** the solo violin is on its own except for downbeat woodwind chords; the pace lessens a little but picks up positively at **44**, where the accents change from half-bars to every beat, the tempo continuing to press on until the last crotchet before the colla parte, where there is a pronounced hold-up. For two bars the opening of the main theme carefully spaces out the background for the soloist's rising double-stopped enunciations before he again careers forward on his own, the conductor merely holding a sustained C♯ which descends to *pp* and then grows. There is no beating during this long projected tone until, at the 10th bar of **44**, the soloist responds to the molto largamente and the moment arrives for strong indications on the third beat (lower strings) and fourth beat (woodwind).

Then the soloist is away yet again, with all the strings hastening to stay with him. At the third bar of the a tempo a quaver figuration in the accompaniment demands a sharply syncopated beat until the last crotchet sforzato. On the soloist's arrival at his top B the full orchestra has to burst in with the utmost forcefulness until, against a sudden drop to *pp* on the brass, the violin seizes the foreground for the last time, taking the vehemence through to the conclusion. There is no mark in the score for a final pull-up, but in practice the quavers in the third-last bar are enunciated within the beat together with those of the soloist, and the two concluding chords are paced with great weight even if kept near to full tempo.

II

After such a grand, extended symphonic structure there will of necessity be a hiatus before continuing, during which the clarinets change to their B flat instruments. This central slow movement is the spiritual heart of the concerto, more even than the famous cadenza.

A particularly dangerous feature of the Andante is its propensity for becoming too static amongst the many fermatas and hold-ups of various kinds. It is, moreover, a perfect object lesson in flexibility of beating, the 'Andante' indication itself, and especially the metronome mark $\quarternote = 52$, being the merest half-truths.

The soloist indicating that he is ready, the conductor starts the opening theme, which must not be too slow although its essentially introspective character will always tend to dominate the music. The quaver phrases must flow towards the crotchets, which are held tenuto, this shaping being adopted each time and leading to the wind chords which act as markers to the sentences.

The fifth bar is appreciably quicker, although handled in the same manner, but the sixth is already steadier again so that the initial calm is restored at the a tempo in preparation for the soloist's entry. As he joins the texture, the strings drop to a hushed pianissimo, allowing his tone to take priority. The third pair of bars presses forward and back with the soloist exactly as before, after which a last statement of the melody sends the violin wistfully aloft against a succession of imitative phrases ending with a muted horn.

The strings now introduce a new motif in which the tenutos on the fourth beats lead to a ritenuto and *pp* subito. The reserved quality of this theme calls for a pulsing all of its own, and the 'a tempo' marking has hardly any relevance. At the 4th of 47 an eloquent new phrase on the solo violin is ushered in by a *ppp* chord on wind and timpani, whose swells, independent of that of the soloist, need sensitive handling. At the same time a subsidiary role is always maintained with respect to the placing of the chords, so that the cellos' phrase, in particular, needs sympathetic control during the rit. The strings take over at 48 for a repeat of their rubato theme with its tenutos and an even softer *ppp* subito just before 49.

The a tempo at 49 corresponds with the colla parte 2 before 48 except that, with the triplet figurations in the violas, the tempo is kept moving, even leading to an animato. The rit. into 50 is only marginal, and the whole passage leads to a short but full-blooded tutti, the first of the movement. The new theme appearing here has the peculiarity of a unison turn notated in demisemiquavers for the orchestra but by the conventional symbol for the soloist; patently the latter is merely an abbreviation for the former, and there can be no question of any difference in intention.

Within two bars the soloist re-establishes his supremacy in a strongly evocative passage which builds to a brief fermata. Here the trombones are quickly cleared to allow a little time for a perceptible crescendo in the wind before the music returns to the opening melody once more in its original tempo.

After only a single phrase, however, a scurrying chromatic scale carries the violin up to the next motif at 52, the conductor's role being purely one of background accompaniment throughout. This is the central section of the movement, and it consistently shows the greatest degree of animation and colour with its string tremolos and timpani rolls in alternate bars. The soloist decorates the melody given to the oboe and thereby controls the tempo, which is more positive and flowing than hitherto.

In the molto allargando before 53 a subdivision is necessary for the wind's two pronounced forte quavers which join the top notes following the soloist's demisemiquaver ascending run. In the 2nd of 53 the three accented quavers, marked with strong timpani strokes, also need vigorous quaver subdivisions after what has been a powerful if terse period of tutti writing.

Once again the orchestra retreats to a hushed pianissimo, but the solo violin is projecting in a rich enough timbre to allow imaginative touches of scoring to make their point, from the placing of exquisite bassoons in thirds to the horns' soli swell and the slight, but supporting, crescendo in the strings. Though suddenly carrying the sostenuto melodic line at the Nobilmente, these should begin discreetly, making allowance for the soloist's demisemiquavers, but with a surging crescendo they will start to overtake him in importance. At the beginning of the new bar the orchestral re-entry should expect to be held up for the strongly evocative triplet figure, but it then plunges into a commanding fortissimo. This soon deflates, however, the soloist emerging accompanied by a horn solo whose double-dotted descending figure is shortly to return as a prominent repeating feature.

The climax occurs at 56 with a considerable, but again brief, orchestral outburst, after which the horn solo, with its descending motif repeated three times, gently brings the intensity down to the reprise. In the last bar the orchestra has a composite fourth beat, both quavers being sustained while the soloist holds. This is an affecting return in **ppp** and must be allowed to take its time as the violin guides the music back to the opening melody.

The sequence of events from 57 to 61 broadly follows that of the exposition from 45, with fig. 59 corresponding to 47 although the horn solo upbeat is embellished with a fermata swell which has to wait for the delayed fermata in the solo line as this soars to his D♭ *in alt*.

Fig. 61 starts the coda, with a sparkling woodwind passage at the fourth bar calling for a light, almost giocoso, beat style. The horn's descending octave makes a last reappearance as the soloist lingers ad lib., the music becoming softer and softer. After a brief recovery of tempo at 62 an ascending scale on clarinet and bassoon restores the tranquillity, and their last four quavers into 63 are beaten out.

The remainder of the movement is profoundly thoughtful and drawn-out. The cellos' *mf* pizzicato in the bar of 63 has a certain shock quality, and so, to a lesser extent, does that in the following bar. The two pauses over the quavers are then beaten out and judged for length before the soloist continues.

There is a strong flavour of *envoi* at 64 (the second bar being given four quaver beats during the rit. with its two pauses), and the return of the theme with the demi-semiquaver turn is most tenderly phrased. Yet one more reminiscence of an earlier theme contains a lunga fermata, and only in the last three bars do we reach the final resolution.

So many degrees of lento, with colla partes and fermatas, have there been in this coda that when the end is at last reached the conductor has to compensate to some degree, however subtly. The woodwind chords in the third-last bar move gently but firmly, the flutes and horns make their poco crescendo without losing time against the slow spread of the violins' and violas' triple-stopped pizzicato, and the subito *ppp* clarinets and bassoons in the final bar are not held over-long, always being gauged with an eye to the soloist's bow, before the strings alone are left supporting him as he dies away.

III

The clarinets again have to change instruments, but more hastily than before as the last movement should follow without too much delay if the audience's concentration is to be held. Marked 'Allegro molto' at ♩ = *c.*138, it begins as if it is to be a really lively successor to the previous long-breathed movements, but the quick tempo is short-lived and recurs only sporadically.

Only the first, introductory, bar is beaten in full, after which the events are merely marked as they happen. The entry of the soloist is pointed by the double bass pizzicato, and regular beating then ceases until the clarinet crotchets in the third bar and the strings' 4 : 1 at the end of their phrase. A succession of 4 : 1's, alternately *ff* and *p*, follows, the beats in between not being given at all; after **65** these brusque interjections are gradually extended until the crotchets are continuous and begin to broaden. They become so emphatic that, as **66** approaches, they turn more and more into sideways slashes, and the last is taken right off before the strong syncopated downbeats of **66** and the bar after. The soloist fills in the beats between with virtuoso passages at a much steadier rate while the horns are bounced in and almost immediately taken off in preparation for the next upbeat.

At the 3rd of **66** the rhythm of the soloist's elaborate double-stopping passage has to be caught for the accompanying string syncopations, but 2 before **67** the background changes to an anticipatory preview of a strong motif not otherwise due until just before **71**, while at **67** the pattern (and speed) of the solo line changes totally. The score shows the a tempo at the new pattern of continuous semiquavers 3 before **68**, and this indubitably gives it an attractive scurrying quality, but in the solo copy it is marked already at **67**, with a further poco allargando two bars earlier; conductors need to be warned, therefore, that soloists not unnaturally tend to obey the injunction of their own copy.

The *ff* chords of **68** are immensely energetic, the Allegro pace having splendidly recovered since **67**. A little upward sweep is then important in handing over the tutti to the soloist while the accompaniment semiquavers, though pianissimo, anticipate the battle scene from *Falstaff*, where similar figures are played spectacularly by trombones. The idea passes to the soloist and leads to another mighty tutti articulated with consecutive down-bows, which must indeed be observed for the 1st violin chords to be sufficiently truncated.

This one genuinely vivace section of the finale now slows up for the theme, which has already been suggested in accompaniment but now finds its proper location and is handled alternately by tutti and soloist. At **71** itself, however, the orchestra takes the initiative and can be given its head at a more stately pace which will accommodate the elaborate fortissimo figurations.

Suddenly a quick, almost violent cadence reintroduces the soloist, who careers upwards with precipitous scales which, not being beaten through, have to be caught at the top. The oboe must just be heard between the Brahmsian solo phrases, hinting at the second subject, which, after two fermatas in a subdivided beat, appears in full at **73** at a markedly slower tempo, the rhapsodic side of Elgar taking over once more.

At **75** there is a brief altercation between orchestra and soloist in which the wind's forte phrase is answered by a most evocative drop to pianissimo in the strings. This leads at **76** to a lengthy discourse, the second subject being pursued in the orchestra against syncopated semiquaver passage-work which has to be implicitly followed by the conductor in all its elaborations even though it is the orchestra who has the melody. It is therefore particularly worthwhile to have sorted out at **77** the few beats with which the accented octaves coincide, that is, beats 2, 1, and 4 in each pair of bars.

The passage reaches its conclusion at **78**, where the solo violin phrases from **72** return, this time even more reminiscent of the Brahms concerto, punctuated by snap first and third beats marked 'allargando', so that much foresight has to be exercised over the placing of the snap in the middle of the bar. The tutti a tempo is then played at full speed, the soloist fitting in at the third beat. This sequence is repeated; in the bar before 79, corresponding to the 2nd of 78 the a tempo preceding the poco rit. is missing, but although there is little time for so rapid a change of pulse, confirmation can be found for it in the bar before 93, even if the passages are not quite identical.

The four bars between 80 and 81 would seem to suggest a calando, but this would be a mistake as the passage leads directly into the reprise (there being no development at this juncture), and an accelerando quickly takes the tempo back to the initial Allegro molto.

From this point the course of events is broadly the same as from the opening of the movement as far as 79 but with some significant variations, such as the complete cut-off at 82. The solo violin precipitoso, continuing to the very brink, makes for a quite different situation from the molto allargando into 66, even though the music which follows is essentially the same as before.

The background anticipatory reference to the strong figure of 71 is naturally omitted, and it is interesting that the passage corresponding to 67 is now a colla parte, the soloist being marked with considerable rubatos before the abrupt change to a precipitous a tempo at 83, relating to the previous passage 3 before 68.

In the brief tutti which follows, the scurrying semiquavers are now transferred to the upper strings with a plethora of flats, while the solo violin tries to emulate the effect of the tutti with con forza triple stoppings entirely unaccompanied and pointedly not beaten. Even the barlines have no need to be marked, the soloist taking his own time with much bravura and the conductor and orchestra plunging in at the a tempo vivace *ff* without even a preparatory downbeat.

Fig. 85 corresponds with 69 except for the short cut to the maestoso theme of 71 now effected by a brilliant solo violin excursion, via the quintuplet semiquaver groups of the opening bars, all the way up to his very highest E. The violins join him on the fermata, growing to a huge elaboration of the tutti at 71 and ending with the same abruptly rapid cadence as had led into 72.

The second subject follows as before, 88 to 93 running essentially parallel with 73 to 79. But here a major change occurs, for the gentle più tranquillo of 79 turns into a vast, but brief, largamente followed by a subito a tempo in which the powerful figure at 93 gradually dies down. The solo violin's ascending trills are bridged to the coda by horns in octaves, and these must be given ample time at such a significant moment, though there is no indication in the score.

'Tempo I (Allegro) Nobilmente' is hardly an adequate direction for what initially takes place in the coda; for here comes a substantial reference to one of the more important motifs from the slow movement, transcribed into doubled notation and accordingly beaten in 2 at a stately tempo, though gathering momentum after 95. Its thematic sequence reaches a climax at 96, where the second bar develops a strong rhythmic answer requiring a subdivided half bar for the 2nd violins and wind.

This happens four times, the last subdivision adding trombones and a pizzicato for the violins before suddenly changing back into a beat of 4 crotchets; the rapid semiquavers in the strings from earlier in the finale return with the sequential theme which they have accompanied all along.

The quick crotchet tempo broadens again at 98 for the theme of 71, which soon leads to a virtuoso exhibition for the soloist in double-stopping while the lower strings hold semibreves. Here they need no beat, but the passage gives way to a substantial orchestral descending tutti in which the same theme from 71 is repeated many times to prepare for the cadenza, the rising interval of a minor second imperceptibly coming to the foreground in order to turn into the opening notes of the concerto's primary theme.

A fermata on a muted horn links into the cadenza in which the disentangling of the beats is so involved that it will be necessary to go into greater detail than usual. In the first place it is well to establish throughout this extra-ordinarily complicated accompaniment that the divisi upper and lower lines of strings are best effected by desks and not at the desk.

The cadenza accompagnata is unconventional not only in its formal placing near the end of the finale, but in its function of meditation rather than the brilliance and exhibitionism of most concerto cadenzas. It begins with two bars of the theme from the first movement on the strings, answered by the soloist with the subsidiary first subject of the same move-ment. All these recollections of earlier material are played ruminatively by orchestra and soloist alike, and the violin soon comes to rest on a fermata with an air of expectancy.

The 1st beat of 102 then starts the famous thrumming tremolo, whose execution is explained in a footnote. Not hard to produce, it has, perhaps curiously, set no precedent either for Elgar himself or for subsequent composers.

There are four spaced beats placed out of tempo in the bar of 102, the 1st establishing the background for the soloist's rising flourish, somewhat in the manner of Vaughan Williams's *Lark Ascending*. A second flourish, rising in the same way but less rapidly, begins just before the laying down of the 2nd beat, this changing the setting of the thrummed chord in the accompaniment, the cellos ceasing briefly.

The 3rd beat is placed together with the soloist's last high fermata C♮, releasing the 1st violins and reintroducing the lower line of cellos. The 4th beat is planted just before the soloist's last fermata of the bar and brings back the lower line of 1st violins as well as changing the chord structure of the other players; the 2nd violins are also signed off.

The conductor now has to watch the soloist assiduously as the next bar starts together with him, the 1st beat making a crescendo from piano to reach forte on the 2nd, which also coincides with the soloist's second high note of his row of figures. The upper lines of all the strings, which have entered at the beginning of the bar, come off dramatically at this forte 2nd beat. The Più mosso does not relate to the orchestra at all, and can thereby cause confusion or misunderstanding.

The 3rd beat falls with the low G♯ after the fifth of these figures. Despite the rit. marked in the solo line it is necessary to be very much on the alert, as this G♯ is apt to come suddenly and the changes of thrummings are substantial, all the players except the lower lines of violas and cellos stopping and even these few changing their chords. The 4th beat is also perilous as it comes unexpectedly soon during the soloist's rising phrase, though not together with any particular note. It also brings the violas off but ushers in the lower line of basses, who have so far not taken part at all. They are to play very softly, and their pause is surprisingly short, the second-line players of the violins and violas, as well as the horns, having to be alerted for the next bars.

These are virtually in tempo, only the chord resolutions needing to be indicated. They are therefore much simpler to shape, as is also the 3rd bar before 103, which brings in all the basses for the first time. The upper lines of all the string departments now play without tremolo, and this must not lead to the resolution at the 3rd beat being delayed. An eye is kept on the soloist's bow, so that all the players can be taken off in good time for his next phrase.

This bar, 2 before 103, is more hazardous than it appears at first sight. If the 1st beat has cleared the string chord with a quaver overlap for the upper lines, there is then no 2nd beat, nor is there time for one as the soloist passes quickly through his quavers before arriving at his E. The second line of 2nd violins enters on the 3rd beat, and an extra half beat, the necessity for which must be made clear in advance, brings in the upper line of 1st violins *pp* non tremolo. But there is an additional complication in that the 2nd violins, who are indeed tremolo, have a rapid swell. The 4th beat clears the sound altogether; all the previous manœuvres having to be accomplished in hardly any time at all, the soloist's half-bar fermata being excessively short before he is ready to proceed unaccompanied with the subsidiary principal subject in the bar before 103.

Only barline markings are given here, the orchestra entering in the 2nd of 103 with relatively conventional beating, ending with the lower line of cellos' pizzicato; this brings back the horns, who again need to be well alerted.

The 5th of 103 presents no problems if it is kept moving, but then the troubles start. The next bar, 8 before 104, is very long, with no fewer than 5 beats needing to be shown with the stick. The downbeat is marked with a fermata, but where the strings are concerned this is simply not valid; the soloist proceeds almost at once, and the conductor has to be prepared to put down his 2nd beat very soon, initiating a resumption of the thrumming *ppp* while releasing the sustaining lines.

The four demisemiquaver groups of the solo line are easily followed, and the 3rd beat falls on his arrival at the trills. This changes the thrumming to a new and more elaborate chord but with the same players (though the cellos drop out briefly), who now have to make a pronounced bulge, indicated with the left hand, while the soloist changes bow on his trill.

At this point the extra beat is inserted (hence the 5 beats mentioned above) as another 3rd beat or half-beat as the soloist reaches his fermata, needing sharp eyes and ears as it is not easy to catch; it is important, however, as the thrummed chord changes again, though still with the same players. Finally, after the soloist's *Nachschlag*, the *fpp* 4th beat changes the thrumming to a sustained chord, now with the upper line of each group of players. Care should be taken lest this 4th beat take on too committed an upbeat character; it must not pre-empt the placing of the next downbeat, as the soloist needs freedom to finish his flourish with a rubato lead into the sustained B.

The strings change their chord at the barline, and there are again two pauses at the beginning of the bar, of which the first has, like that in the previous bar, no validity for conductor and strings. Even the second pause, over the 2nd beat crotchet, is short, barely allowing time for the thrumming swell in the lower lines. This is cleared with the 3rd beat as the soloist moves up a chromatic scale, the upper lines continuing to hold; the 4th beat then merely marks the point at which, as before, he stops on a long trill.

The lead into the next bar (6 before 104) is prepared by the soloist's *Nachschlag*, which is convenient because the 2nd horn has to be ready to join when the strings change chord. Of the veritable succession of pauses, the first comes over a minim so that no 2nd beat is called for, but just before the 3rd beat there is a trap, for the soloist's group of harmonics proceeds without warning into the demisemiquavers of the 3rd beat, and the way the harmonics are inevitably notated gives the eye the false expectation of a leap up at the end of the group which, of course, never comes, and it is easy to be late with the spread pizzicato when the violin takes flight.

The crescendo in the sustaining upper lines has reached *f*, and now subsides through the 4th beat, which places a piano pizzicato for the lower lines coinciding with the soloist's four diminuendo semiquavers (though the 'diminuendo' marking is lacking in the solo part). These again lead back to a sustained B, this time on the 3rd horn.

Another *fp* marks the beginning of the bar (5 before 104), and here again, as also in the next bar, no 2nd beat is given, as the pauses on these 1st beats are excessively short, the soloist often being on his way before the conductor has had time to be prepared. The diminuendo is therefore made quickly, and turns into a ponticello tremolo on the 3rd beat, the upper 2nd violins and cellos joining the 3rd horn in a bulge (which needs to be clearly indicated) while the soloist negotiates a chromatic rise of triplets in double-stopping. The following bar (4 before 104) is similar, like an echo;

again the pause is extremely short, but reintroduces the thrumming in the lower cellos together with ponticello tremolo on the upper violas. At the 3rd beat the thrumming retreats to *ppp*, but with another swell as the soloist manœuvres his way up the next octave. Meanwhile the horns have again changed personnel, the 1st and 2nd having replaced the 3rd. All these rises and falls are, as earlier, indicated only by the left hand, leaving the stick free to give just the 1st and 3rd beats of both bars and no more than a simple downbeat in the subsequent bar, whose pause is by contrast a long one, leaving only the upper cellos and basses sustaining infinitely softly.

After a wait the soloist embarks on a new pattern, the conductor marking each of the four beats out of tempo and one at a time; they are registered by elaborate pizzicatos in the upper lines while the lower reinstate their thrumming *ppp* with a rise to the 2nd beat and a fall thereafter. Moreover the *ppp* entry of the thrumming basses on the 4th beat is not to be missed. This 4th beat is another long pause, the soloist taking his time over the four groups which constitute the end of the allargando.

The last bar before 104 gives the ending of the sequence of pizzicatos with a rise and fall up to the 2nd beat and back to the 3rd, these points of reference not relating to the solo line and all his pauses. The 3rd beat also clears the strings for a moment of silence before the entry of the three horns at 104, which should not be delayed.

They too have a swell of their own, the soloist choosing his moment to introduce the second subject of the first movement during their phrase. After the pause on the 1st beat the pace moves appreciably forward before settling back onto the fermata in the third bar.

This is yet another long one, the strings changing bows as necessary before orchestra and soloist move off together into a longer reference to the first movement. This droops, however, in the 2nd of 105 and ends with a *pp* pizzicato as the soloist continues to meditate around the second subject.

The timpani, a new voice since the first bars of this cadenza, start **ppp** after a pause on the 2nd beat and follow the soloist's expression marks as he proceeds heavenwards.

The 5th of **105** is another involved bar, full of pauses on each beat, none of them long, and the initial pause on the downbeat has yet again no significance at all, the soloist's quavers being fully in tempo. The pizzicato, the thrumming, and the chord on all four muted horns come unexpectedly soon on the 2nd beat, after which the pauses on both 2nd and 3rd beats have to take into account the soloist's bow: the accompanying strings finish with him, although the horns can just overlap by a quaver before being given their own take-off.

The conductor's involvement in the cadenza proper thus ends, and he only has to be ready to join again at **106**, some ten bars further on. When the soloist at last arrives on his trill the orchestra creeps in **ppp** Adagio with a reflective reference to the slow movement. The pause in the third bar, after the horns have handed the chords back again to the strings, comes on the 4th beat and is again long for the soloist's extended trill and slow *Nachschlag*.

The orchestra's fermata in the following bar accommodates the two pauses of the violin, and after the colla parte just before **107** a slow cadence brings back the orchestral opening of the concerto in an unexpectedly rapid moment of recall including, after a reverse mark of ritardando molto, a long drawn-out answer by the soloist; the strings merely place isolated **ppp** chords on the 2nd and 4th beats and, after a hiatus, on the 2nd and 3rd beats of the bar before **108**, no other beats being given.

We are back in the finale at its full speed and impetus, even though there is an unmistakable quality of aftermath about both the soloist's figuration and the orchestra's harmonies, for all the brilliance and vivacity of both. The renewed reference to the slow movement at **111**, analogous in a way to the passage at **94**, is kept in 4 with the soloist bursting in continuously on the second and fourth beats. The alla breve is this time kept in reserve until 112, from which point the movement races to its end, interrupted only by the strepitoso, where after a pull-up for a flamboyant gesture by the soloist, the music plunges forward in a vigorous crotchet beat lasting four bars. Fig. 115 is again in 2, both soloist and orchestra making a great nobilmente feature of the first sequential theme of the movement and taking all the time in the world about it.

In the last bars the horns spell out the notes of the very first motif without pulse and merely allowing for the spectacular upward gestures of the soloist. It is imperative therefore that there is no pull-back or hiatus in the three last bars, nor any hesitation before the last bar of all which would lessen the panache at the close of this great and majestic creation.

Cello Concerto in E minor, Op. 85

◄►

THIS extremely popular and widely played work was written in 1919, immediately after the end of the First World War. It was Elgar's last full-scale orchestral piece and his final composition before Alice's death the following year.

The soloist at the first performance was not Beatrice Harrison, who became so closely associated with the work and recorded it with Elgar himself, but Felix Salmond who immediately prior to the Concerto had played in the premières of both the Quartet and the Piano Quintet.

In every way slighter and more autumnal than the fully-fledged Violin Concerto, it is appreciably shorter at only 27 minutes, though laid out for much the same orchestral forces. However, these are handled in an entirely different manner and for the most part delicately, the heavy brass in particular being used only sparingly.

The dedication to Elgar's oldest friends Sir Sidney Colvin (Keeper of Prints and Drawings at the British Museum) and his wife Frances was one which meant a great deal to Elgar, as Colvin had become very close in recent years and especially during the war.

The plan of the Cello Concerto is totally unlike that of the Violin Concerto, with no orchestral ritornello, and in four movements instead of three, played nearly without a break; only the miniature Adagio is completely detached from the Scherzo, the other movements being played segue.

I

In the very first bar the cello takes the lead, the conductor placing the downbeat with the soloist's nobilmente *ff* chord and then releasing it once the next one has followed. The score gives Adagio ♩ = 56, but this is entirely the cellist's province and bears little relation to the complete freedom he enjoys, the conductor merely marking the various punctuations as they occur. When at the end of bar 2 the soloist has changed finger on the A, the bare fifth of the tutti cellos can be quietly but firmly planted, only to be released again after exactly three quavers have elapsed; the solo cello then landing on the *sf* minim C, the two staccato crotchets are given with lifted beats.

The last staccato quaver on the fourth beat comes relatively freely during the soloist's long crescendo and can be a fraction delayed, there being still time in the fermata to prepare the wind for their two minims in bar 5. These are marked with lines and should be clearly articulated, the second being held a fraction to encourage its crescendo to forte before being cleared with a composite gesture which also contains a sensitive preparation for the pianissimo subito. The clarinet quavers in bar 6 are then appreciably slower, the last of the four being subdivided to coincide with the bassoon.

Again a single gesture serves both to take the wind right off and to prepare the strings, whose pianissimo chord creeps in up-bow and is held until the soloist is ready to continue. As he starts, the strings cease and the conductor's only function is to maintain the atmosphere of mystery and stillness until the Moderato ⁹⁄₈, where the gently swaying violas merge with the cello as he dies away. Curiously the score shows no metronome indication here; the solo part supplies the marking ♩. = 66, but this is altogether too restless, whereas the mood should on the contrary be wholly undemonstrative and easy-going at about 50, the whole movement giving the impression of being itself introductory. The feeling of relaxed melancholy is peculiarly English, so that continental interpreters find it hard to come to terms with its total detachment and gentle sadness and may sometimes therefore have a tendency to overplay.

As the swaying melody reaches down to the low E of the cellos the soloist, with infinite patience and toleration, takes up the strain to the slenderest of accompaniments on two clarinets and a horn, all pianissimo. A third enunciation of the melody is presented by the strings at fig. 3 after a slightly extended upbeat, but they should resist the temptation to play any more warmly than their restrained marking of **pp**, for the soloist now takes a forward role with expressive playing, rising above the orchestra even in its increasingly fervent crescendo in the bars before 4. However, the beat can become quite demonstrative here, first for the pizzicato/arco of the upper strings and then for the weighty duplet in the lower.

Fig. 4 is on an altogether more evocative scale, with the soloist marked 'sostenuto' (though this is not to mean slower) and with the accompaniment in block chords on woodwind and horns. After the sforzando in the fourth bar the accompaniment again drops to **p** and **pp** until the soloist climbs the scale to the top E and the full orchestra gathers itself for the first of the two full-blown tuttis.

Though the bar before 5 is marked 'poco allargando', soloists usually make little of this, reserving the main approach for the return of the passage later in the movement (fig. 16, which is actually printed 'in tempo'). Consequently the beat needs great flexibility with only the barest hint of subdivisions, the bassoons, cellos, and basses experiencing no difficulty in following the soloist's semiquavers once they have been alerted to his intentions.

For so reticent a work the 6-bar tutti is surprisingly sonorous, with the theme doubled first on all four horns, then on trombones and even tuba (whose 'ad lib.', like that of the piccolo, is not to be considered). The elaborate rhythm of the basses should be fairly spectacular and causes much glee among the players if waved into prominence.

Fig. 6 brings back the soloist for a last statement of the theme with only the slightest of backgrounds, although in the first three bars the second and third beats on pizzicatos and timpani are interesting enough to be picked out by the stick. From the fifth bar the cellos and basses ghost along in unison with the soloist until the end of the section in the bar before 7.

The movement is in what is described as 'ternary song form', and the central portion follows immediately, led by clarinets and bassoons. Changing to 4 in a bar has no impact on the tempo, which is exactly the same as before, and the main difference lies in the style, which is somewhat perkier, although still laid out as a peaceful conversation between orchestra and soloist. In the 5th of 7 the violins are linked to the solo cello in a way which makes the ensemble a trifle hazardous if the soloist takes any unexpected liberties.

The conductor needs to be alert for a rubato at the end of the bar before 9, the following downbeat being purposefully placed, but the poco stringendo . . . rit. between 10 and 11 is even freer, the alternation between strings and wind being subsidiary to the expansive forte line of the soloist, whose semiquavers can be extremely fluid and need skilful accompaniment. This is similarly the case at 12, where the soloist's semiquavers, especially in the second bar, are sometimes taken very broadly.

In the two bars before 11 the rit. is only gentle and must not pre-empt the corresponding lead into 13, which is much more extrovert and accordingly harder to judge, so that both beats of the very free $\frac{6}{8}$ bar should be placed with pointed stick gestures, neither of which presupposes where the next must come. The strings are then cleared, and the closing paragraph of the central section sets off at 13 (where a misprinted D in the 1st bassoon can be confusing to spot).

After a hushed but strict bar, the 3rd of 13, the next is the most wayward of all, and the five quavers leading to the fermata must all be beaten out. Nor is the act of coming off the pause a simple matter, the conductor needing to lean forward in sympathy with the cello rather than clearly marking a sixth quaver beat, so that the resumption of pulse merges into the a tempo at the half-bar with dotted-crotchet beating as before.

The last bar before the return to $\frac{9}{8}$ is one of quiet relaxation back to the introspective mood of the main section, the violas having the primary line with two phrases, each with a bulge. It is unfortunate therefore that the word 'dim.' is omitted from the part, especially as it implies a partial contradiction of the rise of the swell on the third beat, which seems an important element in the interpretation of the expression in this exposed linking bar.

In a tranquillity so total as occurs at 14 no pulse beating with the stick is necessary for two bars except at the barlines; the words 'come prima' refer to mood and not at all to tempo, which has never altered, the cello meandering in the $\frac{9}{8}$ as in the earlier section without any need for a beat.

In the 3rd and 4th of 14 the wisps of semiquaver scales on the flute and 1st violins call for the gentlest of guidance from the left hand, as does the horn 2 before 15. The beat takes over again at the upbeat to 15, the strings giving a shadowy recollection of the swaying theme, whose to-and-fro is emphasized within the prevailing pianissimo by the violas and 2nd violins.

The soloist soon joins the stream of melody, quickly building up to the second full fortissimo tutti. The ascending scale corresponding to the bar before 5 is this time marked 'in tempo', but as on the previous occasion soloists do not observe Elgar's instructions and here tend to take plenty of time to complete the climb, no doubt influenced by the largamente in the previous bar.

Like the first, this new tutti is massively orchestrated, but it is even shorter and comes to a brusque end in the third bar, the soloist re-entering to bridge the continuity into the final pianissimo of the movement. After signalling the short and sharp third beat, therefore, the conductor has to be ready immediately to bring in the muted horns and strings quietly in order to give backing to the soloist as he leads into the last statement of the main theme at 17. A slight rubato into 17 is also conventional, but it must be only marginal.

The first four bars of 17 are dominated, however quietly, by the timpani figure on each second beat. In the score these are given as two semiquavers before the crotchet; but Elgar's autograph, followed by the orchestral part, has two demi-semiquavers, and this can moreover also be heard on Elgar's own recording.

In carrying the $\frac{9}{8}$ theme downwards, the soloist is joined by the orchestral cellos and basses in *ppp* all the way to the last pizzicato notes, although they alone hold the bottom E arco on a fermata, which should only just be audible.

II

Following without a break, the second movement begins with a considerable preamble in the form of an accompanied recitative. The conductor takes his cue from the soloist's pizzicato chords, echoing the opening bars of the concerto, of which the first needs marking only for the basses' rise up the octave on the second beat; the third beat belongs to the horns, while the fourth gives the cellos and basses their crescendo to forte.

In the second bar the events are entirely controlled by the conductor, on whom the strings depend for the speed of their semiquavers and demisemiquavers in what is a pronounced and vivid accelerando. The second beat launches the tempestuous rise with a clearly marked syncopated direction; the strings rise from this to the *ff* snap on the fourth beat, which contains more than an element of finality about its fermata.

Neither conductor nor strings must be unprepared, however, for the soloist is immediately ready to proceed and will normally take the downbeat from the conductor for his motivic bar of quick semiquavers, pointed with a short *pp*

chord and caught at the end by the solo muted horn. The
stick plays no part in what follows, and an unobtrusive
finger is all that is needed in the dialogue, especially as the
quick pattern always slows, enabling the horn to hear clearly
when he is to join with his sustained F♯'s.

The beat's responsibility is purely to mark the horn's
entrances and exits, plus the rise and fall 3 before **19**, for
which the left hand joins in order to synchronize the horn
and clarinet in their swell together. The *pp* horn in the bar
before **19** comes off with the following downbeat, the pizzicato crescendo molto crotchets then being conducted with
great vigour and with an almost hectic rush crowned with
trombones, tuba, and timpani.

'Lento, ad lib.' is misleading for the soloist's direct continuation, which is only two crotchets in length and leads quite
precipitately to the conductor's very strong upbeat to the
cellos and basses and a really powerful short downbeat *ff* to
the tutti before the long cadenza bar. There is the risk of
misadventure here, to avoid which it is clearest to direct the
entry to the cellos and basses with the stick and give the tutti
crash chord with the left arm.

There is a complete restart for the Allegro molto, exactly
as in the 3rd of **18**, but this time the second cello pizzicato
(taken quite slowly) is the cue for the horn to make an
evocative swell, at the top of which the strings enter with the
fourth beat as the horn subsides.

A final bar of introduction, though occupied with the
same semiquaver motif, is much steadier; the horn comes
off with the downbeat, but the strings are cleared after
the second beat. There is then a short hiatus before the
scherzo proper begins with a soft but pronounced timpani
stroke.

All the Allegro moltos of the introductory recitative-like
section came under the general tempo of ♩ = 138 marked at
the 3rd of **18**. The main body of the movement is a great deal
faster, however, and it is established at ♩ = 160, with all 4 beats
given in this opening bar. Once the soloist has accepted the

flying pace and set off on his semiquaver ostinato the conductor's role is greatly reduced: in the 2nd and 3rd of 20, for example, only the first and fourth beats are given, the crotchet rests needing no indications; and in the next two bars only the third beats are tossed to the clarinets and bassoons. The sixth bar is beaten through for the horns' entry and the ascending clarinet and flute line, but then the violins need only the lightest syncopated downbeat to set their *pp* staccato quavers in motion with no further beats to disturb their concentration. The same music is repeated two bars later, all the downbeats being given for the horns, lower strings, and the little woodwind flip. The descending clarinet has to be guided under the figuration of the soloist lest the crotchets fall behind, and a touch of anticipation is even appropriate and helpful here.

The soloist's arrival at 21 is even more perilous, the beat for the lower strings needing to be excessively fluid and nimble in a similar way to the last movement of the Mendelssohn Violin Concerto. As there, so here the conducting is primarily of tiny 4-in-a-bar crotchets, but with only the essential directions thrown to the players, any other beats always suppressed in the interests of maximum clarity. Only the lower strings, therefore, require the clear 4 beats, the 1st violins and clarinet imitating the soloist's line needing only to be cued, each in turn. The beating is a little more involved from the 4th of 21, however, as the flute, pizzicato 2nd violins, and especially horns and trombones all need attention for their microscopic entries.

With the horns' *sf*, the cello reaches the apex of a phrase, often sustaining his long F$\sharp$ a fraction extra before setting forth once more on the semiquavers, and the conductor should be especially alert at this corner. Thereafter the accompaniment consists only of isolated crotchets with the pattern 2; 4; 2,3 repeated, the 2,3 two bars before 22 being more colourful with an isolated *mf* woodwind chord. But in each case only these beats are actually conducted, thus lightening enormously the process of accompanying.

The cello puts the brakes on quite violently in the poco allargando and has to be caught with the impassioned wind minims, which mark a complete change for the second subject. In the next bar the forte pizzicato is followed immediately by a short but significant comma, after which the pick-up with the 1st violins is effusive. The 3rd and 4th of 22, the alternating tutti repeating phrase, then conceal a problem for the conductor, for in the absence of any colla parte and comma these bars would seem to be in full tempo; but though they are often played so, this is somewhat insensitive, and the 4th of 22, a good healthy forte cadence, calls instead for a degree of weight in the second and third beats.

The soloist takes up a repeat of 22, but the 'largamente' marking is absent, so that some cellists continue the a tempo in direct contrast with the earlier statement. In Elgar's recording, however, the rubato and a tempo pattern the first time, if to a lesser degree, despite the omitted directions in the score. But in any case there is no need for a parallel weighty cadence before 23, and the lead-in is this time kept moving so that the Tempo primo and the cello's resumption of semiquavers merges naturally out of the to-ing and fro-ing of the unusual second subject.

The music which follows 23 is to a large extent recapitulatory, there being no development. Only a few new features should be commented upon: in the bar before 24 the humorous woodwind slither is worth describing graphically with the stick, and the eight newly interpolated bars at 24, in which the divided 1st violins soar ecstatically in octaves against the continuing ostinato of the solo cello, need an almost feathery quality. There is also an extra bar before 25 (relative to 21) for the orchestra to wait, which does not need to be beaten through, although the entry of the lower strings will have to be the more clearly indicated.

Three bars before 26 the orchestra gives an unexpected explosion which is not to be underplayed. The orchestration is deliberately violent and can be vigorously portrayed. Elgar's favourite use of two low flutes in unison (as in the

Enigma Variations) is added to the background after **26**, but the lead into the second subject is otherwise as before, and the second subject itself (**27** to **28**) corresponds in all essentials with **22** to **23**, merging into the semiquaver ostinato of the Tempo primo in the same way.

This time, however, the coda follows immediately, the soloist's pattern moving forward into an animato. The conducting is again fluid, the accented violas in the alternate bars being positively marked, even though in *ppp*, and answered by the equally distant cello pizzicato, all with the most minuscule movements of the stick. Fig. **29** represents a repeat of the animato sentence but with the soloist an octave higher, so that the figurations of the accompaniment, which are all a little more elaborate, have to be treated with the utmost delicacy. But the flutes, suddenly marked a sharp forte and staccato in an uncomfortably low register, can still be encouraged to tongue for all they are worth lest the effect be lost entirely.

There is a doubtful timpani note at **29**: in the score all three crotchets of this entry are A's, but in the part they resolve to D in the new bar, a natural reading always adopted. Though the drums are still tuned to A, B, and E, there would have been ample time, even with Elgar's old-style kettledrums, to make the change.*

The cello needs plenty of scope for the two bars before **30**, and the bassoons and horns should be prepared for the colla parte, which signifies a considerable slow-up, just as the clarinets must be ready for a resumption of high-speed thinking at the $\frac{3}{2}$. This is often conducted in minims, but if the beat is kept small and swift enough 6 crotchets are more appropriate for this variant of the second subject, going into

---

* A glance at Elgar's autograph reveals that the original note (in ink) was D; this was changed in pencil to A (doubtless in order to conform to the actual tuning of the drums), but the corresponding alteration in the part was evidently overlooked. It would seem, therefore, that both readings have something in their favour: Elgar's final published text was A, but the note he really wanted was D. (J.R.D.M.)

4 at the 4th of 30 and keeping the change of pulse for the più mosso of 31.

If yet another change of beat can be made deftly and without fuss, a suggestion of 4 crotchets for the first two bars of 32 is actually better in controlling both the strings' crotchets and the soloist's ostinato, but at the third bar a minim beat again becomes self-evident and remains to the end.

A confusing misprint in early printings of the score places fig. 33 five instead of four bars before the end. A bar earlier again (six from the end) there is another misprint, this time in the 2nd violin parts, which place the *pp* B on the fourth instead of the third beat of the bar.

The muted horns at 33 should produce a distant mysterious quality depicted by an outstretched left hand rather than a conventional beat of the stick, and the ending must be feather-light, like Mendelssohn's *Midsummer Night's Dream* music. For the soloist it is a finish of great virtuosity, and the conductor's style can contribute significantly to his success.

III

There is a substantial pause (the only one in the work) before the Adagio, and the signal to proceed devolves entirely on the soloist's judgement that there is a sufficiently rapt atmosphere in the auditorium, for this little movement is one of intense *Innigkeit*.

It is scored for only six wind players—clarinets, bassoons, and (for a very few bars at 37) horns—apart from the strings, who might well similarly be reduced by a desk all round, though this is rarely done. The cello plays throughout except for a single bar where the orchestra bursts out, only to subside again almost at once.

The soloist starts the movement, the strings playing with him by watching his bow, and the conductor always putting the beat down slightly ahead, especially for the *pp* subito in the second bar. The take-offs in bars 2, 4, and 6 are tiny freezes taken as the cello moves onto his last tenuto quaver, and the silent downbeats in bars 3 and 5 are then the merest preparations for the respective second beats, which again must not be late. The *ppp* in bar 7 is portrayed by no downbeat at all and two exaggeratedly spaced quavers.

These first seven bars are in principle introductory, and proper flowing beats begin at **35**, where the soloist introduces a new and salient motif. This is particularly important since it will represent the movement when the Adagio returns near the end of the concerto.

The printed tempo of ♪ = 50 is perfectly appropriate and can apply from the start. It is now established largely through the violas, who work with the soloist's dynamics, always poco marcato, adding a little extra stress on the espressivo semiquavers in the 3rd of **35**. Two bars later this stress is no longer marked, as all the strings are about to shrivel to quasi niente, but an element of it will always survive, as also later after **37** and in the violins before **40**. The semiquaver rest before **36** amounts only to a slight hiatus; the downbeat must be placed quite quickly, allowing the soloist's more impassioned phrase the flexibility to travel freely, encouraged by the agitato quality of the syncopated background in the strings with its tiny crescendo thrusts in alternate bars. At first it might seem as if the slurs across the other barlines have been overlooked, but in fact their absence, wherever the hairpin is similarly absent, is quite consistent and is corroborated after **38**.

The bar-long crescendo in the 5th of **36** builds to a curt *f* in the strings, capped with a distinct pizzicato in the basses, and there is no alternative to conducting it thus, only the eyes giving the sign to the wind that their very first note (to which the crescendo equally leads) is, on the contrary, *pp*. The left hand is also useful, however, being free to direct the wind to this effect as soon as the moment of the barline is over. The soloist makes a real forte climax here, matching the strings; but this changes to *pp* subito when the phrase repeats 2 before **37**, and the wind downbeat is correspondingly a fraction delayed.

The minuscule tutti is introduced by the cellos and basses, who can afford to start their crescendo a little early, playing poco espressivo already from the E♮. In the following bar the swell, of which this orchestral interpolation entirely consists, appears in the score to be staggered, the wind reaching the peak a quaver before the strings; but no positive purpose seems to be served by this, and in practice the phrasing is directed towards the new barline as given in the violins and violas.

The orchestra drains away, and the soloist takes up the same principal melody, so that we seem to be back at 35 once more, albeit in A major instead of B flat. But this time it builds in a stringendo molto (not always observed) to the appassionato at 38, which, with its throbbing accompaniment, is the central high spot of the movement. As at 36, the strings return to the initial dynamic (here *mf*) after each of the little hairpins; but the phrasing is intensified, the soloist's largamente being launched by a poignant *fpp* which itself needs to be prepared in the previous bar with a degree of breadth.

The woodwind meet the apex of the cello phrase as before, but then the new colour is added of two low clarinets in unison, their portentous semitone rise to A♭ being placed by the conductor for maximum expressive effect while the solo line ties over the barline.

As the clarinets drop away, the cello climbs to an ethereal subito *pp* which needs to be reflected by the accompanying violas, though nothing is marked; then in the 4th of 39 there is a misprint of alignment in the score at a place where ensemble, with the gently syncopated 2nd violins, is important. But all the time the accompaniment is fading as a mere memory of the main theme returns, and from the entry of the basses it reduces to hardly more than a whisper.

At 40 the clarinets creep in again, but the beat turns instead to the cellos and basses for their pronounced stepwise descent, quaver by quaver. The fermata in the third bar is a little confused by the addition of an extra pause over the clarinets' rest, which is redundant; they are merely held with the soloist on a sustained third beat, while the cellos and basses need no instruction in order to come off short. In the next bar there is again a misprint of alignment, for the clarinets are cleared only at the last moment as the solo cello melts into 41.

In all essentials the coda of the last eight bars parallels the opening of the movement, except for the extended swells on the cellos, which are shown with a prolongation of the stick, five and three bars before the end. The quavers in the penultimate bar are again exaggeratedly spaced, as in the bar before 35 but even more so on account of the rit.; and in the final bar, again as at the beginning, the 2nd violins have to be released while all the others hold for the fermata, whose length is determined by the cellist's bow.

IV

As the last note is extinguished, the conductor picks up the Finale forthwith. Though not marked in the score, such an awakening from the deep meditation of the Adagio is made virtually implicit by the inconclusive dominant chord with which it ended.

Like the first two movements, the Finale again has an introduction, built freely and rhapsodically on the principal subject and beginning with a lively Allegro at a considerably faster speed than the movement proper is to enjoy when it sets off at 44. The expectant pause after only eight bars can be dramatic (the conductor's arm and stick ending aloft) but not long, for there is no relaxation, and the orchestra must be ready at once for the strong phrase with which the solo cello begins his recitative. The tempo is entirely different (Moderato $\downarrow$ = 72 being exactly right), and after the emphasis of the forte strings at the start, and of the basses' *fp* in the second bar, the beat is purely concerned with the quiet strings for two bars. The placing of the imperious accented minims in the wind seems to fall into the conductor's domain, but is in fact closely bound up with the soloist's panache as he prepares for the onslaught of his *ff* appassionato quavers, and the conductor needs to be alert and sympathetic as he slots the various punctuations into the cellist's very free rhetoric.

Two bars before 43 the strings' crisp forte pizzicato coincides with a subito *pp* in the wind, giving a similar situation to that after 36 in the Adagio; but here the wind can be assisted with the left hand before the barline, while the stick gives the strings their pizzicato. In the next bar the clarinets and bassoons need to be prepared to hold their tied notes for longer than they expect before the change of chord, to give the cellist room for ample freedom of expression. Then the barline of 43 simultaneously clears the woodwind and reintroduces the hushed strings, the orchestral cellos having the important line as they climb chromatically to the meaningful D♯ before coming off with the 2nds and violas at the end of the soloist's phrase. A short cadenza follows, in which the two silent barlines should not be given; all that remains is the stance of preparation when the soloist starts his upward flying leap, and when he reaches the top the crash must come almost at once.

Again it is essential to be poised for the continuation which the soloist gives with the fling of his bow. He controls the new and steadier tempo (♩ = 108) which is to be the main pulse of the movement.

The effect of the colla parte ad lib. bar before 45 is a delaying of the second beat, some intimation of this being present already in the firm placing of the downbeat; but 45 itself then bursts in precipitately for a short and boisterous tutti. When the soloist rejoins, the orchestra drops back except for a series of sudden explosions on the half-beats of 5 and 3 before 46, which turn into a more general crescendo in the woodwind greeted by a joyous timpani stroke, suitably anticipating the grand tutti at 46.

This is the most substantial the orchestra has had in the whole concerto and corresponds with the similar passage which breaks out later at 61. Conductor and orchestra need no longer be restrained for these few passages of exuberance, in which the colours are suitably extrovert and brilliant.

A subsiding link, in which the principal theme is started three times as if attempting to recover its momentum, lands instead on a surprise *fp* in the horns. This must be given true shock value, since it introduces the second subject, which Tovey aptly described as 'dignity at the mercy of a banana-skin'. The conductor must allow plenty of time for the horns to resolve onto their pause, having expected the bar of 47 to expand and contract though their swell is rarely emphasized enough.

The 'banana-skin' in the 4th and 5th of 47 should not fail to take the ground from under everyone's feet with the utmost swiftness and good humour, the stick finding no embarrassment in making great play with the timpani's bumps as the cello lands at the bottom, while the woodwind float alternately downwards and upwards in their glee; it is rare to find Elgar enjoying himself so overtly.

Playing with the second subject motif, the soloist climbs skywards, interrupted by downward slithers in the clarinet, a feature to be brought out strongly. Fig. 49 brings a new swagger in the solo line, whose quavers may even take a fraction of extra time, for which the conductor needs to be prepared. The colla parte bar is quite steady, even with a hint of subdivision in the first beat before the emphatic sforzando which brings the orchestra off short.

As the cello plunges down through three and a half octaves, the orchestra dies away, leaving the soloist alone to bridge into the central episode, the conductor's only remaining function being the marking of the barlines. From 50 the barest necessities are thrown to and fro into the orchestra while the soloist cavorts around his semiquaver passage-work; if he is secure and strict in rhythm this can be simplicity itself, but cellists may on occasion be somewhat cavalier in their treatment of this episode, and a débâcle is by no means unknown.

The 3-horn crotchet chords in the 2nd and 6th of 50 should be amply sustained, and the bright semiquaver flips on the upper woodwind, transferred four bars later to the lower strings, may be tossed aside with good-humoured nonchalance.

Two bars before 51 the 'poco allargando' marking is not given in the solo cello part, and nor is the 'accel. . . . a tempo' after 51. It may be assumed that Elgar wisely thought better of these constant adjustments of tempo, for Beatrice Harrison ignores them all in her recording with the composer, and it has become the custom for present-day soloists to do the same. On the other hand the allargando . . . a tempo and animato before and after 52 continue to stand, but the allargando and calando before 53 are once again scarcely obeyed, only a hint surviving in their first two, and last, bars respectively.

The divided string lines (violins and violas) are to be played with the lightest of bow arms and portrayed float-ingly with the stick. Soloists usually make a meal of the rubato 5 before 52, but fig. 52 itself acquires considerable momentum ahead of the 'animato' mark controlled only, but firmly, by the pizzicato violas. It is the violas again who monitor the delicate lead into 53, where the wind's juggling with the principal theme takes precedence over the long notes in the solo part, and all the wind are cued in turn until, with two strong pizzicatos, the soloist triggers off the tense build-up of 54.

Here is the true development, built entirely on the main theme in one way or another, the cello being mostly sub-sidiary. The theme is used in a modulatory capacity, so that the conductor has to keep a shrewd eye on the architectural aspect of the movement, the tempo at last being stable for a considerable period. The short outbursts use full brass, who have to be alerted in good time (after 54, for example), as they have been resting since before 47.

A more consistent rhythmic pattern is then presented by the cello with virtuoso triplet passage-work across the strings, and the conductor accordingly takes charge of the animato and its alternating solo entries of wind and violins until the boisterous 4-bar tutti of 56. The whole section from 54 is then repeated more or less in reverse order until shortly before 59, when the soloist, marked 'feroce' and with emphatic offbeat accompaniment in brass and timpani, seems to become impatient with this recurrent alternation of events, and at last the whole orchestra rears up for the fortissimo rit., the bar before 59 being subdivided dramatically before the comma, which is regulated with due panache by the solo cello.

Barely eight bars earlier the development section had seemed to be still in full swing, the tonality passing through such distant regions as B flat minor, and although Elgar has ingeniously and surreptitiously taken a surprisingly short cut to the home key, 59 now appears to carry the discourse forward logically and seamlessly, for all the grand gesturing in the previous two bars. Yet it must in fact be clear that, though greatly transformed, and presented in entirely new guise, the Tempo primo actually represents the recapitulation, corresponding directly with 44.

Perhaps for this reason (however subconsciously), the 'nobilmente' marking in the solo part is occasionally taken to imply a full-blown meno mosso e grandioso. While such an exaggerated view should be discouraged, the tempo does in the end remain very much the soloist's province, however much the dialogue with the orchestral cellos (likewise marked 'forte') may seem an equal one; and some degree of compromise can reasonably be made so that all the elements in the solo can be stressed without having to battle against the orchestra.

The bar before 60 should be portrayed graphically with a splendidly stylish stick manœuvre, and 60 itself is then a full-scale repeat of 59 with trombone glissandos and pealing horns, so that the conductor can hardly solve the soloist's problem of balance without diminishing Elgar's whole vision.

From this point the cello takes the field again and leads the unison forces, who continue to escort him in a grand crescendo and affrettando to the mighty tutti of **61**. Soloists vary in their management of this build-up, and it requires much insight and alertness for the conductor to seem to be led and yet to lead. It may indeed be as late as the last two bars before **61** that the soloist really takes the pace forward, although the growth in intensity must be apparent from the 6th of **60**.

Here is the best place for the 2nd flute to take the piccolo, using his 3-bar rest to change instruments. He should play an octave lower than printed (so as to be in unison with the 1st flute) until the 6th of **61**, where Elgar prescribes that the piccolo be heard in its own right, and the part is obviously played 'loco'.

The tutti at **61** corresponds to a large extent with the earlier one at **46** but is even more flamboyantly scored, with the brass given its head to an almost outrageous extent. The trombones at the seventh bar and the trumpet semiquavers four bars later are so unashamedly brash that it would simply be self-defeating to underplay them in the least degree, and the only possible course of action is to accept Elgar's single moment of unrestrained vulgarity and conduct these intrusions of ebullience for all they are worth.

As before, the brief outburst leads instantly to the reprise of the second subject, with all its concept of pride and the banana-skin relived, after the short hold-up at **62**, which is handled exactly as at **47**. The continuation at **63**, however, is relatively half-hearted, since it is soon to give way to the substantial coda which forms the emotional climax to the whole work. As it winds down, the horn notes in the allargando are placed punctually and with deliberation as the soloist broadens, culminating in the bar before **64** with the four woodwind quavers all beaten out as they take over from the soloist.

The conductor picks up the tempo at **64** for the theme on the wind, the soloist fitting his syncopations to the firmness of the beat, whose forcefulness is exaggerated in the second and fourth bars by the fortissimo pizzicato of the full strings.

The continuing offbeat pizzicatos in the solo cello keep the tempo absolutely constant, and this has to continue even after the ostinato has ceased. A short passage in which the soloist rests allows the theme to be quietly carried upward by the orchestra, but when the cello re-enters the tempo must still be very strict, any temptation to ease it already being resisted. At last, in a passage occasionally still played by cellists an octave too low, owing to a misprint in the first edition of the cello and piano score, the coda is brought down to a low point with a gradual 4-bar rallentando in which the principal theme seems to bid farewell on 1st violins and then clarinet.

Now comes the chief surprise of the movement, a Poco più lento marked ♩ = 88; and it is important not to overdo the rallentando, so that a smooth transition is effected, the crotchet pulse remaining the same as it had become in the bar before. This whole section is in effect an epilogue, even though not so described in the score, and almost amounts to an additional slow movement in itself, being of considerable stature and possessing themes of its own. A totally novel feature in a concerto such as this, it strikes deeper than anything in the work so far, though as the soloist plays throughout it is hardly the conductor's task to reflect this, the strings generally keeping a low profile. Most important for the conductor to bring out at first are the flutes and cellos in the 3rd bar and again in the 2nd of 67; the **ppp** at 67 itself and especially the subito in the 5th of 67 are of salient importance, and the flexibility of the beat, with so many variations of tempo, is a major preoccupation in following the solo cello. A good artist can make this epilogue quite heart-rending in a four-movement concerto not particularly noteworthy for its profundity. We do not know what was in Elgar's mind, but the strain of the war years and the fragility of Alice's health (she was to die the following year and leave him totally desolate) may have been contributing factors to such a sudden emotional end to what had primarily been a light-mannered work.

Two bars before **69** the orchestra bursts through with a stringendo as well as an abrupt forte rising to *ff*. Here, as again at 4 before **70** and at fig. **70** itself, the sheer degree of contrast is the more poignant after so much excessively restrained orchestral writing, and all the weight and grandeur of the assembled forces, including trombones, can be unleashed each time, even if only momentarily. But where the stringendo was concerned the resumption of the soloist's line at the end of the bar of **69** immediately reins the tempo in, this upbeat already being drawn out for the soloist's ardent *Ausholen* in which the orchestra plays no part, recoiling instead into the background. From the 3rd of **69** the *fp*'s in the lower strings in each bar are then contributions to the 'passione' with which the soloist is instructed to play, whereas the doublings of the cello line in 1st violins and woodwind are mere echoes.

As the second short tutti subsides, two clarinets wistfully hand over the melody to the solo cello. After the last of the outbursts (at **70**), as the tempo slows right down, the clarinets' lead is given again even more quietly, and the misterioso string accompaniment of tremolo 2nd violins and violas, with pizzicato cellos marking the downbeats, all needs handling with considerable delicacy. This melts into a magical fresco in the quietest colouring, and amid total calm the solo cello floats ethereally above a series of exquisitely placed pizzicatos, some merely doubling (and kept extremely discreet) but others suddenly unexpectedly important, as at the beginning and end of the second bar. The 1st violins' change to arco is also a moment of tender expression, as it subsides into the Lento and we realize that ever since the $\frac{3}{4}$ two bars before **69** we have been merging into the Adagio slow movement.

Now the allusion becomes overt, and in a mood of deepest meditation the cello continues the reminiscence until the epilogue dies away. At **72** the soloist returns to the evocation with which the work began, and the first beat is directed to the lower strings, including the entry of the basses. Though the primary consideration is then their strong bulge towards the middle of the bar, the second beat also requires a degree of definition, showing the violins where to cease. In the next bar, the remainder having been cleared with the barline, the conductor simply waits to place the two heavy staccato crotchets for the full orchestra, followed by the two *pp* staccato chords on the strings; all that then remains is to watch for the cello to descend to his low E before starting the final Allegro molto of 73. This corresponds for the first time with the tempo of the finale's opening and is kept moving with a firm beat which sets the rhythm for the syncopated basses. Only the first two bars of the theme are used, repeated many times while the cello rises upwards with no more than a skeleton motif, and in the rit. bar before 74 the beats are spaced out so as to allow the cello to manœuvre the last ascending interval to his high E.

The soloist then joins the tutti for the ultimate a tempo, the full brass taking the syncopation against strings and wind, who give a final statement of the main theme in an upward sweep. The cello's closing semiquaver flourishes may take a fraction of extra time but are simple to catch, and the work ends with a tutti crescendo on the tonic chord building to a short *sf*. The timpani has the last word, and it is unfortunate that the sharp staccato dot which ends his roll so rivetingly is missing from the part, as it adds substantially to the brilliance of the figure. Short as it is, this final coda is far from unimportant, successfully restoring a spirit of *élan* to a movement which has indeed been predominantly lively, for all its heartfelt and introspective moments. In such a remarkable range and contrast of emotions, perhaps, lies the reason why this inspired concerto is found so perennially and deeply satisfying by cellists and audiences alike.

Concert Overture Froissart, Op. 19

◄►

THIS overture, composed in 1890 when Elgar was 33, was his first orchestral score of any size and importance to be performed and published; previously he had composed a succession of small salon pieces, but nothing of any consequence. The inspiration to tackle a work of this stature came as a result of a commission from the Worcester branch of the Three Choirs Festival, and armed with this encouragement the composer addressed himself to several publishing houses, an arduous and dispiriting task. However, the commission stood him in good stead, and Novello decided to take a chance on condition that the young Elgar agreed to assign the copyright to the publishers without payment.

The opus number indicates the quantity of miniatures which had preceded it, and the assurance, as well as the individuality of style already in evidence from the first bars, is quite remarkable, bearing witness to the day-by-day support his new wife Alice gave him at a time when she herself was shortly to bear their child.

Alice was nothing if not high-minded, and the subject and programme of the work were undoubtedly the product of her idealisms. Froissart was the outstanding chronicler, or one might say journalist, of the Middle Ages, and in the novel *Old Mortality* by Sir Walter Scott, which Elgar had been reading over the previous few years, there was just such an idealistic concept attached to Froissart's Chronicles as the composer and his wife were looking for: '. . . with what true chivalrous feeling he confines his beautiful expressions of sorrow . . . such was his loyalty to his king, pure faith to his religion, hardihood towards his enemy, and fidelity to his lady-love!'

This was meat and drink to the budding composer out to make his mark with the festival dignitaries, who had put their faith in him to supply an inspiring orchestral work for one of their concerts. All that was needed now was some equally high-flown motto to head the score, short enough to give the essence of the above but less verbose and yet of strong poetic origin. At last, he found what he was looking for in a volume of Keats. A poem entitled 'to * * * *' contains the lines:

> Hadst thou liv'd *when chivalry*
> *Lifted up her lance on high,*
> Tell me what thou wouldst have been?' (my italics)

from which he extracted the central phrase, added it to the simple title *Froissart*, and all was ready for the heroic music which was bubbling within him. In a matter of months the work was complete.

It is to be expected that the format of this first orchestral venture would be less ambitious than Elgar's later mature scores. But the accomplished instrumentation is full-blooded even if not extravagant, with twofold wind except for a doubling piccolo and an ad lib. contra, which can hardly in the event be omitted; but it uses only two trumpets, the usual three trombones without tuba or harp, and apart from timpani no percussion except a single cymbal stroke marking the high spot of the coda. This too is marked 'ad lib.' but is as essential as the famous ad lib. tam-tam near the end of Tchaikovsky's *Symphonie pathétique*. Two of the four horns (the 3rd and 4th) are pitched in B flat basso, a rarity with Elgar who habitually wrote for F horns; and for the bass clef old horn notation is used throughout, which he was before long starting to shed.

The overture is thus immensely practical, lasting just over 13 minutes, a fact which, together with the high quality of the thematic material, explains the work's continuing place in the standard repertoire, which would otherwise be unusual for so early a piece.

Froissart starts, not unlike *Cockaigne*, with three silent beats, which must be beaten out and will help to establish the vigour and knightly bearing of the opening theme. The silent beats are, as often in other works of the repertoire, an important part of the performance and are not to be omitted on any account.

In the absence of metronome indications, the 'Allegro moderato' marking might seem a little cautious despite the strings' brillante semiquavers, which are taken off the string. The tempo might be in the region of ♩ = 112, which is eminently suitable for the majestic pageant-like announcement by the trumpets and trombones.

The following rit. dissolves into wisps of phrases that want to be floated upwards with a *Wand of Youth* lightness of the left hand, leaving the cellos and basses to manœuvre the introduction into its Andante at letter **A** with semi-subdivisions, especially for the *pp* subito in the middle of the bar.

There is a true Elgarian nobilmente flavour about the first theme of the Andante, which may be taken at ♩ = 88 and needs a broadly flowing beat, changing to a brusque military style at letter **B**, where the 3rd and 4th horns set a march in progress with drum-like figures in the lower strings. This too is short-lived and a lyrical beat introduces the cantabile violins and cellos, the latter no longer divisi with the basses. The detail here is of particular interest, with the pizzicato triplet quavers on the violas and the rhythmic pattern on the trombones rising to a *ppp* subito. Elgar's colouristic imagination in the orchestral palette is already in full swing.

The change from one style to another, as in the 5th and 6th of **B**, can be effected without variations of pulse, and so too the build-up to a return of the march at **C** must not anticipate the accelerando four bars later. Here the beat changes again from march style to one of considerable jerkiness until the fanfares of **D** prepare for the Allegro moderato of **E**. This is clearly presented as being the main section of the exposition, everything previous being primarily introductory, important though much of it subsequently turns out to be. The tempo is ♩ = 104 despite the interruptions of the repeated allargandos; when the passage returns for the reprise at letter **R**, one of these pull-ups is unaccountably omitted, but whereas this could cause some confusion, the rather fussy to-ing and fro-ing both here and at **R** was omitted *in toto* by Elgar himself in his recording and is thus best ignored, making a more cohesive continuity of the symphonic structure.

The fanfare figures inaugurated at **D** continue as an accompaniment throughout the principal Allegro section and indeed sporadically until **G**, during which time it should be a major feature of the texture and be brought out in the beating. The spectacular semiquaver arpeggiandos up and down in the violas and cellos in the 4th of **E** and 1 before **F** look forward to a similar virtuoso passage for these same instruments in *Cockaigne* and justify corresponding sweeps of the beat.

The after-phrase at letter **F** starts with quite a short first note taken with a staccato up-bow, after which a very soft and magical passage follows, the tempo, however, remaining constant. A chordal pair of bars for divisi 1st violins with wind melts into a ***pp***, the violins continuing their octave divisi (not well indicated in the score) until they reach their high E♭, after which the fanfare motif reappears on solo trombones. A pizzicato rising figure is under-marked here with a diminuendo from, instead of to, ***pp***.

The new exposition material comes to life again, quickly building up with the jerky figure adapted with accented quavers, culminating in a universal quaver rest before **G**, much as at **D** although with the beat lifting everyone off this time. Letter **G** is a greatly inflated and quicker version of the Andante at **A**, also with a spattering of rests calling for lift-offs in each bar.

Six bars before **H** great energy is generated by a working
of the march-like theme in which the repeated sforzando
phrases on the violins are themselves so organized with
vigorous beats that the two bars leading up to **H** have
considerable momentum with their third beat accents, the
strings emphasizing the sforzandos of the wind figurations.
In these a real point is to be made of the difference between
semiquavers and triplet quavers; the wind is controlled by
the left hand, the stick giving great emphases to the half-bar
unison string entries.

Letter **H** presents yet a further version in *ff* of the
Andante theme already heard in the Allegro tempo at **G**.
The unexpected drop to piano is followed by a vehement
resuscitation of still further references to the Andante, while
the left arm again comes into its own, encouraging the
upward demisemiquaver sweeps on violas and violins in
turn and building once more to *ff*. Soon, however, the
music subsides with the aid of the cellos' new counterpoint;
this gradual calando calls for a legato-style beat, leading to
the modulation and second subject in a meno mosso tempo.

So peaceable and melodic a subsidiary theme introduced
by the clarinet inevitably recalls Mendelssohn's *Fingal's Cave*
Overture, but is much more prone to exaggerated rises and
falls, together with a two-bar rit. The strings then pursue the
melody in soaring cantabile style; though at first still in *pp*,
this expanded statement again grows to forte before both
retreating with another rit., then adding an effusive one-
bar surge on horn and cellos. These fluxes in tempo and
dynamics need care and tasteful handling, the end of the
sentence coming soon after **K** on a pianissimo oboe marked
'semplice' to contrast with the very strong *fpp* accent in the
accompanying violins.

The cadence at the 4th of **K** produces perhaps the most
memorable passage in the overture, winding its way, always
in *ppp*, and making an elaborate closing phrase which is
initially in the 2nd violins and then taken up by the 1sts with
violas. After sinking right down, the violins climb slowly,

but in crescendo molto, to a *pp* subito on a fourth-beat fermata marking the end of the exposition.

A lift of the stick releases the violins from their fermata, and the development is immediately launched by the trombones, though they must not give more than the prescribed mezzo-forte. Where the violas, and later the 2nd violins, answer with the second subject, Elgar found he needed the contra to complete the accompanying chords, cueing the line into the cello part with little notes in case the instrument was unavailable; but it is a rare emergency that would today call such a necessity into operation.

The accented quaver passage in the cellos is an obvious feature in the forward progress of the accel. poco a poco, as are also the repeated sforzandos, which must be strongly marked in the beating. Before **M**, however, the cellos are interrupted by an important figure with swoops in 1st violins, clarinet, and bassoons, punctuated by articulated groups in pizzicato lower strings. These require very strong syncopated beats at the half-bars and lead to the sinister drama of **M**, where the contra is again a prominent feature, more so than the basses it is doubling, and the snaps on the brass can be quite startling. The string tremolos are unmeasured until 5 before **N**, where they play semiquavers; this is confused in the score, since the third stroke is missing already 6 before **N**. The change must come dramatically in the following bar, making a significant point in the build-up to the fortissimo.

In all this the accelerando has persisted, so that the giusto at **N** creates a powerful pull-up after the climactic strings and brass *ff* fanfare, which had reached at least $\downarrow$ = 112. There is no indication of tempo here, but letter **N** must clearly return to the basic pulse of $\downarrow$ = 104 in its full power.

This is the peak of the development, the knightly march-like motif of letter **B** being inflated to the maximum and building to a majestic unison take-off. These features are, however, to be kept in tempo so that the contrastingly lyrical con fuoco plunges forward, restoring the element of fervour with the surge of melody emphasized by the lower string triplets' offbeat sforzandos, these complicating the shape of the beat correspondingly with varied and curving signals.

From here the intensity diminishes to letter **O**, after which a gradual series of climbs and sudden drops carries the development forward, still with no change of tempo, through the succession of *fp*'s, these increasing in frequency. Eight bars before **P** the fanfare motifs return and always need cueing, as they come from numerous and unexpected quarters of the orchestra, including not only horns and trumpets but cellos, timpani, and lastly violas. The cellos have to keep the figure sharply at the heel, like the violas, who should emulate the imperiousness of horns.

After a short burst up to forte, a chordal progression in the trombones leads with a rit. into the reprise at letter **Q**. Of this the first two bars are derived from the introduction before **A**, albeit here in a sudden Tempo I, but thereafter the corresponding section before **D** is very closely followed, with a touch of extra brilliance at the strings' con fuoco rush of semiquavers into **R**. The *ff* snap in the brass and timpani is another highly effective touch given with the left hand while the stick is busy controlling the strings.

Like the one 4 before **E**, the allargando at **R** is not observed, while the one marked at **E** itself is now in any case missing, as mentioned above. Otherwise the return is quite strict and gives very much the feeling of familiar territory.

However, the stirring music around letters **G** and **H** is omitted, and the reprise passes quickly to the second subject, this time introduced soaringly by the cellos. The tempo is marked 'tranquillo' as at **I**, though not 'meno mosso', so that the sense of continuity is greater, especially at the expansive repeat of the melody with a busy semiquaver counterpoint on the 2nd violins. The characteristic cadential quaver phrase duly makes its appearance exactly as in the exposition, leading at **V** to the coda with a similar drop to *ppp* subito, but this time without the fermata.

The coda starts dramatically with the march-like theme on the 3rd horn, but in augmentation so that it acquires an ominous flavour accentuated by a violent *sfpp* tremolo on the violas. This is picked out by a strong downbeat which is the more effective in that the surrounding beats are not given at all until the tempo picks up in the 7th of **V**, with its gentle upbeat for flute and clarinet.

From here to the end there is a continuous accelerando, the rising string semiquaver groups being very skilfully dovetailed with the opening bars of the overture. These in their turn lead, by way of a brilliant woodwind chromatic scale punctuated at the half-way point with a powerful *sf* pizzicato, to the solitary cymbal clash which marks the culminating climax of the whole overture, and thence to the last invigorating tutti.

The second subject, pealed out by horns, plays its part in this splendid closing passage, each phrase answered enthusiastically by the tutti. The crotchet movement in the region of letter **Y** might suggest alla breve beating, but this is in fact never necessary, and the music builds instead to the triumphant brass theme, once again recalled from the opening bars but here given a molto stringendo lest its stateliness has the undesired effect of pulling the tempo back.

The final cadence comes at **Z** with great pageantry in the brass, strings, and timpani flourishes. The jerky motif closes the work with another stringendo, the tempo by now having reached $\downarrow$ = 132 before the last tonic unison B♭. This could have been crowned with a fermata, but instead is merely marked 'allargando' with a crescendo hairpin. However inexperienced Elgar may have been when he presented himself with this first orchestral work, he certainly did not lack self-confidence and originality, and it is a tasteful close to an exciting piece, avoiding the overstatement and banality which a pause would inevitably have created. There is mastery here, and the Worcester committee may well have congratulated themselves on recognizing and encouraging what at the time may have seemed a purely local talent. In the event they were giving the first big opportunity to a man who was to become Britain's greatest composer.

Serenade for Strings in E minor, Op. 20

◆▶

ELGAR wrote his String Serenade in 1892, two years after *Froissart*. He is supposed to have derived the material from three earlier pieces, but there is no evidence to corroborate this or to show which fragments these may have been. Elgar himself only wrote at the head of the manuscript piano duet arrangement a note to the effect that the themes were to a large extent the product of his wife, whom he describes as 'Braut' (literally 'bride', and his pet name for her), though this should be taken with a pinch of salt, however much Alice may all her life have been a source of inspiration.

Novello were offered the little work but turned it down ('there being no sale for such pieces'), a decision they soon had cause to regret because, although making no great stir at first, it came before long to rate as one of Elgar's best-loved and most frequently performed smaller works. Passing through London later, he visited Breitkopf & Härtel, who accepted it immediately, and to this day it remains one of the only two pieces by Elgar in their famous orchestral series. (The other is also for strings, the slight *Sospiri*, Op. 70.) Moreover this edition remains the only one in existence, so that its rehearsal letters are standard, though it is worth knowing that recent printings of both score and parts carry bar numbers in addition.

The Serenade works well for quite a small string ensemble though requiring at least three cellos. For all its three movements it lasts little more than twelve minutes, most of which lies in the deeply affecting central Larghetto.

I

The Allegro piacevole is marked at ♩. = 96, but there is a danger that at this tempo the movement may seem a little hurried, and it will flow more naturally at 88. Beginning in an easygoing ⁶⁄₈, the viola figure should be set in motion with the bowing *sf* / ⌣ ᵛ ⌐ ᵛ in each of the two bars. The dynamics in the score are not entirely reliable: for example, in bar 5 the 2nd violins lack their *pp*, and in the following bar the violas lack their new sforzando, as at the beginning. (The latter, however, is correct in the parts.)

The ³⁄₈ bar arises quite naturally as a result of the dovetailing of the two phrases, and needs no emphasizing; if anything, it is at the resumption of the ⁶⁄₈ in the following bar that a point may be made in the beating, the 2-bar phrase descending from there into letter **A**. But at **A** itself the beat-style changes from a lateral to a more vertical shape, characterized by the quaver rests interspersed between the pairs of quavers, each 4-bar sentence rounded off by cello/bass pizzicatos.

The violas should be prominent in the 11th of **A**, their *mf* contrasting with the *p* of the violins, whose sforzando two bars later, however, can afford to be quite weighty. The beating stops at that point, giving instead a pesante piano to the cellos and basses in the next bar, but resumes with a 2-bar reminder of the opening theme which leads to the 4-bar cadence rounding off this first statement.

Letter **B** starts the after-phrase, beginning in the middle of a bar with a strong up-beat. The double bar before **B** has ended well below pianissimo, and a general new mark of at least a single 'piano' is needed to correspond with the balancing *p* five bars later. The 2nd violins have a primary role here, as again 4 before **C**, the 1sts being concerned with the little cadential *mf* figures which lie between, and the violas with their initial staccato motif.

The change to E major at letter **C** provides an interruption to the more poignant forte phrase which had seemed to be leading to a further development of this first section. Instead the mood is changed utterly, and a rubato lead into **C** is warrantable on the upbeat, whereupon all the voices are suddenly *pp* with a little extra warmth in the 1st violins, and a lilting beat is brought into operation for the 2nds and violas, leaving the 1sts to find their own legato phrasing.

The brief interlude in the 7th and 8th of **C** should be clearly identified, especially as the 2nd violins take over the violas' staccato figure. The lilting beat resumes for a varied repeat of the pianissimo secondary melody, which then expands perceptibly at **D** before subsiding into a version for solo violin answered by tutti 1st violins divisi in octaves. Here a certain planning is required for the layout of the players, as it is not obvious which line the sub-leader should play. The conductor may take a decision dependent upon the total strength of the 1st violins in both quality and numbers, for the two lines should be as equal as possible.

After **E** the movement quickly builds to a climax, and the sforzando 3 before **F** can be interpreted a little expansively, returning in the next bar to tempo primo for the violas, who initiate the reprise. This follows the exposition very closely, so that a number of details can be correlated, such as the violas' *sf* in the 4th of **F** (cf. the sixth bar of the work), the missing *pp* at **G** (cf. letter **A**), and in particular the curious substitution of lines for dots in the 2nd violins and violas 4 to 7 after **G**, of which those in the second pair of bars, at least, seem to have no clear purpose and may not have been intended by Elgar.

The coda begins 5 before **H** and contains another outburst of emotion, which for so slender a work can be extremely effusive, with a strong imitative line for the 2nd violins and violas (whose double strokes are of course measured semi-quavers and not tremolo). The cellos divide front and back, and there must therefore be enough cellos for a complete desk to play alongside the 1st violins; the situation will recur in the Larghetto.

The surge of emotion collapses after the diminuendo, though the little stress in violins and violas should still have a degree of poignancy. There can then be a relaxation of pulse before the last ***ppp*** bars, which are, on the contrary, played in strict tempo.

II

Like that of the first movement, the metronome mark for the Larghetto is substantially too fast. The deeply introverted character of this kernel of the Serenade needs a great deal more latitude than may be provided by ♪ = 80, and a very thoughtful 60 is more likely to catch the mood of intense meditation which suffuses much of the movement, though equally it should not be allowed to drag.

At the start the 1st violins should seem to materialize from nowhere, an almost ethereal beat discouraging any definition to the beginning of their note; moreover, once they are installed no further beat is necessary until the G moves to A at the end of the bar. But thereafter normal beating becomes essential for the manœuvring of the other parts, from their ***fp*** entry through to the 2nd violin imitation in bars 3 and 4 with its further corresponding ***fp***.

The crescendo molto e stringendo, amounting in its urgency to a considerable advance in tempo, begins at once in bar 6 and can even attain a speed of ♪ = 92 by the time the ***sf*** is reached in bar 8. From here, however, it falls away into the a tempo, which once again picks up the opening theme just as at the outset but now on 2nd violins. Similarly the imitation is transferred to the violas, and in an extended diminuendo the opening sentence is rounded off with a pianissimo cadence. In the bar before letter **I** a clear but gentle downbeat releases the lower strings, and the 1st violins are left holding by themselves, the beat having ceased once more in preparation for the secondary melody, but maintaining strict tempo.

The subordinate theme which follows at **I** is of such length that it even reduces the first subject to an introductory role. The beating should be immensely reserved with no rubatos whatever, and the expression, apart from sheer quality of tone, devolves upon the pianissimos 8 and 4 before **K**. Two bars before the end of the sentence the quavers are marked with lines to indicate the separation between them rather than their length, though also to differentiate from the bars before **M** near the end of the movement, where they are transformed into dots.

Between **K** and **L** comes a central section, with varied texture but in exactly the same tempo, except only that the demisemiquaver turns can linger a fraction. The importance of the 2nd violins, who link the phrases of the 1sts and violas, is reflected by their prominence in respect of intensity of tone, and they should be positively emphasized with the stick. Elgar will have expected them to be seated on the conductor's right, though such a formation can by no means be taken for granted today.

In the 8th bar of **K** they grow to forte, which is an unexpectedly strong mark, especially with the arrowhead accent, but if treated as a firm, rather than a rough, indication this need not seem out of context, despite the prevailing dynamic of *pp*. The phrase is then transferred to the cellos just before the section reaches its climax, only yet again to drop to a most tender *pp* and thence to a breathless *ppp*, though with little hairpin bulges which must be nursed with great delicacy, particularly during the poco rit. leading back to the reprise.

Here Elgar inverts the order of events, and letter **L** gives a fully laid-out version of the subordinate theme. There is no printed change of dynamic, but it cannot be played at less than a single *p*. The elaboration of its treatment confirms the tempo as being ♪ = 60 rather than 80, and the cellos divide, as in the first movement, so that in performances with the smallest complement of players the whole front desk takes the top line and the single no. 3 cello the lower, alongside the basses.

The rustling semiquaver triplets in the 2nd violins and violas need not be too soft and should produce a magical background over the whole length of the melody, in which from the 5th of **L** the upper line of cellos joins the 1st violins. (Four bars later there is a misprint in the cello parts, the *rf* being printed in the wrong place.)

The accents in the accompaniment are subtle and important, requiring substantial emphasis so that when the whole episode is dying away the 2nd violin stresses 3 before **M** emerge logically and expressively. In the following bars all the notes corresponding to those 2 before **K** are marked with dots instead of lines. This should not be taken to mean that the notes are played off the string, although they are certainly shorter than before and well detached from each other. They also continue over two bars, this time descending to the closing paragraph in which the first theme returns, starting on muted violas and imitated as before.

Elgar asks for mutes in all the strings (except basses), and the greatly hushed closing section is pursued without variation of tempo until just the last three bars. The final chords are again separated very clearly, a longer gap being appropriate before the last chord of all.

III

The last movement is the slightest of the three, having very much the character of an epilogue or *envoi*. It should come nearly segue after the Larghetto, although time must be allowed for the strings to remove their mutes. The marking in the score is Allegretto ♩. = 92, slightly steadier than the Allegro piacevole of the first movement, and by analogy ♩. = 84 is likely to prove the most suitable tempo for the Allegretto as long as the beat is kept buoyant and fluid.

The first three bars are introductory, and full tempo is established only in bar 4. The 1st violin parts are marked with a harmonic 'o' sign over the A in the first bar only, but it is likely that those in bars 2 and 3 should also be taken in the same way. A slight lead is desirable into bar 4, where the violas start the main theme, though this should not be taken to mean that bars 1–3 are markedly slower, their introductory character being more a matter of suggestion and feeling before the movement takes wing with the violas in bar 4 followed by the 1st violins a bar later.

As at letter **L** in the Larghetto, there is no new dynamic marking here; yet this primary material can hardly be presented softer than *p*, and on the contrary warrants a real *élan* in the beat, almost of enthusiasm where this main theme of the Allegretto rises to new heights as at **N**. The introductory phrases then return with the harmonics, though again they are not in the score. The bar before **O** seems to languish but immediately gains new heart; **O** itself is then at an altogether new level of boisterousness for a short space before rounding off the paragraph with a full pianissimo return to the opening of the movement (harmonics and all), but now retreating even to *ppp*. The tempo should not, however, be slackened, and a last rising viola passage (again with a harmonic, on the high D) is greeted by the violins with a sudden *mf* chord followed by a *pp* pizzicato which contains an element of surprise.

This surprise is real, moreover, because instead of leading to a new section of the finale, which has after all never properly got into its stride, letter **P** takes us back to the first movement at the corner before letter **C**; and as there, so again here the lead into the new major tonality needs a rubato.

'Come prima' is an appropriate mark, as it transpires that the two movements are virtually identical in tempo, and the little $\frac{6}{8}$ figure, with which the whole work started, can be made to arise happily out of the link into **P**. There is a difference in this return, all the same, for the gracious subsidiary melody proves to have lost its accompanying lilt, the background now consisting purely of short crotchets placed gently on the beats. It has also grown a little turn, to be taken as a quintuplet of equally measured semiquavers, for which there should be ample time; an extra feature is also revealed in the form of a piano subito, which can be sufficiently exaggerated to be quite dramatic.

In the violin solo which follows as in the original movement, a suggestion of the lilt returns, but when the tutti 1st violins make their alternation they now lead with a quick crescendo to a strongly accented forte cadence. This indeed might qualify as the climax of the whole work, with an emphatic broadening over the two bars before **Q**.

Letter **Q** itself is then suddenly back into tempo for the coda, all in the happy tonic major and dominated by the opening $\frac{6}{8}$ figure. The pulse is now kept stable until the poco rit. of the last bars, as a new and descending cadential theme* is handed down from group to group in 4-note phrases.

On arrival at the bottom the violins start the ultimate ascent, cellos and then violas supplying the slightly tricky rhythmic pattern helped by the stick until the apex is reached. The violins are left alone on the top E, which swells until the full ensemble enters on the three closing ritenuto chords of E major, of which the last is the only one to be slightly separated as well as bringing in the basses, here divisi for the only time in the work.

An admirably economical as well as unproblematic piece for listeners and performers alike, the Serenade's present popularity is well established in the repertoire of string and chamber orchestras, being additionally enhanced by its easy availability in the Breitkopf catalogue.

---

* Jerrold Northrop Moore's derivation of this idea from Wagner's *Parsifal* is fanciful in the extreme. See *Elgar: A Creative Life* (Oxford University Press, Oxford, 1984), 160.

Overture, Cockaigne
('In London Town'), Op. 40

◀▶

THIS is not only one of Elgar's happiest, but also one of his most overtly popular pieces, taking its place entirely successfully as the opening item in any orchestral concert. The instrumentation is standard with the exception perhaps of the 4th trumpet (i.e. two trumpets and two cornets) and a considerable array of percussion, but it has no harp and only an optional organ part which, though not essential, adds immeasurably to the effect, exactly as in the Enigma Variations.

Lasting fifteen minutes, it is quite unproblematic to any orchestra and conductor conversant with Elgar's style, and has not infrequently been given by a London orchestra without any rehearsal at all. A thoroughly mature work, having been written shortly after *Gerontius*, it is full of virtuoso passages for the various sections.

The subtitle 'In London Town' naturally gives the clue to the programme of the overture, and the elaborate title page of the original edition is even illustrated with vignettes portraying characteristic features of London from Big Ben, St Paul's, and Piccadilly Circus to activities such as archery and golf, with a long panel at the foot showing an army unit led by a military band, bass drum and all, marching through the streets in full ceremonial kit; the Edwardian flavour of the whole design is irresistible.

The Cockaigne of imaginary medieval legend was 'a Utopian land of luxury and idleness where the rivers were of wine, the houses built of cake and the shops supplied goods for nothing. Roast geese and fowls wandered about inviting folk to eat them, and buttered larks fell from the skies like manna.'* There is also a well-known Bruegel picture of Cockaigne showing the inhabitants lolling about, but all this has nothing to do with the Utopia of Elgar's score, which is overflowing with energy and good humour and larded with an element of native vulgarity, such as the whistling of errand boys and glissando trombones.ß Elgar was not unique in connecting Cockaigne with the city of the cockneys, although their etymology is quite different. He loved such wordplay, and to him London was an endless source of delight, as the music makes plain.

The dedication of the overture to 'my many friends, the Members of British Orchestras' would imply that he had already in 1901 conducted more performances than are documented; but in any case it is amply justified by the grateful writing for so many of the players across the orchestra.

Cockaigne is one of the few works which, like the *Sea Pictures* and the 'Pomp and Circumstance' marches, were not published by Novello but by Boosey, the predecessor of Boosey and Hawkes, who now handle these works. For many decades the material was available on sale, but sadly this is no longer the case, and an eye has to be kept open in hired copies for misprints, which are not uncommon.

One odd feature of the Boosey house style was their use of the old-fashioned crotchet rests, exactly like quaver rests but facing the other way. These are prone to cause doubt and hesitation among players (indeed, they were presumably superseded for this reason), and some of the best orchestras have been known to take the trouble of rewriting every one in the parts, or else highlighting them in some way to ensure confidence and security of execution.

---

* *Encyclopaedia Britannica*, 14th edn. (The Encyclopaedia Britannica Company, London, 1929), v. 941.

ß The little pointing hands and their explanatory footnote on p. 3 of the score recommending the doubling of the trombone parts are, of course, always ignored.

The overture is one of those works beginning after three empty beats. The question is often posed whether the beating should start with the music; however, as in similar instances (e.g. Berlioz's Overture *King Lear*), not only does this create confusion, but the empty beats themselves should be made to set both tempo and style. Here the three crisp preliminaries are already part of the work and establish the cheerful scherzando of the violins' opening staccato. There are no metronome marks, and the simple 'Allegro' tends to cause unfamiliar conductors and orchestras to begin in too relaxed a tempo, which should on the contrary be no steadier than $\bullet = 104$.

The opening, with its fermata on the half-beat of the third bar, needs confidence to conduct effectively; even after this hurdle the clarinets tend to be a little stodgy unless the beat is consciously springy. The bouncing quality must be implicit from the very beginning, affecting not only the 1st violins but also the syncopated lower strings. The fermata is then caught on the bounce and after only a short hold released to carry forward the remaining semiquaver of the first beat before indicating the continuation of the bar.

The horn's *fp* should spark the clarinets into a real show of vivacity echoed by the violins in the following bar. The opening motif is used as a background to the rising line of the 2nd violins and clarinet, which, until fig. 1, is the basic shape of the music and therefore dictates the direction of the beat.

At 1 new figures are launched through the orchestra with a great sense of bustling. Elgar uses one of his familiar devices by which the 1st and 2nd violins change places in alternate bars, and this will be depicted in the beating, the principal line coming on the 1st violins in the first and third bars, the 2nds taking over in between. The tenutos can be allowed to take effect but they must not hold up the basic tempo.

The entry of the trombones with their short snaps presents yet further material on the 1st and 2nd violins in turn, while the second-beat sforzandos in the next bars are given with a flourish. A vehement unison passage follows, beaten with great panache, the strings surging upwards to the *fff* of **2** which is a full-blown restatement of the opening subject and is presented with all the *élan* at the conductor's disposal, side drum and cymbals added to the already brilliant instrumentation and a tuba solo supporting the bright upper strings, all to be characterized in the presentation.

Three bars before **3** the brass take over the theme in a brash version separated by half-bars of string pageantry. The brass are to be under-conducted, the strings on the contrary given their due, especially for the trill, in which they are joined by flute and piccolo and which can be perceptibly extended as it leads into the Nobilmente transition melody.

This is marked 'Vibrante' as well as legato and must unquestionably be taken at a steadier pulse of $\downarrow$ = 96. The beat has already had to change to a more effusive style, especially at the 3rd of **3**, where for the first but by no means the last time, a wide sostenuto is substituted for the perky manner suitable for so much of the overture. The strings play with long sweeping bows and the brass with weight rather than punch on their rows of accentuated crotchets; this is a work which can too easily be made to sound raucous instead of impressive.

If the occasional misprints are sorted out, the strings' slurs can be treated as bowing as well as phrasing and will work perfectly. The typical fourfold sequential repetitions before **4** should move forward supported by the horns and trombones, and end with a slight tenuto on the final crotchet introducing what is patently a vigorous a tempo at fig. **4**, though nothing is marked in the score.

This is short-lived, and after only two bars an accelerando, centred on the trombones but with a sforzando on the second beat featuring the timpani, takes the tempo forcibly forward until cut off with a cymbal clash. The link to the second subject resumes peaceably at what is in fact another unmarked a tempo. The woodwind dynamic of *mf* is missing at the 5th of **4** but is self-evident, and the pedal A♭'s on

the trombones will need to be more than **pp** if their splendid
rumble is to speak. The tempo then eases gradually, having
to be very carefully graded until the più tranquillo of 5,
where the second subject, with its characteristic octave leap,
is only a very little slower than the original speed.

There are a number of interpretative details which should
not be passed over in the beating of this transitional passage
between 4 and 5. In the 4th of 4 the **ff** triangle should be
heralded with an upheld arm; all too often the player remains
seated with his instrument hidden behind the part, so that its
ringing turns out to be disappointingly subdued. The trombone crotchets in the following bar have tenuto marks, but
these should not be construed to imply a broadening of the
pulse, which by this point has a considerable forward thrust,
as indicated by the 'bright' before the accelerando. Then in
the 5th of 4 a return to tempo must nevertheless not rob the
strings' downward swoops of their brilliance despite their
mark of **pp**, and a graphic swish of the stick can be exercised
to feature this additional touch of colour.

At the change of key signature the strings' triplet quavers
become primary in the overall calming of the music's flow,
but once established they should not continue to dominate
the beating, which will rather turn to the woodwind, making a point of their weak-beat stresses 5 and 3 bars before 5
and, in the in-between bars, of the scherzando element of
the staccato figures in the flute and oboe. In the bar before 5
the horn should broaden perceptibly, especially on the last
tenuto quaver at the end of the bar.

Elgar marks the gentle second subject 'a tempo' as well as
'più tranquillo', and this is important for the life of the piece;
it cannot be allowed to linger, lest its romantic overtones
distort the overall drive of the movement. A speed such as
♩ = 88 would allow sufficient elbow-room to the many
lyrical touches in the string writing, such as the violas in the
3rd and 4th bars of 5, or the espressivo passage in the seven
bars before 6 where the interplay of polyphonic string
writing is so effective.

The bar before 6 is one of those crescendo bars needing a pull-up before the piano subito of fig. 6, where a more inflated repeat of the second subject features a counterpoint which, seemingly of little consequence, will register more strongly at its return before and at fig. 33 and must therefore be given enough emphasis already here.

The pervading mood of gentleness is disturbed 3 before 7, the accelerando starting imperceptibly a bar earlier than marked so as to arrive at the very different idiom and tempo of 7. The errand boy's whistling on his bicycle in true cockney style is a diminution of the transition theme (fig. 3) requiring a perkiness easily adopted by the clarinet and thereafter, in 2-bar phrases, by other departments in turn. These are joined by a chromatic counterpoint first heard on cellos and horn, which is equally important and can be additionally delineated by the conductor.

From here the momentum quickly builds up, the beating increasingly concerned with the short rhythmic quavers which, from the 3rd of 8, feature on every beat so that the diminution theme marked 'brillante' on violins and flutes can safely be left to shape itself. Nevertheless when the 2nd violins and violas take over the pattern, joined again a bar later by the returning 1sts, sharp cueing is essential for their sforzandos. Most striking, however, are the four horns in their *ff* unison entry 2 before 9, which can afford a fair brashness, encouraged by a raised fist.

This leads into a brief reprise of the *ff* tutti from just after fig. 2, but that is interrupted 3 bars before 10, where, the timpani marking the beginning of each bar with *ff* figures, a series of rising scales takes the continuity into a return of the second subject, conducted with a suddenly broadening beat in an appreciably steadier tempo.

The phrase repeats at a lower octave on the horns, who appreciate a gesture inviting them to bring out the first deep sforzando note before the rising octave. A 3-bar pattern of overlapping lines building upon one another at half-bar intervals then forms the cadential close to this episode at 11 with an evocative ascending passage on the cellos needing delicate handling.

Figs. 11 to 12 then produce a quite unexpected and deeply poetic vignette for the strings alone in which, at the more relaxed tempo, the grand transition melody of fig. 3 is given dolcissimo, rising yearningly in both pitch and intensity before subsiding in a passage entirely built out of sequential repetitions, as in the bars before 4.

This romantic episode must be most sympathetically woven in its curve up and down, with no vestige of dragging or of rubato over its thirteen bars (six up, one at the top, and again six down) until it turns the last corner into 13. The whole passage, marked 'legato e dolce', is additionally inscribed **ppp** at the head of the score as if to emphasize the peacefulness of the idyll. Elgar was able, with his personal knowledge of string technique, to write into the 1st violin line exactly the way he wanted it played, with which finger on which string, and these indications should be honoured meticulously, string crossing, harmonic, and all.

With fig. 13 the busy streets are quietly re-entered, and faint touches of the distant hurly-burly should be picked out on bass drum **ppp** and pizzicato basses. The gentle tranquillo tempo is resumed as the clarinets' and bassoons' quaver arpeggiando, extending across the gamut of their instruments, alternates with a melodic idea from the second subject on the strings. The spell is broken by a sudden **mf** burst on all the cellos, quickly followed by a virtuoso exhibition for just the solo cello, marked **f** with a further rise and fall into 14. The stick of course has a strong purpose in identifying with these graphic passages as they melt into the new section.

In the whole preceding section, the conducting should aim to be absolutely undemonstrative, especially in view of what is soon to come. With the change of texture at 14, some suggestion of this becomes distantly apparent, although the pulse remains constant, as the clarinet gives a forte premonition of the still far-off military band against an exaggerated vibrato on 2nd violins and solo cello and **pp** pizzicato quavers on tutti cellos and basses. The triangle, though *pp*, also hints at a whiff of excitement in the air. (It should perhaps be added that the hairpins in the vibrato lines are wrongly shown at the 2nd of 14, but correct after 15.)

The tempo begins to pick up soon after 14, and then again especially at 15 after the short 2-bar return to rhapsodic material, where the pulse cannot be relaxed or the ricochet figure on the 2nd violins and violas will become clumsy. Also there must be no doubt that the fever is mounting, so that both the cellos' and 1st violins' allusions to the second subject can afford to be adequately effusive.

By now the pulse will have regained its original ♩ = 104 in preparation for the marching soldiers who are fast approaching. The four trumpets proclaim their proximity with a *f* crescendo fanfare, which will sound quite abrupt in its aggressive noisiness, while the effects mount with cymbals and side drum, both still soft, backed by sharply accented trills in the woodwind. But it is to the hand-stopped horns of 16 that the beat is aiming, and their snarling quality should then be quite startling.

The rushing, chattering figures which surround the brass punctuations, then further fanfares, could suggest the enthusiastic gathering of the crowd as it collects to line the procession. This is mostly a phenomenon of the past; military formations led by a band rarely strut through the streets of London other than for changing of the guard at Buckingham Palace, the Lord Mayor's Show, or similar festive occasions. Elgar's depiction of a feature familiar enough at the turn of the century therefore has a strong period flavour.

When the tuba joins the fanfares the approach is about to reach its apex and a glittering cymbal clash, with jingles and triangle, frames a pageant of trills on woodwind and strings and a rousing peal on the four trumpets. Conducting this should be nothing short of exhilarating, the principal voices being the cymbals and the crescendo of the trumpet chord, depicted with a steadily rising arm until abruptly taken off.

The new episode is of course exclusively concerned with the military march-past, and the cornets and trombones, with timpani and bass drum, are the heroes of the hour, given their head without fear of the resultant vulgarity. The brass are evoked with the stick and the percussion with the left hand, leaving the wind and strings to trill away happily.

A long-limbed march tune, it contains a subtlety not always adequately observed. The semiquavers at the end of the first full bar often sound the same as those before and after, whereas they should be closed in to make two notes of a triplet after an ample semiquaver rest, giving a much more arresting, and sophisticated, effect.

Two bars before 18 the horns and trumpets warrant an evocative lead where they join in for the climactic high A, before the trombones slither down *fff* to a great bump on the percussion, given graphically in the conducting.

The strings and side drum now take over, the violins attacking their G strings at the last possible moment before 18, and the sentence builds, after a couple of offbeat cymbal clashes, to the Grandioso tutta forza for the whole orchestra, which is a little steadier. It is here that the five additional percussion players are fully employed to stunning effect, especially with their three accented quavers.

Two bars before 19 the brake comes off, and from 19 itself the tempo edges forward once again, motivated principally by the brass quavers, which have enormous cumulative power. The whoops on the cornets are a noteworthy feature, as are the running triplets on the cellos, while the 3-note figures on the upper strings and woodwind might well represent cheering among the crowd and should be given with enthusiastic gesturing.

In the three bars from the 5th of 19 it is most effective, despite the second-beat sforzandos, to conduct only the downbeats with their *fff* side-drum figures, resuming full crotchet beating for the trombones (also *fff*) 4 before 20. The upper strings and woodwind here repeat sequentially the errand-boy diminution of the transition theme no fewer than eleven times during the descent into the Tempo I of 20.

The animato of 19 has been carried through to the peak of the whole episode 4 before 20 and the two bars of poco rall. are now necessary in order to restore equilibrium in the ensuing interlude. At 20 it is unexpectedly the semiquaver rises and falls on flute, 1st violins, clarinet, violas, and ultimately the two bassoons in turn that have to be featured: the first subject references which they cover are treated as purely incidental except for an augmented statement on the (unmuted) 4th horn, the player enjoying a moment of glory not to be underestimated despite his mark of *pp*. The *fp* in the bar before 21 can be quite strong, also helping his preparation for the plunge to the long pedal at 21.

An interesting feature of the horn writing already from the 3rd of 20 is Elgar's return, for bass-clef passages, to the 'old' notation otherwise abandoned since the Enigma Variations (where it was used only sporadically), though there can be little doubt that for these pedal notes the deep-looking bass-clef notation is beneficial. The lack of any mark for the unmuting in the 4th of 20 can only be an oversight.

Fig. 21 represents the long retreat and disappearance of the band, whose march step is portrayed by quiet tambourine and bass drum in addition to cellos and basses. Elgar's repeated tambourine crotchets are implemented with the words 'battuto col mano', that is, struck once on the parchment, whereas the sign ⌄ on each note often leads players wrongly to shake the instrument or to use the thumb.

The strains of the band itself are heard primarily on the clarinets in echo-tone (ghosting) with an espressivo after-phrase on the violins. The clarinets present no problem except that they have to be frozen into a true *ppp*, being the one instrument that can really achieve this effect. The violins' phrase has another of Elgar's favourite tenutos, which obviously conflicts with the continuing, but ever softer, march step, whose inflexible progress is nevertheless not to be interrupted; the tenuto therefore has to be skilfully negotiated.

The rise and fall at 22, though marked 'poco', is perceptibly more than that of the cellos and basses two bars earlier, dropping to near inaudibility. The three further violin afterphrases, with their tenuto rubatos, are additionally interesting for their varied dynamics, the middle one in the divisi 2nd violins being the strongest, and the third (returning to the divisi 1sts) as soft as possible. Elgar says nothing about the lead into the Più tranquillo of 23, but with the faltering in the far distance of the march step a calando is patently required, and we are in another pastoral scenario at the halfway point of the overture.

This is a leisurely section on, for the first time, quite new ideas. The tempo can be as relaxed as ♩ = 72, which will allow for the conductor's main preoccupation: the fact that, of the two strands being constantly juxtaposed, one is a smoothly flowing row of quavers, while the other is expressively rubato with a tenuto over the first note of its triplet every time. The latter should not disturb the calm progress of the former even though the tenutos must always be positively observed, and this therefore calls for a sensitive flexibility of beating in which the players have the responsibility of listening to each other as the two motifs wander from section to section across the orchestra. The tenutos are apt to come and go in the score, but this should not be regarded as significant, and the shaping of the motif should be regular and constant through the accelerando after 24, where it is joined with other and earlier themes. Even the tuba has its turn just before the end of the section at 25, where the increase in pace will have reached tempo primo.

Fig. 25 marks the beginning of the link back to the reprise, which is extremely ingenious and makes for great interest in the conducting. The principal theme, starting quietly, is reiterated five times but on different instruments and irregularly spaced, being separated by varied numbers (three the first time, four the second, and so on) of, again, sequential phrases with syncopated accentuations. The result is that the second and third statements of the primary theme, on horns and trumpets respectively, start in the middle of the bar, making for splendid variety.

The trombones and trumpets are uniformly piano, the horns a single 'forte', whereas the woodwind whoops which punctuate the theme are always strong, *ff* or *f*. The balancing should emphasize these irregularities, not only the half-bar horn and trumpet entries, but also the dynamic oddities which contribute to the building towards the reprise at 27. Five bars before this arrives there is great play with the horns, of which three present the theme *f* in unison answered in the following bar by the 1st player, who can be an impertinent *ff*. The humour of this is often lost and needs to be stressed in the conducting.

Figs. 27 to 28 correspond directly with the 4th of 1 to fig. 2, but at the 3rd of 28 the horns take wing and join the semiquavers of the upper strings and woodwind in a passage of high hilarity and virtuosity, the tempo having surged in the excitement to ♩ = 112. Nor has Elgar overreached his imagination by any means: an extension of development using the opening bars with great ardour leads to an elaboration of the material at 30, which the conductor can sweep along with immense joviality for the trombones' *glissez fantastico*.

The end of this outburst comes at 31, where, recalling the broadening at fig. 10, a wide and effusive beat slows the headlong pace for the second subject with its rising octave. In the 3rd of 31, moreover, the violas and cellos should be alerted for a huge downbeat to send them on their way up the nearly 3-octave *ff* arpeggio.

Suddenly all is calm once more for a resumption of the lyrical second subject's full reprise, much as at figs. 5 to 7 though with more fervour than that first time, as witness the fine solos on horn and trumpet, the latter needing extreme delicacy.

The stringendo can start earlier than marked, much as in the bars before 7, leading at 34 to a similar a tempo for the perky diminution of the second subject with its chromatic counterpoint. This quickly builds to a fortissimo with trombone snaps corresponding to the passage after 8.

As on that previous occasion the tempo here remains stable, but instead of the horns pealing out, the 3rd of 35 abruptly doubles in intensity (so that 35 itself should not be too strong; the four horns with their chromatic descending phrase in octaves are only *mf*), and the *ff* can be very sharply accentuated with a suddenly vicious beat. The 1st cornet must raise the bell for his solo semiquavers in the fifth bar in order to obtain maximum projection; it is surprising how often this penetrating instrument can nevertheless be covered in an isolated bar of brilliant solo writing.

In a trice all is quiet in preparation for the fanfares, which relate to those at 16 but have less sophistication, the band bursting in much more abruptly than before. Otherwise everything is very similar, *fff* brass with *fff* trills on upper strings and wind, triangle jangling and all, but greatly curtailed and with less show of enthusiasm, so that the conducting should be less ebullient, once again bearing in mind what is to follow.

The bars before 38 are clearly equivalent to those before 19, but instead of the flag-waving and crowd noises (cello triplet semiquavers) leading to the climax of the band tune, this time there is a pronounced allargando followed at last by the solo entry of the organ on a low A played on the pedals, with 16-foot and 32-foot stops against the trilling upper woodwind and strings.

So striking is this effect that it is disappointing not to find Elgar making provision for the frequent absence of an organ, and many conductors invent some more or less appropriate substitute in order to cover at least this important first note, usually a tuba playing an octave lower than printed. The trills break up into crotchets with a molto rit., and the peroration follows in grand style, consisting of a vastly inflated version of the romantic second subject.

This has of necessity to be broader; what Elgar says is: 'Tempo, Nobilmente (con molto espress.)', and then again— another of his favourites—'vibrante', but if the organ should happen to be present this will automatically pull the tempo back. In any case, even without the cohesive legato of the organ, the texture is massively opaque, and it is fascinating to find Elgar advocating in a footnote that the cornets, of all instruments, are not to be prominent.

Even the largamente in the 8th of **39** must not be overdone, and only substantiates the side-drum roll that culminates in the cymbal clash of the following bar. On the contrary, the descending sequence of seven repeating phrases should at first be allowed to move forward lest they sound heavy-handed. Here, as earlier in the work, the inconsistent use of 2-note slurs can be observed meticulously for the bowing and will be found to work perfectly as it stands, arriving at the sul G $\frac{3}{2}$ bar down/up exactly as marked over the slur.

This $\frac{3}{2}$ is the only other place in the work where the organ is intended to be heard separately from the orchestra, its two minims overlapping the quaver rests of the tutti. It has to be admitted, however, that the gestures taking the orchestra off for their quaver rests too often also bring the organ away, and the effect—acoustically subtle at best in most halls—is generally lost, especially as the organ part adds caesura marks (//) between the minims.

The last brilliant, even hectic, bars of coda relate back to the passage before **10** with the double counterpoint of the principal theme and the ascending scales, here marked 'a tempo, stringendo'. The timpani then dominate the close of the work, slowing the tempo from the very beginning of the *ff* solo. The conducting is mostly done with the eyes until the marked molto allargando, which needs a strong degree of auto-suggestion rather than subdivision. When the timpanist has arrived on the sixth quaver of the second-last bar he has a hiatus while the remainder sustain: then the conductor addresses an intensely vigorous 4 : 1 to the trombones, who also play the last group of rapid semiquavers, and to the solid block of percussion, who meet them on the last note.

Such a highly original and effective coda to a wholly successful piece needs great assurance and panache from the conductor if it is to achieve its intended flamboyance.

Introduction and Allegro for String Quartet and String Orchestra, Op. 47

◄►

THIS larger and more important of only two string orchestra works by Elgar of any consequence came into being as the result of a suggestion that the composer should add another piece to an all-Elgar concert he was to conduct in March 1905 with the newly formed London Symphony Orchestra.

The Introduction and Allegro is a substantial item lasting just under a quarter of an hour and elaborately set for a string quartet seated at the head of a double string ensemble. This can cause seating complications, especially with any but very large groups, for ideally the double formation ought to be laid out with twice the usual number of front desks, that is, a desk of upper 1st violins sitting beside a desk of lower 1st violins, and so on. In this way, passages like the bars before fig. 12 (and correspondingly 27) would be fully represented in all the lines without any loss of intensity in the lower parts of each section.

To arrange this satisfactorily needs a very wide platform, unless the work is played with a small group, as is sometimes done; but the additional arc of the string quartet in front of the main body then broadens the circle to an inconveniently wide extent. It is, moreover, rare to have the possibility of two files of cellos, who need a great deal of space and for whom the musical necessity is far less urgent. The basses are sometimes ranged along the back, which can be very impressive.

The string quartet was always intended to consist of the leaders of the orchestral sections and not, as has become more fashionable of late, an imported established quartet, which has obvious derogatory implications with respect to the orchestral leaders. Nor is there any need for this, as the writing is far from virtuoso and should blend with the other players through familiarity of tone and style.

There are no metronome marks in the score, and indeed much of the time the tempos are so fluid that any fixed indication of speed could be as hard for the listener to establish as recognizing (without the aid of a score) the exact point where the Introduction gives way to the Allegro. On a first hearing, the transition often seems to be at the semiquavers of fig. 10, but it is in fact fig. 7.

The opening bars have the character of an *intrada*, and the massive writing is handled almost in recitative style, the conductor articulating the triplets as well as guiding the pacing of the crotchets, which, marked 'Moderato', are in the region of $\downarrow$ = 44. However, the accentuation of every fortissimo note, as well as the great double-stopped appoggiaturas in the first two bars, can pull the concept of tempo back still further. The quaver rest in the second bar is covered by the 2nd violins as well as the sustaining basses, but in the next bar the players all come off together after the first short quaver.

In the fourth bar the largamente weighs down the progress of the triplets to the point where subdivision could be implicit, although inner pulsations to each main beat are more demonstrative without resulting in too great a ritardando.

The fermata has to be long enough for the *ff* to come down quite gradually to the very soft background over which the quartet starts at fig. 1. The marking here is no less than 'Allegretto poco stringendo', although this only lasts six beats before a rit. brings back the Moderato with which the tutti takes over. The Allegretto starts at $\downarrow$ = 112 and the Moderato at 80; the rallentando then takes the flow back to 50 for the so-called a tempo, though not, of course, the very broad enunciation of the opening bars, which should be kept in reserve for the succeeding largamente.

So many and such a variety of tempo changes means that rather than taking them too literally, a sense of continuity has constantly to be borne in mind when shaping this opening section. The 5th of 1 is led by the quartet, the tutti being kept to an echo quality against the *mf* of the unison soloists; in the next bar the 2nds and violas of the tutti are addressed, with their sudden *ppp*. However, the repeat of the phrase is not merely a simple largamente but is fully reconstituted with a significant dolce harmonic taking time on the fourth beat, although the after-phrase is repeated with its drop to *ppp* exactly as before.

Fig. 2 then goes through the same motions as 1, with the Allegretto intensified to a molto stringendo in forte, and with the variant that there is no 2-beat rit. into the Moderato. Hence the tutti which now enters emphatically on the fourth beat, taking over from the sforzando of the solo quartet, brakes abruptly at the double bar.

The upbeat is therefore strong but quick, the slower tempo of the Moderato beginning at once at the new bar and steadying further in the continuing forte with a heavy bulge in the lower instruments. The poco a poco rit. arrives at an a tempo which is the first in the work to remain stable for any length of time, and can be established at $\bullet$ = 80 as the solo viola embarks on the motto theme of the work accompanied by very quiet lower strings. It is best not to conduct the viola but rather to place the dotted minim/crotchet of the accompaniment and sketch in the occasional phantom-like doublings on sections of the violins, which should hardly be noticed as they creep in and out.

At 3 the quartet can be left to itself both for the two bars of broadening and for the recovery at the third bar; the beating concerns itself purely with the shimmering tremolo on the violas and the pizzicato basses. But from the fourth bar the tutti join in and need full-scale conducting even though their marking is at first only *pp*; in the 5th and 6th of 3 the 2nd violin triplets confirm the moderato tempo of the whole, which persists until 4.

Here the tutti largamente corresponds exactly with 3, despite the vastly increased instrumental setting and the accelerando to which it leads, with collapses to *ppp* and *pppp*, needing extremely evocative conducting. An enormous swell then takes the music back to the beginning of the work.

Before leaving this motto theme it is worth noting a point which is often overlooked, especially by the tutti: this is the dots under the slurs, which should be carefully observed, though not overdone, by the 1st violins with lifted bows during the eight bars before 4.

The tempo primo of 5 is self-explanatory, with its great enunciations of the opening phrases, even if these are differently laid out. The majestic declamation, now supported by dramatic cello/bass tremolos, is conducted as before even without the largamente of bar 4. The *sf* fermatas must not be too long, and the quaver rests between them only just enough to banish each tutti chord and prepare for the next. There should be a calculated impression that it is only half-bars which are being extended and that the mightiest of the chords, which brings in the quartet once more, is a clearly contrasting full bar with a long diminuendo of the tutti to *pp*, leaving the solo ensemble prominent. The più mosso is then essentially cautionary, lest the theme should drag, amounting to a Mahlerian 'nicht schleppen'. The tutti pizzicato in the bar before 7 is marked *pp* but should be firmly placed for its obvious significance. Then, when the quartet has settled onto its lunga fermata, the 2nd cellos still have to be cleared in preparation for the Allegro.

This turns out to be an extension of the Allegretto passages of figs. 1 and 2 at a slightly brisker tempo and in more elongated sentences. The Allegro is about ♩ = 112, with the isolated poco allargando bars suddenly dropping to 76 but returning immediately to the Allegro tempo each time. They are always the exclusive domain of the solo quartet and thus do not directly involve the conductor, who merely picks up the second a tempo bar as it is handed to him, in pianissimo with an abrupt swell to forte and back.

From here to fig. 10 the quartet and the tutti are handled as self-contained units, the quartet generally amplifying the tutti at high moments of the forte argument, except 3 before 10 where it is used antiphonally in piano. The phrasing is at first directed towards the third beats, but as the forte reduces to piano or pianissimo the first beats become more significant until 10, where, the quartet having momentarily dropped out, the surging tutti arrives at a complete lift-off.

The semiquaver passage-work of the second subject is utterly different in style and texture, amply befitting the principal motif of a completely new section. In the first three bars for quartet alone the conductor merely marks the barlines, so that the solo ensemble controls the speed which is in fact identical to that of the preceding passage, but, because of the detail, must not hurry. When the tutti violins take it over, the irregularities in the pattern should have time to make their points clear, such as the accent in the crescendo molto bar and the sudden change to long bows at the forte.

Again the quartet takes a turn, but this time the second line of tutti violas enters to double the solo cello so that only the one bar is marked, though it still needs hardly more than a strong downbeat for the barline. Fig. 11 returns to the tutti exactly as before but in forte, and this can bring up the question of bowing style, since there must obviously still be a contrast with the long bows where the lines are marked in the third bar. Elgar indicates no dots, but the bows nevertheless come heavily off the string.

The entry of the basses at the 5th of 11 should be thunderous, and the fortissimo of first the solo, then the tutti violins immensely striking. The beat will need to give the syncopations to the quartet and to the tutti 2nds in the 5th and 6th bars before 12, this taking the impetus up to the first of the scale passages, which, being broken between the sections, have to be played as strongly and vehemently as possible. The inner 2nd violins, the inner 1st violins, and the outer 2nd violins all need specific forcefulness, and care will have to be taken to place these sections as prominently as the platform will permit.

The downward rush into 12 is precipitant with a quite sudden broadening for the nobilmente itself, which is a positive degree steadier than the preceding Allegro, at ♩ = 92. The beat here concentrates on the pounding cellos and basses, against whose regular and relentless quavers the great triplet crotchets of the opening motif battle with formidable energy.

Five bars before 13 gives another characteristic lift-off for the whole ensemble, and in the subsequent release from rhythmic battling the sempre *ff* con fuoco can forge ahead at not less than ♩ = 100 in one of Elgar's most flamboyant tuttis, which is delivered with energetic beating to bring out the second-crotchet *fff*'s at and after 13.

The style changes with the rising syncopation 3 before 14 and the antiphonal entries which leap-frog over one another, leading to the first of the great scrunches. The massive pillar-like tutti chords are brought in by the left arm, while all the violins combine in a spectacular semiquaver unison controlled by the stick. The pile-up into 14 will have brought the tempo forward so that this 'brillante con tutta forza' arrives at a very strict ♩ = 112.

The zenith comes at the 5th of 14, when the violins are joined by the upper members of the quartet as well as by the tutti violas, the lower instruments taking over the semiquavers. The sudden piano has then to be indicated dramatically, followed by the universal crescendo molto requiring a violently accented beat.

'Rit.' now signifies 'ritenuto', not 'ritardando', the pull-up being sudden and all but beaten in 8. In the event it is only the last two quavers that are actually subdivided with the stick; the penultimate is perceptibly the longer, being specifically marked 'tenuto'.

The a tempo at 15 clearly relates to fig. 12, with a pronounced edge to the first note and the tremolo as close and thick as possible. Although triplet crotchets are pre-eminent until the return of the motto theme, 4-in-a-bar beating is maintained, the triplets broad and firm against the basic pulse as they tail away through the violins and cellos.

A somewhat sharper beat is necessary in the 3rd of 15 for the 1st violins' semiquavers at the end of the bar as they conflict with the cellos, but otherwise the beat is wide and sweeping as the drama subsides and the exposition draws to a quiet close with the combination of the two themes, the triplets now in pizzicato, the motto on the solo quartet. Nevertheless an emphatic downbeat delivers the ponticello *fp* in the penultimate bar, the passage then dying away altogether onto a fourth-beat fermata in preparation for what should normally be the development. However, Elgar had decided instead to insert what he described as 'the devil of a fugue'.

This is given as 'Allegro (tempo primo)' but in the event it has to be a degree less furious, nearer ♩ = 92, in view of the Più animato to come and allowing for the considerable complexity of detail. The beating is fundamentally straightforward and concerned mainly with leads for the fugal entries, but there are some more expressive features which need to be portrayed, such as the cello/bass upsurge to a momentary *f* just before 16 and the equally unexpected change to a brief lyricism 5 before 17.

But generally the dynamic remains uniformly at degrees of *p*, so that when the quartet enters in unison it easily dominates the texture, combining a motif from the start of the Allegro in easy counterpoint with the fugue subject.

Suddenly there is a change and the tempo enlivens markedly to ♩ = 104, the 2nd violins and violas alternating the opening figure from the fugue in a vigorous build-up over three and a half bars, the 1st violins joining them as they progress. The quartet, reinforced by the outer line of tutti cellos, interposes a fanfare-like phrase which is conducted with striking emphases.

The beat then follows the alternating figure as it descends through the tutti strings down to the basses before fig. 18 resumes the fugue subject, now at the quicker tempo and with a new countersubject on the quartet. More important still is a running semiquaver idea which joins the general mêlée.

This goes through the different voices until the climax is reached at **19** for the final *fff* fugal entry with its powerful row of three sforzando quavers in the second bar, all of which should be enunciated with powerful stresses.

This is clearly the high point of the fugue, pressing on to the three bars before **20**, which feature a succession of sforzandos crowding in one upon another so that in these bars only the second and fourth beats need conducting at all. Fig. **20** itself, on the other hand, relaxes the tension as well as the tempo, so that the fugue subject, though in fact persisting through to **21**, can be left to itself and the legato lines more carefully directed, especially since the poco a poco meno mosso is so gradual.

The a tempo of **21** corresponds with the beginning of the fugue, and needs careful direction as it steers the music back to the reprise of the Allegro. The solo cello in the meditative bar before **22** enjoys the maximum freedom, only the second beat, in which the lower tutti strings change chord with his entry, being marked.

From this point the reprise covers essentially the same territory as the exposition with only minor variations. The tempo is, as before, $\downarrow$ = 112, which is quicker than the opening of the fugue and hence than fig. **21**; then the semiquaver section at **25** is as controlled yet excitable as ever.

The overlapping scales before **27** are exactly the same as before **12**, and so too is the nobilmente passage that succeeds them, except only for pitch and key. The violin semiquavers at **28** are also largely parallel although even more brilliant in detail, particularly the ascent to D *in alt* at **29**. But the bar before **30** shows an important difference, with the fermata on the fourth beat and a sustained cutoff over the semiquaver rest, creating a moment of suspense before the passionate and expressive coda is launched.

This is a true Elgarian grandioso consisting of a blown-up version of the motto theme. It is marked 'a tempo', but the purpose of this is to ensure that the additional molto sostenuto is treated as an indication to sustain the actual notes of the theme rather than as a broadening of overall pace. The reference is to the ♩ = 80 in which the theme first appeared on the solo viola before fig. 3, and which therefore must not be too pompous or over-inflated.

Particularly interesting are the dynamic marks of the middle voices, which are notably restrained to avoid the textures becoming over-congealed. The semiquavers linking the phrases at the end of the fourth bar can be hurried a little, lightening the passage for a few bars before it becomes even more full-blooded at the largamente with its sul G colouring.

This, however, lasts only two bars before a stringendo carries the peroration forward once more. No indication is given of where the stringendo leads, but the *ff* con fuoco at **31** can be taken to establish a new and vigorous development of the theme, the orchestra dropping to pianissimo while the quartet continues the evocative fortissimo in a unison continuation of the melody.

The orchestra then swells up in just two beats from piano to *fff* for the final 4-bar enunciation, the tempo remaining forward-thinking though there is no new marking; nor is anything printed to signal the change of tempo at **32**. Here the peroration of the motto theme gives way to an energetic concluding passage based on the Allegro material, necessarily at the much quicker ♩ = 112, the last bars being extremely brilliant.

The whole work concerns itself so much with musical rather than colouristic technique that it is the more welcome when, after a lift-off of the unison low G, the final chord is a mighty pizzicato which, being of itself naturally somewhat less resonant than a corresponding arco would have been, needs to be delivered with tremendous panache.

Concert-Overture In the South (Alassio), Op. 50

◄►

ALASSIO is a seaside resort in the north of Italy which was much patronized by the English at the turn of the century and was visited by the Elgar family in the winter of 1903–4 when the composer felt in need of inspiration as well as new thoughts and ideas. The weather proved a disappointment with ceaseless rain and a bitter east wind, but the change of scenery did him the hoped-for good, and by the time he returned to England a substantial plan of the overture was already mapped out.

The appellation 'Concert-Overture' was given it from the first, perhaps after Mendelssohn's examples such as *Fingal's Cave*. It is, however, a longer piece than *Cockaigne* and a good deal more substantial than *Froissart*, lasting over twenty minutes and scored for a bigger orchestra with triple wind and two harps; with a symphony in the offing Elgar was thinking on a larger scale.

For a time *In the South* was less regularly played than other popular pieces, but in recent years it has come back into favour, as well it might. The impetus of the opening has something positively Straussian about it, and the 'canto populare' of the central section with its viola solo has been arranged for numerous combinations under a subtitle 'In Moonlight'.

Elgar marked the opening 'Vivace ♩. = 63', implying that it might be conducted in 1, but he himself played it a good deal more steadily, with 3 beats at ♩ = 144, which is far more realistic, and indeed exciting. The two silent crotchets of the first bar have to be beaten out, with a tremendous punch given to the violas for their third-beat entry. In the second bar the three pulses have all to be emphatically accented before the main theme starts on the horns in bar 3, thus emphasizing the necessity for a crotchet beat.

This opening wants to be given all the *élan* the conductor can muster, reaching a splendid climax with cymbal clash 2 bars before 1, although the actual peak comes a bar later with the *ff* timpani roll, both cymbals and timpani falling on the second beats of their respective bars.

Nor is the exhilaration to be allowed to drop at 1, despite the reduction in dynamics and the mark of 'sostenuto' in the violins, whose $\frac{3}{2}$ cross-accentuation over the first four bars of 1 carries the music along with ever increased momentum. The harp arpeggios add to the *joie de vivre*, doubling each other as they do virtually throughout; indeed, the work is sometimes mooted to be perfectly practical for a single harp, but this materially disturbs the balance of Elgar's orchestral colouring.

Two bars before 2 a sweep of quaver triplets down and up leads already to the next climax, in which the main theme is transferred to the trombones, pounding out with great weight and, at the same time, considerable agility. On the upper instruments, the new counter-theme demands some sharp demarcation, provided by the staccato crotchets on the first beats. In the 2nd of 2 this is effected by a retaken down-bow, but two bars later it conveniently arrives up-bow, a lifted staccato thus happening automatically instead of having to be artificially engineered.

The excitement builds up further to fig. 3, where the descending octave A♭'s on, in turn, the 2nd violins, violas, and basses cause a pull-up in order that their accentuations can be given extra emphasis. Tempo is, however, resumed at the *ff* surge of a new sequential figure which drives in passionately at the upbeat. A point should be made here of the bassoons, who have a quite spectacular rush of semiquavers, an effect not too easy to bring through with our ultra-refined instruments.

The new melodic figure has a counterpoint on the 2nd violins and violas, each new phrase restarting with a sforzando. These again are effected with a series of down-bows so that the groups of quaver triplets have plenty of attack.

At the 9th of 4 the texture lightens for a short while, running semiquavers in the violins taking pride of place over the leaping principal subject, whose triplet figure is continually repeated, always needing special attention from the beat. But this motif comes vehemently to the foreground during the approach to 5, where, marked by a thunderous crash on the percussion, it is launched on a *ff* restatement against a background of repeated quavers not unlike the opening of Strauss's *Ein Heldenleben*. However, after only five bars the lower instruments run headlong down a *ff* scale while the upper lines have a succession of sforzandos every half-bar, each alternate one having to be indicated with a syncopated second beat.

It is apparent that the suggestion of $\frac{6}{8}$ is already implicit, and at the Nobilmente of 6 this duple rhythm completely takes over as the primary one, the beat changing to two broad dotted crotchets in *fff* molto sostenuto, at $\downarrow. = 96$. This duple beating is sometimes wrongly ignored, especially if the whole opening has been beaten in 1, but it is essential to the proper understanding of the work, relating directly to later passages such as fig. 51.

Four bars before 7 it can be necessary to explain to the trumpets that the crotchets of their $\frac{3}{4}$ cross-references back to the primary motif of the work are proportionately faster, so that the minims in the first two bars come before the second (dotted-crotchet) beats.

Fig. 7 gives the solo line to the four horns, who benefit from a beat given in their direction; meanwhile, the subsidiary $\frac{6}{8}$ theme rises steadily until at 8 the music springs back to $\frac{3}{4}$ for a continuation of the primary theme on the trombones, beaten as before in a quick 3 so as to bring the brillante violin triplets into prominence. These build ever higher with strong accentuations on the third beats (given with the left arm), until the three dazzling cadential bars are reached which bring this whole opening paragraph to an end. Of these the third inevitably takes time, its pesante character anticipating the following bar, which then amounts almost to an a tempo.

Even allowing for the mark of 'Molto espress. e largamente', which does indicate a reduction of intensity, both tempo and energy continue to be maintained in this gradually descending bridge passage. The beating changes to a wide legato style apart from the 2-bar groups of woodwind figurations at the 7th of 9 and 2 bars before 10, which demand clear pulsations, the one *mf* the other *pp*. Even the basic motif needs a smooth treatment during this period of relaxation, descending ultimately to fig. 10.

The transition section is reached with a *pp* low C on two oboes in unison, a hard note for these instruments to sustain so quietly in perfect intonation, but it nevertheless has to persist through nearly to 11 as the new themes quietly announce themselves to an unobtrusive crotchet beat. In the alternations between wind and strings the two most characteristic features are the dynamics, with woodwind crescendos to subito *pp* answered at first by an espressivo swell in the strings (which must all be indicated, with appropriately contrasting gestures), and the ascending scales in the strings, which are later brought into even greater prominence.

Eventually, after a bar in which all movement ceases, a quiet pulsation establishes itself, with pizzicatos and drum taps at the barlines marking off the pattern of the otherwise gently flowing sequences of the transitional melody. For reasons which will soon be apparent, this tempo has to be very precisely judged, as it relates to that of the second subject soon to follow. After the easing of pace at 9 it will have settled down to a quiet $\downarrow$ = 112, and this must be kept unaltered until timpani and basses take it over for the last twelve bars before the $\frac{2}{4}$ as an ostinato of repeating crotchets which, as the clarinets fade to nothing, remains the only perceptible element. For this the beat, which has been legato in style during the lyrical transition, changes again to clear, albeit tiny, pulsations.

With the ostinato established, the time now changes to $\frac{2}{4}$ for the Poco meno mosso of the second subject. The basses and timpani, oblivious, continue their pattern, so that the beat has to catch the rhythm and against it set a new tempo corresponding exactly to the ratio of 2 in the time of the old 3. But from here on, the tempo is by no means as stable as before. For four bars the basses and timpani pulsations continue inexorably, and the beat is of course constrained to fit the new melody with them; but then there is a great surge in pace as the ascending arpeggio of the lower strings presses forward in a passionate forte.

The next allargando bar is then so much broader that it is beaten in a wide sweeping 4, immediately changing back to 2 for the accelerando, where the violas and clarinets are urged up their rising octave at almost double speed; then again the tempo pulls back in the approach to a dramatic pianissimo at another much slower pace. The a tempo 3 before **14** temporarily restores the equilibrium, the melody resuming as before, and even if the degree of intensity is now somewhat heightened, the rubatos and the single bar of subdivision followed by the pianissimo are all conducted in the same way.

Fig. **15** initiates a change of direction, a 6-bar stringendo being pressurized with a succession of second-quaver accents which have to be featured with an urgently syncopated beat. This culminates in an affrettando, the ascending, still syncopated violins moving forward so fast that the quavers of the lower strings at the largamente are suddenly at least twice as slow. Their second quavers are still accented as in those of the stringendo, but now handled with a wide, curving beat in what is a most expressive passage. (The 4th horn here should read B♮ instead of B♭, one of several surprising misprints in a generally reliable edition.) A lead-in bar for the cellos then carries the music over to the closing section of the exposition at **16**, whose a tempo refers to that of the second subject $\frac{2}{4}$, as at **13** but in absolute calm.

A fleeting memory of the original motto theme on the clarinet cuts across the gentle idyll, the $\frac{3}{4}$ (not indicated in any way by the conductor) sounding curiously fast against the prevailing $\frac{2}{4}$ pulse. The exposition then fades right away as the corner is turned to the fragmentary development.

This time the return to an overall $\frac{3}{4}$ for a restatement of the transitional material is made by crotchet equalling crotchet (that is to say, as it was before the rit.), the triple rhythm thus being markedly slower and more relaxed than before. There is considerable purpose here, as a long and gradual stringendo no less than 44 bars in length is soon set in motion, leading up to the first of the two central episodes of the work which take the place of a true extended development. This linking accelerando is entirely devoted to working up the transition themes as they become ever more excitable.

The timpani bulges in the 4th and 8th of 17 are at once suggestive of future tumult and can be exaggerated by the left hand while the stick controls the calm repetitions of the smooth themes in woodwind and violins. The subsidiary rising scale, on the other hand, quickly boils up to violent exhibitions of fervour, the new theme 8 before 18, marked 'con passione', building the stringendo with great impetus in its second beat emphases. The renewed accelerando before 18 is additionally highlighted by a sudden *ff* outburst on all the violins, given with a flurry of the stick.

Yet more excitable repetitions of the transition theme are given fresh vivacity by the fanfare-like trumpets and the upward skirls of the strings, while quaver scales are given to *ff* horns and then trombones, these heavier instruments requiring increasing shows of energy to intensify the continuing stringendo. Even the con passione theme is marked 'con fuoco' on its return, while the scales rise from the trombones through to the trumpets and end with a dazzling flash on the flutes and piccolo as well as, down in the depths, a rearing tuba solo six bars long. At last the whole passage is taken off with a clearance beat, leaving a silent crotchet rest before the next section begins with as forceful a *fff* upbeat as it is possible to give.

The conductor's main preoccupation amidst so much activity is to gauge correctly the degree of acceleration over the 44 bars from the ♩= 112 of fig. 17 to the Grandioso at 20, marked at ♩. = 56. As at the beginning of the overture this seems to presuppose a beat in dotted minims, which is again quite unsuitable for the style as well as being simply too fast.

On the other hand, so consistent and so forward-thrusting has been the long accelerando that it has far overtaken the Grandioso tempo, arriving by the bar before 20 at hardly less than ♩= 152, whereas the 'Roman Ruins' section, which does not go into 1 until 26, should be no faster than ♩= 132, to reflect the weight and majesty of the conception.

Elgar had been enormously impressed by the Roman remains and the echoes they seemed to evoke of past glories, but in particular by a huge bridge, one of many examples which are such a feature of the northern Italian coastline, which he therefore set out to depict in the passage between 21 and 26. First of all the mighty 8-bar theme of fig. 20 is stated twice, the second time with upbeat thumps on the bass drum, all indicated with the left elbow; but this is curtailed by a bar, so that the strange and highly original idea, suggestive of the tall supports of a Roman aqueduct, then bursts in with added impact. This is nearly but not quite conducted in 1, with only a single strong beat given in each bar as the chords build downwards one note at a time.

After the first two such 'pillars', each always eight bars long, they are joined as before by the heavy upbeats, reinforced now by bass trombone and tuba but conducted in the same way. There are eight 'pillars' in all, the heavy upbeats of the first four being at first replaced, then joined, by an ostinato in 'Amsterdam' rhythm. From the seventh, even the pealing horns are overshadowed by glitteringly high trumpets, which can be dangerous unless helped by the conductor's high outstretched arm. The last of all, in which there is uniquely no diminuendo, is extended by a bar to round off the whole sentence with a moment of silence.

Fig. 25 returns to the Grandioso theme, now marked 'largamente' and gradually fading away through the poco rit.

to **26**, where an entirely new and wild episode breaks out, in which for the first time in the work a real 1 in a bar is necessary. The marking is 'a tempo (con fuoco)' but it should be positively brisker as well as rougher than before, at $\downarrow$. = 69. Elgar visualized this section as 'a sound picture of strife and wars', and certainly it is full of violence and syncopated cross-accents.

The background drum roll here produces a possible misreading: for the first eight bars after **26** the roll is given to the timpani in the bass clef, but on turning the page it is suddenly on side drum in the treble, while the timpani play on tonic and dominant with the basses. Moreover when the side drum starts on this next page of score there is no new indication 'tr' as at **26**, and the impression is given that it should have been side drum from the start, the timpani entering afresh with its imitation of the basses rather than changing suddenly from the one line to the other at the turn of the page. The side-drum *pp* is the natural mark after the crescendo from *ppp* on p. 43, with further crescendos to follow on the next two pages, while the timpani continue their own figure.*

The turbulent quaver passage-work builds up steadily with its regular downbeats, every second pair of bars being syncopated with three accents against the two regular stresses of the pounding downbeats. This all comes to an end at **28**, which presents an object lesson in 1-in-a-bar conducting, syncopated tutti crashes coming irregularly on the different offbeats.

A single allargando bar reverts momentarily to 3 beaten-out crotchets, only to plunge forward immediately once more. The violas' triplet quavers are primary in surging forward again, followed by the savage descending trombones who need a strong lunge with the stick.

---

* However, I am aware that the opposite point of view is held by my son Jonathan, who in a closely argued note on the text (unpublished) presents the case that the score is correct as printed, only lacking the 'tr' marking 8 before **27**.

At **29** the whole sequence repeats with, exactly as before, the single bar of allargando beaten out in 3 followed by a precipitous bar of triplet quavers given this time to the 2nd violins, and the formidable accented quavers transferred from the trombones to the horns but with no less panache. A leap up the octave on tremolo 1st violins then brings back the Grandioso theme (now at full tilt) from the 3rd of **30** in a threefold sequence of crescendos each restarting from piano. There are percussion upbeats, side drum followed by bass drum emphasizing the corresponding upbeat groups on violas passing to cellos and basses. Nevertheless the string tremolo crescendo moltos are the leading voices for the conductor's attention, the third of them building to the climax at **31**.

This recapitulates the sequence of **26** but is much more strongly projected, with mighty percussion strokes dominated by cymbals, steadily decreasing in power, however, as the fury begins to dissipate. The essential point of these percussion crashes is that they come not on the first, but on the third bar of each 4-bar phrase, omitting altogether the group at **31** itself. Furthermore they descend to piano just as the rushing quavers reach their most furious fortissimo. The perversity of these irregularities means that very clear direction is essential, not only for each percussion stroke but also for the string and wind *ff* entries, the last of which careers downwards into the calming section of **33** with great precipitation, even suggesting an avalanche.

Elgar uses two motivic elements from earlier in the work for the long transference from violence to the calm episode which forms the kernel of the overture. The first is the passionate 4-bar phrase which, coming just after **28** and repeated before **30**, contains the bar of allargando, originally beaten out in 3 before going back to 1 for the string triplets and brass quavers. Here, however, the tempo quietens steadily, the quaver triplets continuing the uninterrupted flow on first a solo clarinet and then a bassoon.

The other motif follows immediately and comes from much further back. This is the delicate woodwind figuration from between 9 and 10, and for which the beat reverts to 3 directly after the bassoon's descending triplets and for the remainder of the episode, the tempo having in any case calmed to this extent, so that the transition is smooth. (A minor misprint ought not to escape notice here: the timpani rise and fall 7 bars after 33 naturally takes place in a roll, as four bars earlier.)

Recurrent isolated glockenspiel notes give a nice colouristic touch as the string tripartite descending chords fall away to the Meno mosso of 34, and should each be neatly pointed with the left forefinger. The muted viola solo is often thought to be a folksong, and Elgar was on various occasions challenged with this, but he persisted with a denial though it continued to be known as a 'canto popolare'.

The four solo 2nd violins, who from the third bar of the harp chords give them continuity while still ***ppp***, need placing or they tend to lack definition, coming every time on the second beat over the next 26 bars. (The 4th bar of 35 lacks the crotchet rest, a patent misprint in the score.) A crotchet beat is maintained despite the absolute prevailing tranquillity, but the last four bars before 35 should be less positively conducted so as to allow the solo instrument greater freedom, strict tempo being resumed at 35.

A rich low G on the flute engineers the tonality into E, and the new melody passes to a haunting solo horn. In all these events a minimal beat is of the essence, only a faint undulation being perceptible apart from the flute and horn cues, until 36, where a marginally richer string texture briefly replaces the solo viola, who then returns to round off the cadence into 37.

The 32-bar section from 37 to 39 is a kind of entr'acte in which motifs from elsewhere in the work make very quiet reappearances while the viola solo is resting. It should be conducted with infinite tenderness, always in 3 even though the textures are so slender, and with a persistent leaning towards the third crotchet.

At 39 the viola reiterates the opening bars of his solo with 2-bar interruptions which can press ahead, falling back each

time for the viola's next phrase. The first of these **ppp** interjections recalls the theme from fig. 17 with its rising scale; the
second brings back, equally wistfully, the chromatic flute
figure from between 9 and 10. In each case the rubato back
to the viola has to be handled with the utmost sensitivity.

The solo instrument then utters one more phrase to hardly
any beat, the few accompanying lines fading to nothing until
he is left quite alone on a fermata, dying away without any
further indication from the conductor.

Pianissimo, almost apologetically, the reprise creeps in,
but quickly gains confidence and within only seven bars has
attained its original **ff** panache. From this point it repeats
the opening of the work faithfully with only a few changes
of instrumentation and some minor abridgements, of which
the most important is undoubtedly the dovetailing of the
transition by means of a Poco a poco meno mosso after 43
where the staccato wind and 2nd violins need most adroit
control.

The tempo at 44 must of course correspond with that of
11, and it is necessary to maintain control for the second
subject at 46 even though the earlier subtlety of 3 against 2 is
eliminated this time round, the timpani changing to 2 crotchets in the bar with the new pulse. The many varieties of
tempo in this highly imaginative theme are exactly as before
until, instead of the a tempo tranquillo of 16, the closing
motif of the reprise at 49 is marked 'Poco più mosso' so as
not to anticipate the total calm of 51.

Against the quiet forward flow the rising arpeggios of the
two harps are a prominent feature, while the motto theme's
$\frac{3}{4}$ against the prevailing $\frac{2}{4}$ (this time on two clarinets in
unison) is even given a little extra boost to the speed. Then,
in a more extended passage than earlier, it loses all energy,
getting ever softer and the figures on the harps degenerating
from semiquavers to triplet quavers, while the melodic solo
horn and lower strings are marked 'echo **ppp**'.

At 51 the passionate $\frac{6}{8}$ theme from near the beginning of
the work returns in a profoundly meditative guise, still **ppp**

but at a slightly more moving pace despite the 'tranquillo' marking. At last, after 12 bars, the ruminative stillness begins to be enlivened by a gradual crescendo, and after a further ten the accelerando adds to the process, though it will take all of 28 bars for the crescendo to reach the forte tempo primo at 53, bringing back the spirit and enthusiasm of fig. 8.

Consequently the energetic $\frac{3}{4}$ returns, conducted as before, but this time heightened by a notable cymbal clash in the fifth bar, a colour that has not been heard since just after 32. The short extension of reprise is thereby propelled towards the coda by means of a stringendo molto, and 54 is accordingly conducted in 1 to obtain the considerable increase in speed. In the 4th and 8th of 54 the cellos and basses plunge in with great vehemence, after which the horns' quaver passage is the foremost element in the ascent, while the once-lyrical transitional motif is transformed into a sharply enunciated figure growing towards the timpani explosion and the tutti outburst.

The whole grand build-up achieves its resolution at the *Volles Zeitmaß* (as it were) of 55, where the coda begins in earnest. Constructed entirely in regular 4-bar phrases at $\downarrow.= 92$, this development of the opening motif climbs easily with the horns echoing the leading voice, whether on strings or trumpets, with mounting energy through four sequential 8-bar phrases until 57. Here there is a conglomeration of themes, with glockenspiel and harps adding the sugar icing to the cake, and with so many disparate elements being controlled by a single beat in the bar, it can be worth keeping an eye on the duplets (including 1st violins) to ensure maintenance of ensemble with the relatively less flexible lower instruments. The excitement then mounts higher and higher until it breaks off suddenly, leaving only the $\frac{6}{8}$ icing while whirling quavers spiral upwards in groups of fours to the peroration of 58. Though the final approach is again of eight bars, the symmetry has clearly been broken, the bar-groupings being $2 + 3 + 3$; indeed, this conceals a further irregularity, for in each of the 3-bar phrases it is a different pair of bars which contains the twelve 3-against-2 quavers across the barline.

Two of these bars now become one at the *fff* Grandioso in $\frac{6}{4}$ time, thus beaten in 2 though the speed of beat remains the same. Essentially, the music corresponds (in renotated form) with the Nobilmente of fig. 6, but combined from the start with the primary motto theme, here given jubilantly in horns and brass with uplifted beat, until 59, where the texture edges upwards to the climax at 60. The strings now produce as thick a texture as they can for the 6-bar cadence pressing the tempo forward to as much as ♩. = 108.

They come off short, and the stage is cleared for the triumphant crotchets on the brass, who carry all before them for two whole bars before having to be forcibly gestured down to piano for the downbeat of 3 before 61 so that the strings, directed with vehement beats to the lower and upper sections in turn, can be heard to make a powerful attack on each of these half-bar entries. A savage solo timpani stroke is then marked with the left hand and raised in a mighty crescendo roll up to the general fortissimo of fig. 61.

Five last bars provide a satisfactory but more conventional ending than to *Cockaigne* or the symphonies. Yet it can be made highly effective with strong syncopated beats three bars from the end, these last bars making a feature of what was from the start an outstandingly dramatic motif.

Although hardly a major virtuoso solo, the Serenade interlude often earns the viola his own applause at the end, for when played beautifully it can make a most moving effect.

Falstaff—*Symphonic Study,*
Op. 68

◆▶

AFTER the two symphonies *Falstaff* is Elgar's mightiest orchestral work. It was written for the Leeds Festival in 1913 for which purpose the composer even provided a substantial explanatory note, realizing that the piece would be hard to understand without some guide, which, he further conceded, everyone should read if they were to grasp the many and continual intricacies of the score.

His analytical essay, also masterly in its own way, was originally printed in the *Musical Times* but was subsequently published separately by Novello. Yet even so the work proved unfathomable for many listeners, with its basis not only on the Shakespeare of the *Henry IV* and *Henry V* plays, but on many contemporary literary comments about the characters and events, and despite its superb musical qualities the work has failed to capture the wider public's imagination and enthusiasm. It is interesting to note, moreover, that it has acquired a parallel in Orson Welles's equally scholarly but less well-known film *Chimes at Midnight*, based on exactly the same Shakespeare plays, in which Welles himself plays the part of Falstaff.

It is a moot point, rather as in the case of Strauss's *Don Quixote*, to what extent a primarily descriptive score loses validity if performers and audience alike are not fully conversant with what the music is intended to portray. Tovey was courageous enough to write one of his *Essays in Musical Analysis* without reference to Elgar's, comparing his findings with the composer's stated intentions and adding in footnotes the many places where he had gone astray.

To regard this as a shortcoming on Elgar's part is to do him an injustice. Ultimately it has to be the sheer quality of the music which must be paramount, however important a knowledge of its literary background is in its appreciation, and here Elgar cannot be faulted. A continuous 35-minute symphonic span, it is crammed full of thematic ideas of the highest calibre which lead to and from one another as in any symphony. Furthermore, as Elgar's essay explicitly points out, it is in reality built in four clear sections, though the demarcations between them are less musical than programmatic. Moreover, there are no indications in the score either showing where the four sections lead from one to another or identifying the thematic allusions to the different characters and events.

Elgar uses a large orchestra, similar to those of the symphonies, with the two harps and an extensive percussion department. Although the 2nd harp is marked 'ad lib.', in fact it is essential, as is immediately evident in places such as fig. 137. On the other hand, set within the piece are two interludes for small orchestra, which have even been published separately, although they make little sense on their own and cannot be said to have had any kind of individual life, excellent as they are in context.

When in 1931 Elgar recorded the work in the brand-new Studio 1 in Abbey Road (and it was an inaugural recording), the Gramophone Company sensibly included the entire analytical note in the record album. So important an event was this considered to be that a splendid photograph was made (see Frontispiece) showing Elgar standing on the podium, not only surrounded by the London Symphony Orchestra with his friend W. H. Reed in the leader's seat, but with many of his more distinguished devotees draped around the studio steps, including none other than Bernard Shaw and the conductor Landon Ronald, the dedicatee.

I

Without any preamble, the work opens immediately with a character-study of Falstaff himself. It demands a heavy upbeat, but thereafter the printed $\jmath = 92$ is exactly right. Sir John Falstaff is corpulent but not unwieldy, with buoyancy in his sequential motif, so that a degree of momentum as well as humour should be reflected in the realization of his themes; in this respect the bar before fig. 1 can stand out, as will the others a little later. On the other hand, the comodo after 1 itself shows another side to his character and should be gently, even affectionately portrayed. Falstaff is too often taken to be a mere buffoon, and Elgar is at pains to show that there is much more to him than that. He has, however, a strong comedy element about him, and in the bars around fig. 2 there should be quite a ribald suggestion of Falstaff running, to the high amusement of his confederates. Chief amongst these is, of course, the prince, who is graced by the cheerful but dignified motif at fig. 4. The tempo has built up in the preceding bars so that the string trills and riotous trumpet triplets lead easily into the $\jmath = 100$ of Hal's Con anima.

It is particularly important that there be no pomposity as yet in this theme of youthful royalty, broad and extended as it is. Hal and Sir John genuinely enjoy their times together, as is shown by the lightness and gaiety of their conversations. The *ff* restatement by the tutti should have a true *élan* and *joie de vivre*, also a notable absence of snobbishness about the company the prince is keeping, to the despair of his father, King Henry IV.

The hardest passage to conduct in this scene is the subsidiary motif at 7, a fine theme for the cellos where even the lead-in a bar earlier needs a joyful flip, after which the accompanying offbeat staccatos in the upper strings come sometimes on the second, sometimes on the third crotchet of the new $\frac{6}{4}$'s half-bars. The cello section needs to bear in mind the cajoling side to Falstaff's behaviour in this most gratifying of soloistic passages.

By way of a poco allargando, the cellos reach their high E at fig. **8** only to swoop down with a glissando before once again picking up the tempo. The offbeat staccato now comes on the trombones before being pursued by the harp, a particularly hazardous passage with the harp playing together in unison with both flutes and upper strings.

The 2nd bar of **9** returns to the music of fig. **2**, with its alternation between an easygoing motif and animated passages, building at **11** to a boisterous restatement of Falstaff's and Prince Hal's themes. Both these are delivered with enormous enthusiasm until at **14** the cellos' theme is reintroduced in high spirits and at a greatly enhanced tempo on the four horns. At **15** the Allegro molto presses on to a Più animato, and in the hurly-burly Falstaff's themes career downwards to a dramatic cut-off and forte after-sally. This brings to an end the short section devoted to character portrayals of Falstaff and Prince Hal, the two colleagues in mischief.

II

With the next section, which of course proceeds without a break, the action begins and a mass of new thematic fragments is introduced. Although fig. **17** is marked 'Allegro molto', the printed $\downarrow$ = 120 would turn the array of material into a positive scramble, and the relatively sober mood and the fragmented themes might on musical grounds suggest a more practical tempo such as $\downarrow$ = 100. Yet this runs the risk of being pictorially too tame; the motifs are intended to illustrate Prince Hal's tavern life in Eastcheap, in the thick of London's underworld, and the level of sheer ebullience has to be kept to the maximum, even humorous silences such as the bar before **18** or the half bar six bars later not being allowed to defuse the tension.

These Eastcheap themes are splendidly contrasted, and it will be suitable to vary their style appropriately in the beating. They are all fundamentally light in texture but have important elements which make them treacherous to convey. The first groups are overtly scherzando, the staccato quavers in the third and fourth bars running forward into the motif garnished with trills. The bassoons' theme 5 before 18 is one of Falstaff's humorous epithets, and leads immediately into an explosion which seems to lie rhythmically upside-down, both beginning and ending on a strong upbeat. This is followed by a string of little wind phrases always differing in number at their various appearances over the course of the work; and the whole is cut off abruptly in mid-air.

After a G.P. bar the entire sequence is repeated, sparked by an even greater explosion with a longer appendage of wind groups but descending this time into the start of a new and considerable sentence. After so many epigrammatic utterances this lengthy theme takes on an importance of its own even without revealing its programmatic allusion, and it is, hardly surprisingly, the place where Tovey went furthest astray. For the feeling of continuity is one of the theme's main characteristics, whereas its suggestion of wailing is entirely subsidiary; Elgar accepts Falstaff's description of himself as 'a goodly, portly man of a cheerful look, a pleasing eye, and a most noble carriage', and accordingly this theme carries the tempo forward over its 27 bars, leading to a strongly invigorated development at 21 where Falstaff's motifs are combined with the strings' quaver pattern, the tempo having built up to $\stackrel{.}{\downarrow} = 112$.

At 23 the motif with the trills is embellished with ferocious brass *fff* chords, summoned evocatively with the left arm, until an elongated trill boils over into the fragmented figure, itself extended and supported by a meandering chromatic phrase rising and falling in the lower instruments, which must also be driven forward vehemently.

Out of all the turmoil the bassoon motif emerges in the lower strings and, soon broadening, leads to an immensely wide-spanned theme, taken at a slower tempo and intended to convey Falstaff's 'colossal mendacity'. The tempo will have eased to as steady a pulse as $\downarrow$ = 92, and the strings should be encouraged to play with long bows. Wide sweeping beats will give the right character to this generous theme, and even more so when it is transferred to the lower register doubled by bass trombone and tuba.

The tempo picks up energetically 2 before **27**, the beat slashing the pizzicatos forward for the themes to combine at **27** with no feeling of artificiality, and the trombone and tuba work hard to keep the wide-spanned theme consistently sonorous until the climax is reached at **28** with the crunch of the harps.

So long an accelerando inevitably brings a return to the basic tempo of the section, marked at $\downarrow$ = 120 but still in reality hardly quicker than 100. The violins re-enter with the quaver motif in what is an exacting passage, needing ultra-clear springboard downbeats as the 1st and 2nd violins take over from one another, and especially when the phrases in the diminuendo to piano each start after a quaver rest.

The tavern themes return once again for a very quiet extended scherzando, using all the different areas of the orchestra in turn and only reducing the tempo at the bassoon motif, which is here bandied about on the whole department with wistful flute touches given with twists of the left hand.

A more directly descriptive section intervenes, recounting the exploit at Gadshill in which the companions set out to indulge in some highway robbery and the prince turns the tables on Falstaff. The scene is set at **32** with a deliberately innocent-sounding motif on the violins in which the earlier tempo is suddenly restored in the prevailingly deceptive *ppp*. The sustaining cor anglais suggests that the conspirators are holding their breath (no beat for two bars), then the 2nd violins run away with the quaver passage-work transformed into Falstaff's main motif in diminution. The idea is a visual one: Falstaff is panicking, and the tempo can accordingly quicken for the two bars before **33** and again at **34**, the bars in between returning each time to tempo primo.

A particularly comical effect is created at the 4th of 34 where the easygoing 'out-of-door' motif (as Elgar himself describes it) is suddenly played *ff* for a bar and a half before being sternly repressed to *ppp* once more. Without doubt Falstaff has fallen flat on his face and has had to be reproved by the others for his clumsiness.

The G.P. bar before 37 will suggest that the conspirators all keep total stillness until they know the alarm has not been raised and they can continue their operation. The silence is thus indeterminate in length, scurrying semiquavers only starting when the bandits are reassured that all is well. This is a very theatrical section and can be handled in a theatrical way. Muffled horn calls summoned by the left hand are answered by a rush of semiquavers depicted with the stick.

In the score the horns are muted, but in his own recorded performance Elgar has them played 'open', and there is much to be said for following his example; the low G on all four horns at 38 is particularly ineffectual played muted. This is not the only detail in which Elgar's recording departs from the printed score, as will transpire in due course.

Suddenly all is hustle and bustle; against the strings' triplets Prince Hal's theme can be detected in half-bar bursts, though everything is still to be kept on tiptoe until 43, when pandemonium is let loose. Sweeps of the cymbals, given with the left arm alternately at the half-bar and on the barline, are especially important in the depiction of the battle in which the booty, stolen in triumph by Falstaff, is in turn stolen from him by the hooded and disguised prince.

Fig. 44 is a virtuoso fugato pursued with all vigour on the mendacious theme in diminution, at a tempo of $\downharpoonright$ = 112. Too difficult to play well any faster, it is the more exciting if kept clear and well articulated. Harps and timpani are added to the detail and can be given appropriate emphasis.

At last the music builds up repetitively, a syncopated rising line in lower strings taking it again to the extended theme of 19, which repeats at 48 in combination with the wide-spanned motif (from just after 25) on all the lower instruments. The adventurers are back at the 'Boar's Head' tavern, and Falstaff is boasting to the prince, uselessly since that character knows precisely what took place and makes no pretence of accepting Falstaff's preposterous version of the ever more inflated horde with whom he says he fought.

The music quietens at 49, but not the tempo, which is maintained for some way yet. The tambourine is featured here with mordent signs over the *pp* crotchets, which have given rise to some controversy as to whether the instrument should be struck or shaken, Elgar's normal practice being the former, as in *Cockaigne* (cf. p.153).

Once again a crisp beat is necessary, there being a great deal of syncopation in the Eastcheap themes, which are recapitulated in very light instrumental setting as well as quaver figurations in the strings. After 50 the pulse is controlled by the tambourine strokes, the wind playing off the beat and the strings still busy with their quavers, all in *pp*.

A sudden isolated bar of two forte minims brings back the out-of-doors theme, unexpectedly *ff* with *f* offbeat pizzicatos in lower strings. This is a most imaginative passage, and the fact that the tempo has been stable for some time should not mask the complexities to be encountered in conducting it. The horns and muted trumpets, once they have been initiated at 52, need less attention than the violently swooping string groups, which, although only piano, qualify for energetic arm movements while the stick keeps the tempo inflexible, continuing as the distribution of motifs changes and the strings take over the syncopation.

After one last return of the out-of-doors music, the tavern themes build up via their broken phrases to an even more protracted scherzo. The tempo is enlivened to an Allegro molto marked at ♩ = 138, which is somewhat excessive, particularly for some of the more cantabile moments, and 108 will prove more realistic. The whole of this section is characterized by the tendency to work towards the middle of the bars with strong upbeats, giving the feeling of the music standing on its head. This is especially true at the moments leading up to brass and percussion crashes, where the conductor constantly has to remind himself to beat upside-down, with weak barlines building to powerful upbeats.

In an accelerando, the broken phrases on the 1st violins, followed by solo cello, are further hurried between the quaver rests each time, in the manner of a Mahlerian *flüchtig*; the bar before 59 relaxes back to tempo, and the last figure of all is indeed taken staccato as marked. Gentler answers ensue on flute and clarinet, with a con anima to follow in which Falstaff reveals his presence with the cajoling theme from fig. 7, and the *status quo* is then restored with a poco rit., the whole section being marked to be repeated in what is a mandatory return to 57.

After a mighty second-beat crash the fragmentary passages swoop down in another accelerando, the last cello phrases slowing much as before to lead, again with an upbeat, to the recitative-like solo bassoon. Falstaff is in full voice with the wide-spanned theme, a little coarsened and the worse for sack but still articulate.

Despite the 'recitative' marking, the stick needs to keep control, partly because of the complexity of the solo bars with their fermatas, *ff* belches portrayed by grace-notes, *f* pizzicatos on the cellos, and the like, until they merge into 63, where Falstaff's humorous theme leads into a trio-like middle section. Here the inmates of the tavern engage in a major brawl, the hullabaloo being enormous and the tempo riotous, only the harps being withheld from the furore. Until 64 the beating is still quite restrained, but by 65 the conductor can indulge himself in a fine exhibition of temperament, the pace having increased sharply.

Fig. 66 is an emphatic pull-up with repetitions of short phrases, the *fff* quavers building to a huge climax with cymbals and bass drum, before the turmoil breaks out afresh. Only at 67 does it finally abate, gradually easing in both tempo and dynamics by way of the poco tranquillo, and make its way back over twelve bars to the scherzo-like tavern group of themes.

These are recapitulated at **68**, marked 'Allegro molto' as before and complete with the crashes of full brass, harps, and cymbals, always on the upbeats. Falstaff's cajoling theme again leads to a poco rit., this time only two bars long (unlike the more extended pull-up which had occurred after fig. **60**) but otherwise virtually identical. In the same way after the accelerando the fragmented phrases lead by way of the solo cello into the protesting bassoon, although there is no similar attempt at dovetailing, and the state of intoxication has become lamentably evident.

After the fermata the two silent crotchets are beaten out, and the five bars before **72** are all in 4. The belches (especially that of the bass clarinet) are even more pronounced, and at **72** Falstaff clearly has the greatest difficulty in staying awake. Here we go back into 2, and the tavern themes become increasingly obscured with tremolos and pizzicatos, a hiatus on the bassoon allowing it to join with piccolo for a brief drunken phrase before Falstaff's main theme, backed by tremolo triplets, ultimately drops into the most profound slumber.

Fig. **73** returns to a crotchet beat for one of the finest evocations of snoring in the repertoire. The wheezings and gruntings are all conjured to perfection with richly imaginative use of the orchestra, the timpani and tuba needing especial highlighting, until 5 before **75**, when the beat returns to alla breve for the greatly simplified version of Falstaff's theme as he sleeps more soundly. The score seems so uneventful after **75** that it could be easy to ignore the violas' important rise and fall, leading to the woodwind *ppp* chord, the cellos' quaver descent, and the bass drum stroke, also *ppp*. The final fermata comes on the second beat of the last bar, and holds for a long time while we follow Falstaff's dreaming.

INTERLUDE I

The interludes are the only places where Elgar actually identifies his programmatic intentions in the score. In this first 'Dream Interlude', as he himself calls it, his hero is presented as 'Jack Falstaff, now Sir John, a boy, and page to Thomas Mowbray, Duke of Norfolk'. He is thus described by Justice Shallow in the Shakespeare text, but we hear little more of Mowbray, who is, nevertheless, to become the rebellious Archbishop and Earl Marshal of England, nor of young Jack's conduct when in his service. If the portrayal in the interlude is to be trusted, he must have been a very quiet and well-behaved lad, in marked contrast to the old reprobate we know so well. There is no evidence in Shakespeare for the gentleness of the youth, and the whole concept of the interlude is a charming figment of Elgar's imagination.

The conducting must be totally quiet and undemonstrative, in 4 quavers throughout, perhaps with a shorter stick or even none at all, at a tempo a little below the printed $\flat$ = 100, which would give too hurried an effect; Elgar describes the little movement as 'simple in form and somewhat antiquated in mood'. The important passages for solo violin and the delicacy of the whole bring to mind Elgar's style of writing in the *Wand of Youth* suites.

At 80 an appropriate 'a tempo' marking after the poco rit. is patently lacking, and the progress of, in particular, the harp continues undisturbed to the last note, reinforced wistfully by the piccolo. The fermata is sustained by the bows of solo violin and cello before the sharp silent beating of 81 banishes the dreaming and we are back to reality.

III

Rebellion has broken out in the North, and Captain Sir John Falstaff is everywhere in demand. His rank and knighthood are both military honours, and there are repeated references to the courage and resourcefulness which earned them. His immediate assignment is as recruiting officer, and once he is fully awake he tours the country searching for suitable, or unsuitable, material. At first the themes are familiar from the opening of the work; shrill but distant fanfares then break out on the offbeats, alternating with the tavern motifs once more.

The second time the fanfares return *fff*, landing onto a Poco meno mosso where the gawky theme represents Falstaff's 'scarecrow army'. Although marked $\downarrow$ = 104, a tempo of 88 serves a great deal more aptly here in obtaining its true grotesque flavour. The trumpets and horns, who are mostly entrusted with this caricaturing, are all muted in the score, but in his recording Elgar unmutes the horns; moreover, where the percussion instruments imitate the shape of the theme in what could be described as a caricature of the caricature, the bass drum, which takes the low note of the theme, is changed to cymbals. This is an excellent and most effective substitution, which occurs every time the passage reappears (around **96–97**), but it has to be admitted that, as Sir Adrian Boult once expressed it in a letter to the present writer,* the equivalent in Tovey's 'dumb crambo' would doubtless have been the bass drum.

This second and equally gawky theme, describing the presence and activities of Wart, Mouldy, Feeble, and the rest of Falstaff's ill-assorted press-ganged army, also benefits from a markedly steady pace with its characteristic descending sevenths. It starts as an extended march with side-drum strokes to measure the rhythm, but as battle overtakes them the tempo quickens considerably. Before long they are in the thick of it and the excitement has become feverish, the speed reaching $\downarrow$ = 120 and still pressing forward after the downhill stampede to **89**.

Falstaff is clearly heard in the front line of the fighting, which climbs menacingly with the chromatic quavers of the cellos and basses, marked regularly by percussion strokes. At the height of battle the trumpets give strong voice along with the side drum and insistently repeated phrases on the violins. Chromatic *ff* scales on the horns can be exaggerated in the fury, and a splendid piccolo solo adds to the frenzy at

* Letter dated 4 June 1958.

91. In all this a superb downward woodwind rush can be graphically depicted by the conductor's left arm.

The trumpets and the horn chromatics reassert themselves, and at 94 trombones are added to the cello/bass quavers with spectacular effect. This is one of Elgar's most vivid orchestral tableaux and must be given its head to the full.

Fighting dies down and the scarecrow army themes return, but they gradually soften as Falstaff accepts that 'the army is discharged all and gone' and decides to take a holiday himself with his old friend Justice Robert Shallow Esquire of Gloucestershire, who had already collaborated with him in the picking (or 'pricking' as it says in Shakespeare's text) of his ragged soldiers. Now that they are dispersed his business is purely on a civil footing, and the themes take on a rustic flavour. There is another obligatory repeat, though shorter than the earlier one and reduced to *ppp* without the swell to *f* of the first time.

The scarecrow army fades away on the clarinet, and the cheerful out-of-doors theme returns in its own tempo and also *pp*, alternating with languid phrases on woodwind, drum beats, and tambourine. Although this passage is marked 'poco sostenuto', the contrast of pulse should be very positive: if the out-of-doors theme centred round ♩ = 104, the sostenuto (which obviously returns similarly at the 7th of 100) cannot be more than ♩ = 72.

Moreover, the tempo is further instructed to give way from 2 before 101, but 4 bars before 102 the repeated crotchets should gather pace in the approach to the second interlude, enlivened by the medieval tabor which appears for the first time. Though not precisely identifiable, this is really equivalent to the French tambourin, a Provençal long drum usually found with a single snare; the tabor was a local English variety once used for rural activities such as morris dancing. Elgar says in the score that a tamburo piccolo without snares may be substituted, but this is not really satisfactory, and a special long drum is usually found amongst the percussionists' collection of miscellaneous equipment.

INTERLUDE II

Unlike the first interlude this is joined onto the previous section, but the scene is again visually identified: 'Gloucestershire. Shallow's orchard'. Elgar's 'sadly merry' folk-dancing to the pipes and drums is marked ♩ = 88, but the lounging-about in the hay with which this alternates needs far greater relaxation. The tambourine, struck lightly on the parchment as before, very softly stresses the beginnings of the phrases, in which the luxuriating is depicted by divided violas and cellos undulating at not faster than ♩ = 72.

As at times earlier, the fluctuations of tempo which accompany the elements of this interlude are not always clear in the score. The poco allargandos before 104 and 105 are plain enough, the latter needing a little subdivision at the end for the clarinet, but the resumption of the dancing at the 5th of 104 and again after 105 wants to be restored to its natural gaiety in contrast to the relatively languid a tempos of 104 and 105. At last after 106 even the dancing droops and, following a last bar of timpani crotchets beaten out in 4, a fillip on flute and piccolo dismisses the tableau.

The slumberers on the hay try to linger on but are disturbed once and for all by the sudden arrival of Pistol, one of Falstaff's followers, announcing that Henry IV has died and Prince Hal is the new king. Falstaff's tempestuous excitement is carried by rushing quavers on the violins with associated motifs building to an incredulous cut-off and breathless G.P. The news can hardly be believed.

A brief statement of Hal's theme in very slightly broader tempo confirms the truth of it, and under the renewal of cascading violins Falstaff's mendacious theme is augmented to minims marked '*ff* sostenuto e pesante' in all the bass instruments, but primarily the tuba, whose chief solo this is. The old knight's boasting knows no bounds as he cries out, 'Master Shallow choose what office thou wilt in the land, 'tis thine . . . I am Fortune's Steward . . . we'll ride all night. I know the young King is sick for me.' He little knows what reception awaits him in Westminster as he gathers his associates about him, including not only the country Justices but also members of the scarecrow army, and to a hasty stringendo full of recollections of their themes he rides off full tilt into the distance.

IV

There is a silent fermata and a total scene change to Westminster Abbey, where all are awaiting the arrival of the new king for his coronation, and Falstaff with his followers joins the thronging crowds. The eight introductory più moderato bars between 114 and 115 cannot actually be taken at $\downarrow$ = 92, and much the same is true of the new king's stern motif, which appears for the first time at 115, marked 'Giusto $\downarrow$ = 100'; 84 and 96 respectively are more suitable tempos. (There is, by the way, doubt over the bar before 115, where the side drum appears to play on the wrong beats.) 'Giusto' usually means 'precise' in the sense that will hold up a tempo, but here it signifies the opposite, and Hal in his new-found royalty is full of energy. The enthusiastic chattering of the crowd is vividly portrayed as the king approaches, and at 118 a cheer is heard (on the piccolo) followed by rumbustious tub-thumping on the drums, a splendid and graphic moment for the conductor's stick technique.

The loyalty of Hal's subjects is sincere, and their affection for their new sovereign is depicted in glowing harmonies at 119, the tempo remaining constantly flowing while Falstaff's main theme (on the cellos and bass clarinet) joins in the fervent outbursts of allegiance as the procession approaches, greeted by the clear sound of caps thrown in the air and portrayed in each bar by a sweep of the left arm on the upbeats.

Delicate and regular beating returns, the tempo continuing little by little to accelerate, until by 122 it has reached $\downarrow$ = 112, to match the Gadshill passage at 41, where Prince Hal could be heard in the background woodwind against the scurrying triplet quavers of the violins. There the tempo had even been 120, but here it has still to continue increasing until 125; otherwise, the passages are parallel until the Falstaff theme of fig. 7 interrupts twice on the deepest and heaviest brass and in the ever-enlivening tempo.

The 5th bar of 125 heralds the approach of the king in jubilation and flag-waving that know no bounds, with great brass chords and horn fanfares. At last the young monarch himself appears amidst a perfect flurry of acclamation, his Prince Hal theme resounding Grandioso, at first at a steady tempo (♩ = 92 is perhaps not quite steady enough) but soon quickening to ♩ = 104, at which speed (only a very little faster than its original marking when characterizing the prince at the beginning of the work) it continues through until, at 129, it is replaced by the cheering and cap-waving. At 130 the pace increases again for the exultant chords and cymbal clashes, and with a monumental tutti chromatic scale thundering up and down through three octaves Falstaff joins in the celebratory demonstration. The last little phrase of his main theme, which once was jocular, is here repeated like a question mark, and then again *pp* as if bewildered.

Figs. 131 to 134 describe the dreadful confrontation so precisely that one could almost put Shakespeare's words to the phrases '. . . I know thee not, old man . . . How ill white hairs become a fool and jester! . . . I banish thee on pain of death . . .'. Falstaff's endeavours at cajoling, mostly with the theme from fig. 7, are at its original speed of ♩ = 104 and include rubatos on the cellos as before; but the king has no patience (133), and Falstaff's last ill-advised attempt, with the wide-spaced theme on the solo cello, is sadly dismal.

With a rapidly descending staccato chromatic he is swept aside, and the procession plunges on with the cap-waving, brass chords, glittering outstretched cymbals, and all, leaving the poor old man, Shallow and his other associates still standing where their last royal encounter left them. The coronation crowds fade away, cheering as they go, until at a distance their chattering, so noisy and enthusiastic at 116, could be mistaken for falling tears, as Tovey suggests. This is especially so in its new instrumentation, which makes skilful use of the two harps and, with the previous quavers replaced by staccato crotchets, is to be conducted with the greatest delicacy.

At last the tempo falters with backward glances at the Boar's Head theme. The 4th of 139 and the similar poco rit. four bars later are both subdivided at the end of the bar before being left, the one to a silent hiatus, the other a high cello F♯ sustained for two bars, rising and falling. Out of this, fig. 140 is in 4 with the softest possible beating as the violins ascend with gentle bulges until they reach the ***ppp***, here returning to alla breve. The aim is then for an impression of real stillness, the beats being minimal until the forte subdivided upbeat which sparks the violas in their rather pathetic attempt at joviality marked at $\downarrow = 80$.

Another subdivided upbeat for the cellos' triplet prepares the clarinet's slow and dubious echo, leaving him on a lunga fermata as meditation turns to dreaming. The section between 141 and 143 wants to be conducted as if in a trance recalling the luxuriating in Shallow's orchard, but with the tambourine replaced by harp unisons achieved by means of harmonics. These downbeats need great precision, whereas the rest of the passage is evoked by a gentle swaying at an even more languorous pace than it had enjoyed during the Interlude. The woodwind rit. before 142 should be very slight.

The solo violin adds poignance to the last bars before 143, which become increasingly unreal with the background of chromatics in contrary motion against a last memory of the upside-down Boar's Head theme. This needs to move forward to increase its suggestion of Falstaff's mind wandering. One more reminiscence of a tumble in the hay in Shallow's orchard as he 'babbles of green fields' descends to a poco rit. ***ppp***, with the bar before 144 beaten out in 4, and then there emerges a clear recollection of Prince Hal as the much loved companion he used to be, flooding over the consciousness of the dying Falstaff. This is beaten with quiet simplicity at $\downarrow$ = 69, a slightly quicker tempo than most of the preceding memories; Elgar is wise not to let his failing hero sentimentalize over his lost friendship.

Fig. 145 portrays the death scene with broken phrases of Falstaff's first motif, a touchingly beautiful clarinet solo, and a held C major chord on the brass; Falstaff is dead, his passing marked by a muffled side-drum solo.

The story is over, but Elgar with a flash of genius suddenly gives 'the King's stern theme curtly thrown across the picture' as if using the most imaginative present-day film techniques. 'The shrill drum roll again asserts itself momentarily, and with one pizzicato chord the work ends; the man of stern reality has triumphed.'

Without the revealing wording of the composer's analysis the purpose of the last bars inevitably remains to some extent enigmatic, but when explained so masterfully the symphonic study is perfectly rounded and has justified Elgar's confidence that *Falstaff* is his greatest and most perceptive purely instrumental creation. 'I have enjoyed writing it', he wrote to the journalist Gerald Cumberland, 'more than any other music I have ever composed, and perhaps for that reason it may prove to be among my best efforts.'

Elgar once said to Eric Fenby, 'Do you know my *Falstaff*? I think it is my best work,' adding, 'and tell Delius that I grow more like Falstaff every day!'

Sea Pictures, *A Cycle of Five Songs for Contralto*, Op. 37

◄►

THIS song cycle was composed in 1899 for the Norfolk and Norwich Festival, where it was first performed with Clara Butt, a majestic woman who became so closely associated with the work that her name appears prominently on the title-page. The *Sea Pictures* occasioned a dispute with Elgar's usual publishers over the matter of royalties, as a result of which it went to Boosey, who later also published both *Cockaigne* and the 'Pomp and Circumstance' marches.

The poems are all by different authors, the words of the second song 'In Haven (Capri)' being written by Alice Elgar. Although described as for contralto, the songs lie a little high at times, and the concluding top notes to Nos. 3 and 5 have led to a mezzo-soprano being often thought more suitable.

The songs are set for a conventional orchestra, though with the addition of an optional organ in two of the songs. Otherwise the work uses double wind plus contra, normal brass, harp, and timpani with two extra percussion (including a cymbal, concealed in the middle of No. 5), together with strings. It lasts 24 minutes and makes an excellent additional item to an Elgar programme. The five songs are always performed as a unit and in the published order, with Nos. 3 and 5 the largest in scale, Nos. 2 and 4 being miniatures.

1

'Sea Slumber-Song' is a quiet Andantino marked ♩ = 50, though 60 is nearer the correct pacing, as it gently wanders along setting the mood, which is melancholic rather than tragic. The orchestral colour is beautifully imaginative, the wind and harp softly caressing the voice part's subito *pp* on the high D, then the harp glissando ending with a whimsical turn on the flute just before the tempo changes.

The tranquillo of letter **B**, with its cavernous bass drum and tam-tam pointing every half bar, is appreciably slower, though the marked ♩ = 40 should rather be 50 despite the tenutos on each of the two-quaver groups. Nevertheless the beating changes from a flowing style to a heavy, ponderous one, always very reserved despite the brief crescendo to *mf* in the fourth bar before rapidly returning to *ppp*. Suddenly the upbeat to **C** returns the tempo to that of the opening; but after only a bar and a half the woodwind lead with another rit. into the middle section. This contains the most memorable melodic idea of the song, which, however, must not be taken too slowly, but allowed to progress gently with its counterpoint of semiquavers on the lower strings. The marking is once again 'a tempo (tranquillo)'; yet this does not relate either to the beginning or to letter **B**, but somewhere in between, and requires a gentle evocative beat without any suggestion of the heaviness of the previous tranquillo section so that the strings are able to maintain a real cantabile throughout their semiquavers. Much of the voice part lies very low, and the texture of the accompaniment can never be fragile enough.

The bar before **E** is a further rit. bringing the tempo back considerably so that letter E itself strikes the original speed afresh. But the lead-in bar has its own interest which is to return more than once in the concluding song, where the notes are written out in double values. Here, after the shock of the *fp*, the phrasing suggests a beat of 8 quavers, although whether it needs the full implementation with the stick is doubtful, making heavy-handed what is a very gentle context.

The melodic line is then as before, though with extra colouring on the harp and horns. After **F** the voice descends to low **G**, and the background figuration of flutes, a considerable harp glissando rising to forte, and a sextuplet on the 1st violins replacing the flute should again be handled with the utmost delicacy. Letter **G** is an exact reprise of **B**, so that the omission of the bass drum stroke in the bar before **H** would seem perhaps to have been inadvertent.

In the 3rd of **H** the coda brings back the semiquavers in the middle strings, leading to two fermatas at the repetitions of 'Good-night' against string chords of a truly ethereal quality. The first fermata, it will be observed, only occurs in the orchestra, and merely serves to give the soloist time for her ad lib.; but the second is considerable, coming on the fourth beat after the flute and oboe have been released.

The tiny coda brings back the central melody wistfully, with a last memory of the opening bar, and the fermata is taken on the fourth beat after the 1st violins have faded away.

2

'In Haven' is the first of the two miniatures, and is a peaceful Allegretto, marked ♩= 72, which is in the event a little stodgy for so light a piece, 80 being more appropriate.

The song is essentially strophic, the three unsophisticated verses corresponding very closely to one another, and is scored for chamber orchestra using only one of each wind, a single horn, harp, and strings. The quietly cheerful beat, bouncy in style, only needs a little extra clarity for the staccato semiquaver runs in the solo viola and cello which link the tiny stanzas.

In the third strophe soft support to the voice is given by divided 1st violins, but for the remainder of the song the gently swaying motif persists throughout. The movement ends simply, with the diminutive scale in thirds on the divided 1st violins, and is quietly dismissed with a cello/bass pizzicato on the second beat.

3

Next comes the first of the two more substantial movements, using the full orchestral forces including the organ, which gives it a semi-religious flavour only to some extent justified by the title 'Sabbath Morning at Sea'. The voice enters after a 2-bar orchestral introduction marked 'Moderato ♩ = 72', but the metronome has little significance, as the tempo is constantly in flux with repeated interpolations of più or meno mosso.

Equally the instruction 'Quasi Recit.' in the third bar hardly applies, as in practice the voice line continues with little variation of pulse, the beat simply placing the chord-changes in the horns accordingly. But at the first più mosso in bar 5 it is the conductor's responsibility to carry the music forward, if only to the ritardando and fermata barely two bars later. The a tempo then brings a linking phrase to the new più mosso at **B**, whose gently pulsating string crotchets, with semi-staccato separations taken on the string, establish the recurring vein of sadness which epitomizes the piece, though this time with a stronger sense of forward progression.

At letter **C** the 'rit.' marking naturally no longer applies, the return of the opening two bars being taken at tempo primo. A further più mosso is then somewhat quicker still than previously, the wind triplets giving a sense of momentary excitement for the 'new sight, the new wond'rous sight!' But still the tempo does not settle down: the restless violin accentuations in each alternate bar give way to two bars of tranquillo leading into the Tempo primo of **D** and a return to the semi-staccato crotchets, as at **B**.

The word 'glory' initiates a solemn march (somewhat reminiscent of *Die Meistersinger*) embellished with full brass including trombones. This dissolves into letter **F**, whose Poco meno mosso relates to tempo primo, being on the contrary a fraction quicker than the previous, weighty, molto maestoso. But the string triplet pattern gives a more restful background than that of the wind at **C** and is also of longer duration, setting a precedent for the Grandioso after **J** which represents the climax of the song.

Meanwhile there is a respite with again a Quasi Recit. at **H** in which the beating is restricted to the orchestral events such as the accented horns in the second bar. These quasi-recitatives and colla partes (as at **G**, for example) are really overstatements in what is essentially free rhapsody, and the beat has always to be kept flexible for them, even where the semi-staccato crotchets seem to maintain a strict rhythm. At letter **I**, in particular, when they return for the last time, too rigid a pulse will add to the already dangerously sancti-monious atmosphere.

Letter **J** brings the entry of the organ, whose 'ad lib.' marking results in some unfortunate cueing with little notes in the wind at **M**, intended to fill out the missing harmonies in case of emergency. But the very presence of the organ in the score might be considered a doubtful asset: quite apart from adding to the already somewhat pious tone of the song, it could well even be an impediment to performances of the work taking place in a hall which has no organ. In view of this it might seem surprising that Elgar felt the need to bring in this colour just for so few bars in this movement and again for a short boost in the pedals over a similarly brief period in No. 5.

Here the organ does, of course, add intensity to a further repetition of the 2-bar opening phrase at **J** before the Grandioso sweeps all before it. There is even a new metro-nome mark of ♩ = 66, but this offers too little incentive for what is to be a major build-up of the material, as well as the continuing references to the 'Sea Slumber-Song' in which the harp plays an integral part in the increasingly colourful orchestration.

The idea of 'Grandioso' is itself somewhat misleading, because what is needed is a considerable element of *Schwung*, and this should begin already well before the accelerando at letter **K**. With the organ now added, the texture can be a little thick for the voice, which is in the low register. The rejoining of the harp, however, allows the organ to drop out for the four repetitions of phrases from the opening of the cycle, and the song builds to its final culmination using the 2-bar introductory phrase to take the soloist to top G in what is marked in the vocal line as a *ff* passage. But although Elgar is, apart from the organ, economical in his orchestration, it can be quite hard for the singer to penetrate the opaque mass of sound at the low start of her final phrase until she rises to her upper register; the strings should therefore be marked right back to pianissimo from **M** until shortly before the fermata.

The pause signs are wrongly set out in the score: they should be spread across the two crotchets before **N**, as in the organ part. The ritardando is also vocally most unhelpful, and the singer generally asks the conductor to keep moving until just before the top note. The a tempo at **N** is still a danger spot, and only the harp should play as strongly as *mf*.

Once the voice has ceased, the balance is of course no longer an urgent matter, and the massive orchestral sound can be allowed to build towards the forte; but three bars from the end the general drop back to *pp* should enable the harp triplets to come across until the last forte (or fortissimo) crotchet, which is to be well sustained even without an extra tenuto mark.

4

The second miniature, 'Where corals lie', is well placed being, like No. 2, set for chamber ensemble (although this time using the full complement of woodwind and horns) in a gentle Allegretto. The tempo should be no slower than

♩ = 66 and very lightly treated with, from the third bar, an effervescent beat for the persistent syncopations.

Each of the four stanzas ends with a colla parte, and these can call for quite an element of sensitivity in accompanying. The first rubato occurs as an allargando in the 3rd of **A**, although in practice there is normally also a substantial hold-up on the seventh quaver before the voice proceeds into the a tempo for the catch-phrase 'and see the land where corals lie', the words being repeated in the bar before **B**. The opening motif is used here to turn the corner with appropriate elegance.

Letter **B** picks up the tempo with alacrity, and before the second stanza there are three introductory bars (instead of the earlier two), in which a new mannered figure is presented. The tempo is exactly as before and so are the syncopations, so that the beating is entirely straightforward except for the echo effect in the 3rd of **B** and the solo cello, who plays most winningly with the voice.

Another place for an alert stick is the 2nd of **C** with its allargando colla parte, the soloist taking a breath between the third and fourth quavers and a rubato after 'still' before continuing in tempo with the refrain in the following bar. The end of the stanza in the bar before **D** again requires a sympathetic pull-up at the word 'corals', with the last beat subdivided for the solo horn.

The third stanza of the four is the most wayward, with colla partes and a tempos in every other bar, the syncopations being suspended in the 2nd and 4th of **D** as well as between **E** and **F**. In this 4-bar period there is an accelerando which again needs ingenious handling, as it leads to a bar in which the singer descends to the low register and takes a breath after 'shell', and allowance has to be made for both of these. Furthermore the 1st violins, following the voice line throughout this verse, have to accompany scrupulously in the bar before **F**, where the sforzando on the third beat is succeeded, after a brief fermata, by the violas' fourth beat crotchet before the phrase 'corals lie' finishes with the last quaver of the bar.

Letter **F** starts the closing stanza jauntily with the syncopation once more, and the vocal phrases (ghosted again by soft divisi 1st violins) alternate with the mannered figure from **B**. At the colla parte in the 2nd of **G** allowance has to be made for a breath between the two 'leave me, leave me' phrases before resuming tempo at the next bar just as before.

One more fermata occurs in the bar before **H**, the horn following the voice on the last quaver while the strings sustain. The closing four bars are virtually in tempo despite the minuscule Rit. in the penultimate bar. The final fermata, which should be long as the strings die away, lies primarily in the province of the harp, whose closing *pp* flourish seems to be incorrectly notated, and should more probably be unmeasured grace notes (as printed, in fact, in the vocal score). When it is taken freely in the player's own time, however, beginning the upward group after a second beat, the difference becomes academic.

5

The last song, 'The Swimmer', is again on an expansive scale and for the full forces. After the opening drum roll a highly evocative reference to the linking bar from the first movement bursts in *ff*, written out now in quavers over four bars. Its original tempo had been very steady, but now in Allegro di molto ♩ = 116 it takes on an entirely new significance, and its relationship to No. 1 is somewhat nebulous.

As the scales descend to the lower regions with the splendid assistance of the tuba, the main lyrical idea of the present song arises, still in the agitated tempo, quickly building to the sharp sforzando at **B**. Here a period of genuine recitative breaks in and the beating is interrupted, only the sforzato downbeats and the expressive dynamics in the clarinets being indicated. One of their more unusual markings, in the fourth bar, is 'vibrato', which should not be taken to mean any kind of tremolo but rather the continuing intensity of clarinet sound above the piano tremolo of the strings.

Full agitated beating restarts 4 before **C** with the stormy string semiquavers rising to the lightning flashes in alternate bars. At **C** itself the brass and woodwind figurations should receive the greatest attention from the stick, although the trills on each upbeat should also be emphasized. Oddly enough only the first of these, at letter **C**, is actually given the 'sforzato' marking, and only the second the hairpin; but Elgar's intention must surely have been for the subsequent bars to follow simile.

Letter **D** resumes the lyrical quality of the beating, and a broader style is adopted for the Largamente. The bars before **E** maintain the typically Elgarian tutti *ff*, the horns and trombones adding sonority rather than power. At **E** itself, although there is no new mark, the style should change again to one of agitation, the oboes' and trombone's crotchets pressing forward to the strings' *sfp*, which then subsides, like the ebb and flow of the sea.

The bars of accelerando are repeated at **F**, to relax again at the allargando, in which the forte declamation of the four horns' minims takes pride of place. The characteristic lyricism then returns at **G** and continues in 4-bar phrases until **H**, where the pianissimo chorale flavour of the strings and harp inevitably suggest an easing of pace; this is also suitable for the oboe solo quoting from the previous song in notes of double value.

The piano subito in the strings 3 before **I** is important for the voice, the orchestra following through the colla parte. The a tempo at letter **I** is brief, leading already through its second bar to a poco meno mosso which amounts to a substantial quotation from letter **C** of the 'Sea Slumber-Song'. The semiquaver counterpoint is here transformed into quavers, but otherwise the passage until just after **K** is basically as in the earlier song. The quotation ends, as this movement began, with the two bars of dramatic descending quavers (originally, of course, semiquavers) in which, however, most of the dynamics in the violins and violas are missing. A general sforzato and a section of recitative follow as before, with the same vibrato clarinets.

A reprise ensues, conducted in the same way as at letter **B** and with fluctuations of pulse exactly as at letters **E** and **F**, the main difference being the additional 'cymbal' at **M** and **N**, whose unusual nomenclature raises a problem. A soft stroke with the pair would indeed accord with Elgar's normal practice; yet in his scores this would invariably be labelled 'Piatti', and it seems at least possible that he intended a single cymbal struck with the stick, corresponding more closely to the image evoked by the words 'bloodshot sword-blade' and 'death-stroke fiercely dealt'.

The climax comes 3 bars before **O**, where the allargando colla parte is on a grander scale, with the emphatic horn minims additionally stressed in other wind instruments and with percussion on the alternate beats.

After one bar of accelerando at letter **O**, the lyricism of **G** is resumed in fuller orchestration which has to be carefully restrained, especially at **P**, except for the harp, whose triplets add a fine splash of colour. Four bars before **R** the reprise backtracks to **C**, with the alternating woodwind and brass being brought out as before while the strings, who double the voice, are underplayed except for the fourth-beat trills.

The largamente at **R** corresponds with letter **D**, the reprise continuing as far as **S**, where with bass drum and tam-tam, and with the organ reinforcing the low D on the 16-foot and 32-foot pedals, the last climax is powerfully structured until the soloist attains her culminating top note. In No. 3 this had been a G, but now the apex goes one better to A, a note which not every true contralto can boast in her range; some even prefer to take the lower octave, a rather disappointing *ossia*.

In the approach to the fermata, itself marked back to piano, there is wisely no ritardando until just the last crotchet, testifying to Elgar's practical experience in accompanying the voice.

The coda from **U** to the end is an orchestral peroration, marked 'a tempo' but usually taken somewhat briskly, so that (despite a final backward glance to Wagner) the closing statement will avoid too grandiloquent a last gesture in what is, on the whole, a carefully reserved group of orchestral songs which amply deserve their popular niche in the repertoire.

The Music Makers, *for Contralto Solo, Chorus, and Orchestra*, Op. 69

◀▶

FOR a work with so evocative a title, *The Music Makers* is unexpectedly full of melancholy. Composed in 1912, a year before *Falstaff*, this setting of Arthur O'Shaughnessy's 'Ode' was something on which Elgar had long set his heart; he had been toying for the past eight years with the idea of turning it into a major choral work, perhaps unaccountably as the words are anything but distinguished. The 'Ode' speaking, however, with especial relevance to his personal view of the composer and his mission in the world, the catalyst proved to be the Enigma theme, which Elgar had always associated with the loneliness of the composer and which he now felt to be at one with the first stanza of O'Shaughnessy's poem. If this were made to be the mainspring of the entire concept, then as the setting progressed other references to earlier works might find their place in the composition.

On this basis he finally set to work, using the complete words of the 'Ode' as the musical scheme seemed to propose; this was a rare procedure for him, even the text of *Gerontius*, a major religious work in its own right, having been liberally abridged. But here he was upheld with a strong emotional tie through the entire shape of the nine 8-line stanzas, and even though the versifying was in some places more than a little obscure and even banal, the music could, he felt sure, be made to elevate these and turn the whole into a unified creation.

The composition went forward with great fervour, though there were periods of discouragement. Published as usual by

Novello, it was first performed at the Birmingham Festival on 1 October 1912 and conducted by Elgar himself, but received with only partial success. The work undoubtedly contains many moving and beautiful passages, but it has always been thought that its artistic level is lowered by the quotations. It is scored for Elgar's normal large-scale forces, with triple wind, full brass, organ, and two harps, and lasts 41 minutes without interruption, occupying a generous second half to a programme. Unusually, the contralto solo is silent for the first third of the work.

There is a long orchestral introduction based primarily on a new main theme in $\frac{3}{8}$ time but alongside bringing in the Enigma, which is transformed very successfully into the triple rhythm. The Moderato tempo, set at $\flat = 138$, is well chosen, though there might seem a conflict between the swiftly moving quaver beat and Elgar's favourite epithet 'nobilmente'. It is, however, appropriate for the climax at fig. 4, which introduces a further important motif hinting at the prelude to *Gerontius* but here referring forward to fig. 39 ('A breath of our inspiration') and fig. 50 ('the land to which they are going').

The chorus does not stand at the very beginning but is raised at fig. 9 in plenty of time for its first statement, which comes after a silent pause. The voices are given 'Larghetto $\downarrow =$ c.58', with a poco rit. in the 3rd of 10 to allow for 'dreamers of', which needs extra beats for each syllable. The a tempo then quotes overtly the opening theme from *Gerontius*, and 'lone sea-breakers' at 11 is an obvious place for an allusion to the first of the *Sea Pictures*. Three bars before 12 the Enigma returns, now of course in its own duple measure, while the 2nd of 12 leaves the chorus quite alone for three bars ending subito pianissimo for 'pale moon gleams'.

In the huge climax starting at 13 there is a comma after 'Yet' which is not to be found in the full score, though it is clear enough in the vocal score in every stave. The peak of the *fff* comes on the allargando at 'shakers of the world', a very brief high moment requiring no subdivision, the declamation of the chorus quavers being emphasized within the beat, and capped by mighty orchestral triplets which again can be evoked without the use of the stick.

By 14 the momentary show of violence has collapsed and the Enigma reappears once more at the a tempo for the rhyming line 'for ever, it seems', which rounds off the entire section with a fermata on the third beat. The full crotchet upbeat to the next section is given while the chorus and lower orchestral parts are still sustaining, the quaver corresponding to those of 15 so that the return to $\frac{3}{8}$ is again begun in 3. The chorus is brought off with the downbeat of 15.

However, the 4-bar stringendo moves the tempo forward dramatically and the Allegro breaks into 1, the dotted crotchet beats easily arriving in that space of time at the stipulated ♩. = 80. The successive barlines have to be full of energy for the syncopated upper strings, fig. 16 additionally bringing in the chorus once more.

The pace still quickens, so that by 18, when the voices break up into separate strands, the tempo will have reached ♩ = 100 and continually presses forward; even the vivace after 19 is merely a stepping-stone. Hidden in the orchestra are commonplace references to 'Rule Britannia' and the 'Marseillaise' referring to the poem's 'great cities'. It must be confessed that Elgar continued to feel uneasy about these indiscretions, and it is amusing to find him writing to Ernest Newman in defence of the passage: 'You will be interested to see how they go together & the deadly sarcasm of that rush in horns & trombones in the English tune—deliberately commercialising it'.*

By fig. 20 the speed will have reached ♩ = 120 for the rising harp chords of 'One man with a dream'. On the word 'dream' the hairpins peak at the fourth bar, so that the 8-bar phrase may be thought as 3 + 5; fig. 21 is then constructed similarly, though the contrasting dynamics are an additional feature, the continuing *pp* having to be emphasized.

* Letter, 14 Aug. 1912, quoted in Moore, *Elgar: A Creative Life*, 634.

The tenors recover their vigour in the bar before 22, starting forte to lead the different voices of the chorus in a spirited ascent to the *ff* climax at 23 for the word 'crown', after which a brief return to Tempo primo demands renewed energy in the downbeats for the syncopated upper strings, as at the Allegro before 16.

A fortissimo passage leads dramatically to the stringendo molto of 25, a spectacular *fff* débâcle already sparked by the wind flash two bars previously, though the temptation should be resisted to pre-empt the element of accelerando, thereby weakening the outburst at 25 itself. The vehement drum beats graphically 'trample a kingdom down', and a precipitous descending whole-tone scale reaches a return of the 'Marseillaise' on *fff* brass at 26, with a triumphant gesture being called for from the conductor.

The chorus having shouted the word 'down', a tutta forza against C major crash chords on the weak bars of 26, the drum beats are left alone, still *fff* and with emphatic cello support, to descend against a sad viola phrase which is to return later more than once as a refrain. Here it carries through the rit. and più lento to the next melancholy section, an Allegretto $\frac{9}{8}$. This needs to be skilfully handled so that the beat can remain the same for the new movement, which is marked ♩. = 88, the transition being made the more apposite by the continuation of the timpani figure into the bar of 27, overlapping the new entry of the chorus.

'Allegretto' hardly describes the $\frac{9}{8}$ tempo adequately, as the elegant string formulas proceed at a stately, almost funereal pace. But at 28, despite the more elaborate triplet semiquaver groups, and even the 'Maestoso' marking, there is a new feeling of forward movement in the almost spiky dotted rhythms, against which the chorus is conducted with very smooth legato phrases for the word 'sighing', the rest of the orchestra merely punctuating the regularity of the beats.

The style changes materially at 29 with the chorus references to 'mirth', the beating being appropriately more perky, as required by the 'giocoso' indication. The violins' phrases

are here very staccato, and the tempo can even move forward for the descriptive semiquaver descending runs in the
sixth and seventh bars, though it reverts to the earlier
sombre manner when 'sighing' returns before 30.

The momentum picks up substantially, however, at fig. 30
with the basses' forte lead for 'And Babel' while a stringendo
molto quickly builds to a repeat of the earlier vivid downward sweep and a suggestion of the demons from *Gerontius*
at 31, needing strongly extrovert beating at the con fuoco.

The chorus has a powerfully separated upbeat 4 before 32,
the *ff* syllable 'o'er-' being a distinct unit before the rest
of the word, '-threw', follows in the next bar; these two
bars require a steadier tempo. The lead into 32 is, however,
another subtle juxtaposition of ideas, the quaver of the new
Moderato $\frac{6}{8}$ corresponding with the dotted crotchet beating
of the poco animato which follows upon the brief maestoso,
building to $\downarrow$. = 112 through the four beats before 32.

Swift as this is in terms of dotted crotchets, it is admirable
for the new quaver pulse of the lyrical section which, in a
continuing fortissimo, is the next episode in this extremely
varied work. The beating too, from being emphatic, changes
to a legato style with much cueing to the chorus, which
has broken into a more contrapuntal idiom. It is supported,
moreover, not only by the orchestra, but by the organ,
whose first important role this is. Only the entries present-
ing the principal new motif with the words 'To the old of
the new world's worth' are still strongly stressed at each
appearance.

A climax is reached at the allargando before 34, subsiding
to a swaying a tempo that benefits from being taken in 2,
also for the sake of the accompaniment on the harps and
pizzicato strings. The music would be too heavy-handed
beaten out in 6, and by changing into 2 the $\frac{2}{4}$ just after 35 will
merge smoothly. The strong duple rhythm is marked within
the beating for the men of the chorus supported not only by
the cello/bass department but by trombone and tuba, who
lend additional weight to the words 'Or one that is coming'.

The further allargando becomes increasingly emphatic, and the beat broadens to $\frac{4}{8}$ five bars before 36, with a great fermata on the first quaver 2 before 36, the tenors taking over the principal voice before the return to $\frac{6}{8}$ and 6 dreamy, but not too slow, quaver beats. Only at the a tempo, however, is the true pulsating movement restored, with the timpani and basses throbbing beneath a revival of the opening motif.

The a tempo here refers to the speed of ♪ = 112, not to the 138 of the work's initial bars, and there is a retrospective air about the chorus when, after 37, it very softly intones the opening phrase 'We are the music makers' as a reminiscence of the first lines of the 'Ode', interpolated here by Elgar and consequently given in brackets. The orchestra having died away, duple rhythm once more returns for 'dreamers of', and the conductor's left hand controls this with four dotted quaver beats before arriving on 'dreams', a long dying chord which is held together with the entry of the 1st violins for a moment and only then released.

Fig. 38 is a very soft ruminative return to the subsidiary $\frac{3}{8}$ melody from fig. 2, marked in the score with the highly unlikely ♩. = 76, which, in view of the molto tranquillo, is better with the quaver unit as given in the vocal score, though Elgar specifically (in a sketch) marked it 'but not too slow' and 'keep it moving'. It pulls up considerably, however, in the bar before 39 for the *ppp* chorus entry which requires subdivision for the upbeat 'A breath' with its fermata after the strings have ceased; the chorus then continues unaccompanied in the sostenuto 'of our inspiration' which is spread across the voices with a carefully marked angular bracket.

In a piece so full of quotes from other Elgar compositions, it is tempting to light on further passages recalling works perhaps even composed subsequently, and to conjecture whether a quotation from a piece Elgar had not yet written could conceivably have been intended. The present instance, the phrase beneath the bracket, is a particularly appropriate example since it seems so consciously to have been highlighted; yet the Cello Concerto, whose sublime Adagio this phrase seems so poignantly to presage, was written as much as seven years later. A similar example in the two bars 5 and 4 before 30 reoccurs in the opening movement of the Piano Quintet of 1918.

The bracketed phrase is echoed by the clarinet as the chorus prepares for a repeat of the words at a slightly more flowing pace, though still immensely calm. Only at 41 does the tempo really pick up for a new idea, 'Is the life of each generation', which is initiated by the altos in a strong forte and marked 'Allegretto $\downarrow$. = 46'. Despite the metronome mark (only found in the vocal score), the beating is still in quavers until the poco più mosso at 42, which turns into a real $\frac{12}{8}$ conducted in 4. The speed increases from 46 to 60, but this is disguised by the change to dotted crotchet beats so that the effect is essentially one of quaver = quaver.

The removal of constraint eases the 1st violin semiquaver passage which thereby flows naturally as well as allowing the offbeat harp and wind to punctuate their gentle chords effortlessly.

At 43, however, with the transformation to a real $\frac{4}{4}$, the beat quickens for 'impossible seeming' in preparation for the next energetic passage. This begins with the basses' dramatic octave leap on the word 'wond'rous', and the whole chorus takes a mighty breath on a quaver rest in order to plunge *ff* into 'The soldier' at 44, one of the more commonplace of O'Shaughnessy's verses, which Elgar disguises as best he may with an exaggerated full-blooded utterance summoning recollections of *Gerontius* and such jingoistic pieces as the 'Pomp and Circumstance' marches and *The Crown of India* set to the united forces with brass and organ pealing majestically.

After the drop to *pp* at the trombones' sforzato, the chorus's sudden re-ascent towards the Grandioso of 46 instigates a stronger element of sincerity in the setting of 'Till our dream' with the general *sf* on 'shall'. This must not be a slow drawn-out passage, and the tempo marked at ♩ = 100 can still progress purposefully, with renewed but soft drum beats, towards the long diminuendo in the descent to 49, which marks the end of the first overall portion of the work. The harp punctuates the final bars with very quiet spread chords, the violas are left holding a minim which has changed to the minor for the fermata, and the contralto soloist at long last rises.

Her opening lines are uttered seriously and solemnly, a slow crotchet beat accompanying her in the strings, who die away as she reaches the $\frac{3}{4}$, then resurge in a new accel. whose triplet figures hark back to the $\frac{9}{8}$ of fig. 27. With the subito **pp** in the bar before 50 the clarinet and bassoon are thrust into the foreground for their swell to forte before the Più lento. This gives way to a background of soft strings for the soloist's words 'They had no divine', sung to the ruminative violin melody from 38, but at the even slower tempo of ♩ = 72 written out in double notation.

The fermata 7 before 51 leads, as did the similar one at 39, to the 'inspiration' motif and thence, as the tempo slows even further for 'But on one man's soul', to a complete recollection of 'Nimrod' in memory of Elgar's friend Jaeger. Much as the appropriate section in the Enigma Variations was designed to be affectionate rather than elegiac, fig. 51, which is marked 'solenne' and very slow at ♩ = c.46, is indeed sad. Jaeger's death three years earlier had a profound significance for Elgar.

The chorus creeps in at 52, and over the next 14 bars the intensity gradually grows until, at the climax of the 2nd of 53 with its thunderous timpani figure, it has become apparent that the allusion has surreptitiously changed and we are now deeply into the last movement of the Second Symphony.

A consequent allargando, with an additional sostenuto marked in the solo voice, carries the passionate expression to the next pause, which is written purely in the accompaniment of both voices and instruments, leaving the soloist at liberty to indulge the word 'flame' in what is a considerable show of emotion as the chorus enunciate the broken syllables of 'spo-ken'. As she moves on to 'in another man's heart' the chorus bursts in again *ff*, only dying down as 54 approaches and leaving another four bars of general diminuendo before the start of the next contrasted section.

Fig. 55 is an Allegro molto for the sixth stanza and introduces a total change of mood and substance. It is marked $\downarrow = 152$, and since this is certainly a most vivacious speed, it constantly merges into an alla breve, the speed of crotchets always remaining precisely constant. The 5th of 55 gives the first transition, breaking into minim beats with the entry of the tenors and basses as they proclaim 'Today' at the half bar.

At the brisk 'And the multitudes' a crotchet beat becomes essential for the four and a half bars at 56, the minim beat taking over at the half bar for the new phrase, 'today', exactly as before.

A more substantial $\frac{4}{4}$ section begins at 57 in what is a very excitable passage. It is essential to bear in mind that however exactly the two beatings correspond in overall pulse, they are strongly contrasted in manner, the $\frac{4}{4}$ sections being extremely agitated while the alla breve minims are conducted with a wide and sweeping beat. This longer $\frac{4}{4}$ at 57 is therefore especially vehement as it builds towards the fanfare-like horns at 58 and trumpet staccato triplets leading, in an allargando, to the next alla breve at 59.

As on the two previous occasions the return to minim beating comes at the half-bar, here bringing in the entire chorus and marked with not two *f*'s but three for 'The dream that was scorned'. Moreover it leads to a *fff* shout of the first lines of the 'Ode', once again interpolated by Elgar as at 37, with 'We are the music makers' reducing to piano through 'And we are the dreamers of dreams'.

On the word 'dreams' the beat returns to 4 in a bar for a varied reprise of the whole section from 56, with the same trumpet triplets at the allargando and the same half-bar change to alla breve for the *fff* entry of the chorus, leading to yet another insertion, this time of the last two lines of the first stanza. 'We are the movers and shakers' is backed with *fff* brass, the sopranos rising to top B♭, a tone higher than before.

The music passes into a slow $\frac{4}{4}$ in which the crotchet equals the previous minim for a Maestoso of great evocation. The beat accordingly remains the same, although it soon picks up for the poco a poco animato where the brass are strongly featured as the voices take it in turn to enunciate the verse, the soloist remaining silent.

The climax comes at the 2nd of **66** for the Nobilmente, which, after the considerable animato, is suddenly slower. This relates to the Grandioso of fig. **46**, and the timpani *ff* figure at the fourth bar is a truly characteristic touch. The chorus quickly recedes to *pp* for the soloist, who is left almost alone for the descent into a further quiet extension of the alla breve theme from the previous section, now treated very softly and fading further and further away.

To this motif the chorus, having dropped out for three bars, re-enters at **67** with the oft-reiterated words 'for its joy or its sorrow', which are additionally taken up by the soloist before the last chorus restatement. This must be as soft as possible while the orchestra works back to the very first theme.

Yet again the crotchets correspond with the $\frac{3}{8}$ quavers and the beat remains the same. Even when the a tempo is reached after the 4-bar poco accel. the quaver is only marked at 120 as opposed to the original 138. The *mf* recedes to piano and thence to *pp*, while the rit. molto drops the tempo still further to lento espressivo ♪ = 60 for the poignant new motif made from chromatically descending harmonies. This is important as it will become associated with the last words of the 'Ode' shortly before the end of the work. The softest and most affecting bar is the *ppp* (with its upbeat) 3 before **71**, the chorus re-entering with 'But we' to hold a fermata third beat (which releases the strings) before continuing with the Andantino as at fig. **32** although both softer and slower.

This $\frac{6}{8}$ begins by being an almost direct reprise of the earlier similar section, although their ways soon diverge. The 2-bar allargando after 72 takes the crescendo, which had begun as far back as the 5th of 71, up to a peak of forte in expressing the words 'The glory about us'. There have been numerous duplets which have to be brought through the six beats, so that it is no surprise when, at the a tempo 2 before 73, it proves to be more convenient to go over into 2 in a bar, even though there is as yet no great pressurizing of tempo but only a suggestion that it must be kept moving.

The crescendo continues to build, and after 73, at the words 'Our souls with high music ringing', where the upper parts are clearly in duple rhythm, fortissimo is reached although a gradual diminuendo begins soon after. The lower instruments have continued to pound $\frac{6}{8}$ quavers with the whole trombone section as well as cellos and basses, bassoons and organ, until by 74 the level has returned to piano and the beat to 6 in a bar.

A climax in the chorus and upper instruments has for this quasi-$\frac{2}{4}$ brought back a reference to the motif of the passionate alla breve in the earlier section; this gives purpose to the change of beat after 73 in what is primarily an arch of $\frac{6}{8}$ writing corresponding with 32 to 36.

The return to quiet $\frac{6}{8}$ beating is short-lived, however, and fig. 75 is once again in 2 for a reappearance of the Enigma theme, and with timpani punctuations memories of the $\frac{6}{8}$ pattern fade away until by the $\frac{4}{4}$ of 76 the chorus takes 'our dreaming and our singing' into total stillness, ending quite unaccompanied. The orchestra creeps back into the picture in *ppp*, the upbeat quavers needing subdivision for the chorus syllables 'a-part' as the divided 1st violins, playing very tenderly at the point of the bow, introduce as softly as possible a motif from the Violin Concerto, coloured with spread chords on the harps.

At first there is a mixture of thematic references from both the present work and its predecessors, but within a very few bars the themes from the Violin Concerto acquire pre-eminence until, by the silent fermata before 78, marked specifically 'lunga', the whole passage has died completely away. This is a particularly emotional corner of the work and patently one in which Elgar identified the words with his own soul. Treated with the sympathy it deserves, it should bring tears to the listener's eyes, much as the recollection of the concerto will already have done.

Almost unaccompanied, the chorus quietly restarts at 78 with a further subito *pp* at the pause on the third beat for the word 'afar'. As the orchestra joins with a scurrying scale from bottom to top of the string section, the chorus builds quickly and passionately with the phrase 'And the suns that are not yet high', a further rushing scale sweeping up in the string department.

This time the arrival is marked by a pair of soft trumpets in octaves sustaining the B♭ on which the chorus builds the next phrase, whose predominant feature is its use of the motto theme from the First Symphony. The purpose here is by no means clear, and, more seriously, the words do not fit the symphonic theme well, so that it was possibly misguided for this particular allusion to be so vehemently pealed out *fff* by the full chorus.

A 3-bar reference to fig. 65 in the present work, also forcefully projected by full orchestra and organ, links the phrases of the symphony's motif, which is given a martial character quite foreign to its original purpose. In all this the chorus stresses the word 'intrepid', which is delivered with the utmost heroism.

Majestic triplets during the allargando bar before 82, portraying 'God's future draws nigh', connect with the triplet pattern of the succeeding con fuoco. This bar of 82 is one of the hardest to gauge correctly, the first half being beaten out in triplet quavers but breaking into dotted crotchets when the *ff* trombones and bass instruments become too fast to control as they merge into semiquavers. By the middle of the next bar the tempo has reached Allegro, and the beating is by now vigorous dotted crotchets.

At the barline of **82** the motif of the work's opening tops the triplets of the trombones and the lower instruments, this being its first return since fig. **68**, but rapidly leads to the precipitoso as in the earlier episode of **15** but differently handled with a stringendo descending swoop. There is a momentary reference to the theme of fig. **16**, but on reaching the bottom of the plunge, marked by sforzato trombones, the chorus intones the sinister word 'must' on the second beat supported by a *fp* on the horns, leading straight into the *fp* 'die' in the next bar. All this should be explicitly portrayed by the stick, especially the dramatic hesitation of the two silent rests, not beaten, before 'die', where the harps are then pre-eminently important, pianissimo as is their spread chord.

This is a vivid moment, however restrained the conductor's gestures must suddenly be, before the drum beats start piano at the half bar of **83**. Formally it corresponds to the violent passage at **25**, but the background of course could hardly be more contrasted, with its soft but portentous bass drum strokes, harp murmurings, and eerie ascending string scales. The chorus is taken off with the left arm at the 3rd of **83** not to return until **93**, but should still remain standing.

The drum beats and cello/bass rhythmic pattern die away in the 4th of **84**, and there is half a bar of total silence. Then the viola phrase, heard earlier in similar circumstances (before **27**) as a kind of refrain, makes a diffident appearance, but here on the solo instrument dying away to *ppp* and a further silence. The air of expectancy is absolute, amidst which the solo contralto slowly rises again. (She has been tacet since **68** and will have chosen her moment to be seated.)

After an orchestral surge inaugurating the coda, O'Shaughnessy's last stanza is passionate, as befits the words of the singer, 'Great hail! we cry', but despite the mark of 'Allegro', **85** cannot be too fast. It is essentially a $\frac{12}{8}$ in which all the details need to be well articulated until, after the outburst, the orchestra dies down under the voice, with even a pull-up for the violins' diminuendo to piano in the next bar, followed by the wind swell to the crash chord on the third beat.

The soloist's phrase soars up to high G, the strings accompanying her scrupulously through the largamente. After forte snaps on the trombones at the 1st and 3rd bars of **86**, the section corresponding to **42** is then recapitulated though greatly elaborated with harp arpeggios and wind conclusions to each semiquaver arabesque. The molto allargando grandioso of **87** then changes the pattern from the $\frac{12}{8}$ into a strong $\frac{4}{4}$ as it leads, by way of the $\frac{3}{8}$ motif from fig. **38** interposed as triplets within the $\frac{4}{4}$, to a $\frac{3}{8}$ in its own right and beaten in quavers, the last crotchet before **88** being already subdivided.

A succession of colla partes breaks up the continuity of this Arietta, which establishes its tempo only at the 3rd of **88** after the singer has taken her breath between 'hither' and 'your sun', the violins phrasing similarly alongside. The Andantino is marked $\flat$ = *c*.112, which is surprisingly quick and makes little provision for the tender expression of the passage.

Another rubato allows for the soloist's allargando before **89**, and yet again at **90** for her broadening at 'things that we (dreamed not before)'. Otherwise the tempo has to be kept moving, if not quite as relentlessly as the metronome mark might suggest.

The poco più mosso at **92** brings the next change, the beat going into whole bars for 'The glory about you clinging', as both the melody in violins and harp are in duple rhythm. However, it soon returns to 3 for the gentle violin motif at **93**, the chorus having re-entered very quietly in the previous bar. In the allargando 8 before **93**, although keeping the single beat, the harp quavers are so strong that the second player can justifiably be added, and the quavers not so much beaten out as indicated within the whole-bar beats, much as the wind quavers will be at **98**.

Figs. **93** to **99** constitute an elaborate and extended repeat of **88** to **93** with the chorus joining the soloist sometimes alternately and sometimes as a background. Hence at **97**, corresponding to 92, the poco più mosso brings a similar change from 3 beats to 1, violins and harp being in duple rhythm as before. Nevertheless there are triple elements in the chorus (e.g. basses at 97) which need to be kept quietly in evidence.

The combination of duple and triple rhythm persists until 2 before 98, where the three quavers in each bar have to be made prominent within the single beat despite the allargando, only breaking back into 3 beats from the bar before 99. The violins again carry the melody beneath the voice, which they follow carefully through the rit. Despite the soloist's mark of 'semplice' a breath is necessary between 'not' and 'before' while the violins rest, and both have an extended pause in the bar before 100, the soloist continuing with a further pause on the dramatic 'Yea' at 100 itself, for which the conductor must expect to wait expectantly.

There is another breath for which time again needs to be allowed before continuing with the very slow epilogue. This is based on the chromatic figure already heard before 71, which now comes fully into its own, alternately on wood-wind and strings, the latter together with ominous *pp* trombones. Following a pause after 'slumbers', muted horns accompany the line 'And a singer who sings no more', echoed by the chorus.

That Elgar found here a not inconsiderable tragedy is substantiated by the quotation of 'Novissima hora est' from *Gerontius*, the phrase uttered just before the moment of death. A brief memory of the opening motif of the present work follows in a Più lento, and this too fades altogether into a long sustained E♮ and silence.

There is an element of shock in the *mf* wind chord which begins the final *envoi* at 103, leaving only a *ppp* shadow in the strings. The chorus murmurs the opening words of the 'Ode', becoming ever softer and slower. The bulge in tim-pani and lower strings is taken away piecemeal, leaving the chorus to finish the work as their last note dies away, transformed first into a hum, then into a whisper.

It is a profoundly moving end, as well as being unexpected after so long and elaborate a canvas; but for its composer the work is known to have had a very particular and personal significance, and this always needs to be borne in mind in performance in order to do it full justice.

The Dream of Gerontius, Op. 38

◀▶

'THIS is the best of me', wrote Elgar on the last page of the autograph score, and there have been very many who have accepted this assessment at face value ever since, believing *Gerontius* to be his finest work although, as the opus number reveals, it is quite an early achievement.

It was commissioned by the Birmingham Festival of 1900 despite the anxieties aroused on account of Cardinal Newman's poem, which is unashamedly Catholic, cutting against the strongly Protestant background to the festival. To many Elgar devotees the pervading air of piety presented an impediment, and opinion continues to be divided despite the undeniable quality of much of the music.

However, Elgar was himself of Catholic origin and found no objection to the project, which he had indeed cherished for some years. The work is in two parts, exactly like the poem, the first depicting the 'Death Scene on Earth', with Gerontius surrounded by his friends, and the second following the adventures of his soul as it travels, in the company of his guardian Angel, towards the supreme Court of Justice. The first takes rather less than 40 minutes while Part II lasts the full hour, and despite Elgar's instructions 'a short pause should be made between the Parts' it has unfortunately become usual to have an interval. This can only destroy the intensely rapt atmosphere of timelessness, and should be firmly resisted.

Elgar wisely felt it necessary to make substantial cuts in the poem, obtaining permission from Cardinal Newman's

•

friend and executor, Fr. Neville. These abridgements are indicated with dots in the vocal, though not in the full score. The role of the Angel is taken by a mezzo-soprano, Gerontius (and, in Part II, his soul) by a tenor, and the Angel of the Agony by a bass, often doubling with the Priest in Part I.

The chorus is full of every kind of elaboration, from semi-chorus to double chorus (fig. 89 of Part II), for which purpose they are seated mirror-wise with the semi-chorus to the fore so that the antiphonal effects are visually as well as audibly apparent. The result of this is of course that the voices on the outside—usually sopranos—are separated from each other when, as in the bulk of the work, the chorus is operating as one body; this is an inescapable hazard of the piece, and should not be shunned on that account.* The constituents of the semi-chorus are precisely specified in the score; where the main chorus divides, the numbers should be as equal as possible.

Elgar's orchestral scoring includes triple wind, full brass, timpani and the usual array of extra percussion, two harps (the second, though marked 'ad lib.', is an essential ingredient of the texture, and far from merely doubling) plus an obligatory organ part in addition to the strings. These are all fully operational already in the Prelude, which amounts to a kind of pot-pourri of the principal motifs.

PART I

The unison opening sets the atmosphere with its Lento, mistico marked ♩ = 60. This seems a sober enough tempo to establish the idiom of so serious and extended a work, but in

---

* It is certainly the case that many conductors adopt this seating arrangement, or one similar to it. However, I am indebted to Donald Hunt for the fascinating information that Elgar himself always preferred to seat his chorus in flanks, with all the sopranos on the left, then altos, then tenors, and basses on the right. (J.R.D.M.)

practice it will drop to nearer 44, as is borne out by Elgar's own recording.

Already in September 1900 Elgar's close friend and colleague, A. J. Jaeger wrote an analysis, published as a booklet (happily still in print) entitled *The Dream of Gerontius: Analytical and Descriptive Notes* and giving all the various themes of the prelude labels according to their associations later in the work. Here the initial phrases and rising sequences at fig. 2 are called Judgement and Fear respectively. Though Elgar was at first doubtful about Jaeger's treatment of his themes as leitmotifs, he had to admit that Jaeger's conclusions were sound, however 'intuitively' (Elgar's own word) the various thematic or motivic relationships came about during the process of composition.

The Fear motif, then, is enunciated in very reserved shades of colouring, a degree of unease being evident only from the little swells in each instrument in turn. These can be quite hard to bring through, and should be evoked from the very first moment of entry. With the especially delicate statement in the 1st violins the whole idea vanishes, and the tempo is enlivened by a harp arpeggio which marks the further new motif of Prayer in the woodwind.

The alternation of the two themes is repeated at 3, but the sequence of string entries passes over the 2nd violins so that the harp arpeggio brings in the Prayer motif half a bar sooner. Instead of the earlier crescendo and subito ***pp***, the woodwind this time crescendo to a fermata, which must be held with care through the third beat before the cellos drop to their D♯.

After a ***ppp*** 2-bar link, the positive sense of continuity is set in motion at 4 with the music associated with the words 'So pray for me' at fig. 28, where it is marked 'Andantino', giving a better clue to its character than the 'Più mosso (ma poco)' marking which heads the longer initial statement at 4. Jaeger calls it Sleep, which Elgar at first resisted, then conceded 'I suppose after all "Sleep" will be right . . . Sleep will do but it's the ghastly troubled sleep of a sick man.' This constitutes the first main section of the prelude, forming an expressive arch up to the 'Miserere' phrase (which finds its true context between 40 and 41) before descending to 7, whence it ascends once more to the *fff* Moderato of 9.

This will feel a good deal more animated, though once again Elgar's own tempo is markedly more emphatic than his printed ♩ = 92. The powerful downbeats almost give the passage a feeling of 1 in a bar, although there is no question of beating it so; on the contrary it leads abruptly to a *Luftpause*, the upbeat to which needs a vehement subdivision and take-off gesture.

The same happens in the repeat phrase building to 10, and this could be taken as the climax of the Prelude. From here it descends to the Andantino of 12, which presents a threefold statement of the majestic theme capping Part I with the words 'Go forth in the name of Apostles and Evangelists', though here at a steadier tempo than will befit the passage later at 73.

Now it is given a great elaboration with string triplet quavers during its ascent and then a delicate harp figuration as it calms down into the rocking theme of fig. 4, which in its turn gives way to the earlier themes from 2 and thence to the initial unison motif with which the work began.

The Prelude and the Angel's Farewell are the only excerpts which may be performed separately, and with this purpose in mind an extra concluding bar is added after the rit. molto, much like those after individual movements in the Enigma Variations. Here the Angel's Farewell may serve as continuation, the tonality being then uniformly D major.

During the next rising and falling connecting passage the solo tenor stands and prepares to sing. Marked ♩ = 100, this Allegro moderato really needs a more dramatic tempo to break the spell, especially over so short a period, for it only surges for four bars before lapsing once again into a largamente. This theme recurs several times during the course of the first scene and signifies brief bursts of renewed energy in the dying Gerontius.

He reflects on his state of existence in the recitative-like bars at 22. At 23 the tempo recovers for 'I know it now', the molto stringendo culminating in a *sfp* on the violas and wind which amounts almost to a fermata before the Prayer theme returns, to the words 'Jesu, have mercy!' A new burst of energy lasts only half as long as before, broadening already in the third bar. After two quite slow bars the tempo is suddenly much quicker until 25, where the rit. is shaped by the conductor alone. The fermata in the 3rd of 25 comes on the third (not the fourth) beat and leads into the rich *ppp* chord, reflecting the words 'strange innermost abandonment' on 15-part divisi strings. Here the low harp triplets have a solo rise and fall that should achieve real prominence. The string effect is repeated even more softly (*pppp*) two bars later, but the harps remain at their soli dynamic of *p*, enriched by the addition of an even deeper octave. Meanwhile the più mosso in between can be deceptive, for in practice the second bar contains a substantial rit. leading into the fermata.

Trumpets and muted horns support the voice, followed by ponticello string tremolos which remain *pp* even though the tenor is marked with a crescendo to forte and beyond. The double-bar change of pulse to $\frac{3}{4}$ at 26 swells the orchestra to *ff* momentarily with the violent string descending figure at Gerontius's fervent outcry 'Pray for me', and the chorus rises in plenty of time for the 'Kyrie' at 29. The throbbing accelerando builds up to 27, emphasized by the flutes in illustration of Death 'knocking his dire summons'.

Fig. 27 reaches a più mosso, starting forte with the rising and falling Energy motif. This quickly subsides into the theme of troubled sleep at 28, itself growing from *pp* to a desperate, agitated *ff* and back in anticipation of the semi-chorus entry, whose total calm is in dramatic contrast to these emotional outbursts.

The six bars of 'Kyrie eleison' are a *ppp* andante in which Elgar's instructions to the tenors, at one of the rehearsals for the first performance, were happily recorded. 'He entreated them not to sing as if they were in a church. He wanted "more tears in the voices, as if they were assisting at the death of a friend." '* The gentle climax of the phrase comes at the basses' entry, and in the last bar the word 'eleison' is pointedly separated, syllable by syllable, as it dies away altogether into 30.

The full chorus now takes over in more *aperto* style, pleading to all the different ecclesiastical bodies or individuals for intercession. Musically this prayer is relatively conventional in style, though accompanied solely by divided violas and cellos, but once again Elgar's own directions as to the manner of execution have survived. Each entry in turn begins *p* crescendo and then drops to a sudden *pp* at the refrain 'pray for him', so that the next voice is clearly heard. Elgar was insistent about this *pp* (which in the full score is missing in the altos), and also that the first two bars of each phrase should be sung in one breath. The whole lyrical 18-bar arch returns to the calmer semi-chorus 'Kyrie' out of which it had emerged, but this time the *pp* dynamic is quite hushed, without nuance, and the main chorus joins for the final *ppp* repeat of 'eleison', now sung legato. The linking Energy phrase breaks in for a last time with just two Allegro bars, ending forte at 33 to introduce Gerontius's next solo.

His first words, 'Rouse thee', are printed to coincide with the strings' final chord, but Elgar in his performances apparently allowed the tenor to delay his entry, making a long downbeat and placing the change of chord in the trombones correspondingly later, with the word 'fainting'. The Moderato pulsations then start in the 2nd of 33 on cellos and basses, making a huge crescendo before the subito *pp*. The effect is repeated two bars later, but here Elgar gave the added tenuto markings such a degree of weight as almost to amount to a rit. into the following bar.

The *pp* 2 bars before 34 can be allowed to flow, the gossamer harp arpeggios introducing a new element of lightness.

---

* *Birmingham Post*, 13 Sept. 1900, quoted in Moore, Edward *Elgar: A Creative Life*, 325.

Gerontius is calmer, more philosophical now, and there is no particular element of drama about the colla parte bar, in which the *ppp* pizzicato is simply placed on the 3rd beat, and the wind taken off. The succeeding barline is marked, and the beat resumes for the quaver pattern, which starts off in the bar before 35 just as it did after 33.

But the vocal score shows a rit. at the half-bar (followed by Elgar in his recording), and this is the first of a number of significant places where, at some stage, revisions were evidently made to the vocal score which supersede the text in the full score. It is surprising that these appear never to have been documented, and especially that they were ignored in the new Complete Edition score published in 1982.*

At 35 the movement sets forth in earnest, the cello/bass ostinato providing a pulsating rhythm. The supplications are initiated by the tenors, each sentence ending subito pianissimo with a murmured 'Spare him, Lord' and 'Lord, deliver him'. This Moderato is additionally marked 'e solenne ♩= 54' (notably steadier than the previous Moderato); yet Elgar himself took the less static, yet still definitely solemn, tempo of ♩= 66. It is a long chorus, nearly fifty bars, and the soloist would be well advised to sit while preparing for his next outpouring of 'Sanctus fortis' at 40. The ostinato is not without its interruptions, such as the six bars before 36 or the expressive passage between 37 and 38, but it is a well constructed section derived without amendment from Newman's text, and the pace is kept constant and unvaried throughout, the orchestral background merely highlighting features of the choral writing. As it fades away there is another important correction to be made to the full score: in the 3rd of 39 the vocal score shows a hairpin crescendo in sopranos and tenors matching the identical phrase two bars earlier.

---

* Similarly, there are places where the orchestral parts show a superior text to the full score; an example is figs. 5–9, where the cellos' divisi works perfectly in the parts but leaves some loose ends in the score. Again the new 1982 edition makes no comment or alteration.

Gerontius's fervent solo is an Allegro moderato ¾ at almost double the pace. His line is forcefully delivered against tremolo upper strings, with an after-phrase built over the earlier rocking motif. The chorus meantime sits, for this is a major aria, and one of Gerontius's primary utterances in Part I.

His prayer is written partially in Latin, as in Newman's poem, and Elgar follows the original text verbatim, changing to the vernacular after 41 and 48. The tempo flows swiftly at ♩ = 120, with a real feeling of 1 in a bar; but the beat can never actually break into 1, even when after 42 and 48 the trombones softly intone the first pulses of each bar, or at 51 where the stringendo molto places the stresses in alternate bars, thus seeming to suggest such a style.

The lyrical quaver movement in the violins before and after 50 preserves the flowing 3, and this becomes intensified at the fermatas of the colla parte before 52. Here the various beats with their respective events (2nd violins in the one bar, horns with their crescendo in the other) need to be handled sensitively by the conductor without leaving the poor tenor stranded too long on his top notes. Some tenors, indeed, reduce one or even both of the pauses to the most minimal tenuto.

A single bar of composite string writing now collapses into 52, where, for four bars, semiquavers are added in violas and wind for the build-up to the sforzato cut-off. This leaves the tenor dramatically alone, supported by only the most delicate accompaniment in violas and cellos alternating with flutes and bassoons. After the elaborate orchestration of 52, the simplicity and spareness of Gerontius's direct address to the Trinity should be the more moving, the piano subito on 'Son and Holy Ghost' accompanied by *ppp* wind making its own impact after the considerable allargando during 'earth and heaven', with 'Father' being already very slow.

There is a danger here in that Gerontius, already sounding improbably young as a tenor for so old a dying man, can easily become too lachrymose in these bars, which on the contrary should reflect a hidden strength. Fig. 53 contains a wealth of expression in the shimmering background to its repetition of 'Sanctus fortis' turning to real vehemence at 54 for 'Miserere', Gerontius's last great *ff* outcry ending on a fermata. The orchestra then enjoys a dramatic postlude with surges of tempo and ferocious climaxes marked by brass and timpani. The peak is at the 4th of 55 and the rush up to the *fff* at 56, all of which should suggest the paroxysms which beset the sufferer, not unlike those depicted by Strauss in *Tod und Verklärung* eleven years before.

There can, however, appear to be a paradox between the stated tempo of $\downarrow$ = 138 and the brass triplets of 56, which can hardly be accommodated at such a speed. While indeed some subtle adjustments to tempo have to be made in the passage as a whole, these should be perceptible only as degrees of ebb and flow, rather than sudden changes of gear.

Fig. 57 returns us to the sustained *pppp* string chords and three-octave harp triplets with the addition of new woodwind fragments, which, hardly more than shadowy here, are soon to come into their own. In the 5th bar of the Lento the third beat is subdivided so that the pause comes on the half beat, just before the dramatic pianissimo of the words 'and collapse'.

The phrase 'I can no more' suggests that this concludes the aria, but Newman supplied an extra page of text full of such graphic and gruesome pictorial images that Elgar clearly found the idea irresistible and devised from them a climactic section closely related to the Demons' Chorus in Part II. Orchestrally the music is full of dazzling and kaleidoscopic effects which should be hurried along in keeping with the mark of 'agitato', culminating in the bars before 61. The chorus rises once more at 61, sparked by the fortissimo timpani sextuplet.

The tempo changes to Andantino for a further outcry, Gerontius beseeching different branches of the Deity for help and to pray for him, as the Energy theme briefly rears up for one last time in the cellos and basses. The accompaniment has dropped to a soft tremolo ending in a fermata, held as long as the soloist stays on his note. He now gathers his utmost power for the high B♭, which is capped by a harsh, 'appalling chord' (as Elgar called it) in the wind for the words 'Thine own agony'. This turns out to be identical to the chord in Part II introducing the Angel of the Agony himself (1 before 106), something Elgar freely admitted but which, amazingly, seems to have been a genuinely subconscious inspiration.

After the pause on 2, the third beat follows Gerontius through to 'agony' in the next bar while the chorus braces itself for a powerful new attack at 63, the voices entering individually in the same order, and at the same bar's interval, as in the 'Kyrie' of 29. This time, however, an unexpected solo entry is interpolated just ahead of the basses. The sober 'Allegro moderato' marking understresses to some extent the fervour of this brief choral outburst, which, however, does grow from forte to fortissimo at the fifth bar with the added affrettando. At the brief climax the basses' entry is underlined by all four horns, but the orchestra's purely supportive role is otherwise largely neglected during this prayer. There must be real passion in Gerontius's plea for intercession by the 'assistants', which only subsides during the approach to the liturgical section of 64.

This anticipates to some extent Britten's use of the Benedicite in the Church Scene at the beginning of Act 2 of *Peter Grimes*. Here the semi-chorus intones the verses with organ accompaniment, the full chorus taking the part of the congregation in supplying the 'Amen's. There is no suggestion in Newman, of course, that the lines should be handled in this way, but it works well enough and also provides variety of texture. The beating involves, in every alternate bar, a fermata on the downbeat, picking up the semi-chorus each time on the second beat and giving the 'Amen' to the main chorus on the fourth. During the fermatas the left hand can if necessary suggest the phrasing to the semi-chorus, including in each case a definite gap after the names Noe,

Job, Moses, and David. The final 'Amen' in the bar before 65 gives a pronounced ritardando leading into the Andante, in which the chorus very softly echoes the Rescue passage of 63 in an abbreviated form, subsiding into an excessively hushed rallentando for Gerontius's final entry in this world.

The strings creep in with Gerontius for the sublime moment 'Novissima hora est', fading into the last few bars of the swaying motif during which, with the words 'into Thy hands', Gerontius relinquishes life altogether, the strings following him into total extinction.

There is a silence during which the Priest stands, a portentous wind chord preparing his solemn utterance. He declaims at the beginning of the new bar, after which the conductor merely places the wind in their background-like pillars, giving the bass soloist no interference in his pronouncement. The score indicates a tempo of ♩ = 76, but whether or not this is adhered to strictly may depend on the acoustics and resonance of the building.

The words are sung in Latin with horn support, and repeated in English with trombones. Out of this develops a gentle D major processional in slower tempo punctuated by the two harps, timpani, and the lower double basses in a succession of deep repeated crotchets.

Newman had expounded a list of the different Eternals in whose name the spirit of Gerontius should go forth, but these hardly satisfied the demands of Elgar's finale, in which chorus and semi-chorus are added to the Priest in the cumulative treatment of this valediction. At first, with the *f* chorus entry (rising immediately to *ff*), the pulsations give way to a più mosso ♩ = 88, only to relax in pace for the emphasis of the added trombones to the word 'Cherubim', then especially as the *fff* 'go forth!' is hurled out by the full chorus. This gains in urgency, striding forward to the broad, majestic theme already presaged in the prelude (fig. 12). Here it unmistakably forms the climax to the whole first part of the work, fulfilling this function nobly.

Elgar's imagination is splendidly at work between 73 and 74, with string trills building to *ff* pizzicatos and a fine brass counterpoint. The peak is attained with a further largamente at 74, after which the weight of tone evaporates for the Priest and semi-chorus alternating with two *ff* bursts of sound from the full chorus, while harp and middle strings embroider with semiquaver arpeggios.

The mark is now 'a tempo', and it is crucial that, after so many largamentes, the flow should be resumed to the full. At 75 the pulsations return as at 70, but this time most touchingly shrouded by a velvet cushion of soft choral harmonies, building up until twelve independent parts are all interweaving, forming a great arch of tenderness. As this subsides into 76, there is a meltingly beautiful exchange between the two soprano lines, whose words 'thy place be found' may be gently coaxed through in turn. Fig. 76 itself then makes colourful use of the semi-chorus in a long and increasingly reflective passage which was to be the source for many a corresponding idea in Vaughan Williams's *Sea Symphony* only a very few years later. Here the drama is essentially at an end, and the broad sentences can easily become static unless the conductor is positively conscious of the necessity to keep the pulse flowing.

The final più lento combines another version of the first 'Kyrie', the voices always entering in the same order, with a very exposed counter-thread for high divided 1st violins, who need to be nursed carefully round their delicate tracery. From the sixth bar the apparent simplicity of the music can be deceptive, for there is actually a multiplicity of events which need the conductor's full attention. The first beat gives the semi-chorus 'Lord'; the second beat helps the 1st violins, then marks the final consonant 'd' with the fingers of the left hand, while preparing the main chorus and sparing the Priest a quick glance; the third is directed at the full chorus; the fourth is once more concerned with the 1st violins, and waits for the Priest's quaver; and so on, not forgetting a very distinct sign after the next second beat for the 'st' of Christ.

All this must not be allowed to take too much real time, for it is an important feature of this serene coda that it be perceived as coming only to a temporary place of rest. The last bars therefore need almost a sense of continuity, being quietly and simply measured and the harps marking the minim pulsations, with no trace of pull-up after the voices have ceased.

PART II

The opening of the second part is something of a phenomenon, and Elgar handles it with consummate skill and beauty. After death Gerontius has lost touch with time, and there is an atmosphere of total stillness. But it is hard to give the illusion of complete inactivity in terms of music necessarily portrayed in circumstances of measured pace, and Elgar achieves this with music of such calm that the conception of non-movement is nevertheless established, and the conductor's assignment is to conjure the sense of timelessness in such a way that the shape is not lost altogether.

A time signature ($\frac{3}{4}$) and a speed ($\bullet = 48$) are given for the opening unison violas, or they could not play, and the più lento which begins in the fourth bar has to be controlled in its prescribed rubato; but the means by which this is conveyed to the strings should be so intimate (the word 'beat' is quite inappropriate) that the audience is hardly aware that the music has begun, with such subtlety has it been coerced into existence.

The conductor scarcely stirs, the rit. in bar 8 is purely a matter for the eyes and marginal movements of the head, and the communication is excessively slender. Only the balance and degrees of tone-colours in the alternation to and fro between the 1st and 2nd violins after fig. 2, and the handing back of the textures to the rising fourths of the unsupported violas, as at the very first bar, have to be nursed with the utmost tenderness.

All motion comes to rest at 4 on a sustained cello harmonic A, whose emptiness, transparence, and lightness all prepare us for the presence of the new central character, Gerontius's soul, and the state in which he seems to find himself. After his first words in free recitative, 'I went to sleep', the music has to be kept very quietly moving as, alternating with an echoing phrase on clarinets (the first wind instruments to be heard in this part) and *ppp* upper strings, Gerontius attempts to describe his bewilderment.

Fig. 5 changes the pulse to $\frac{12}{8}$, but the actual beat, such as it is, remains constant for the extremely gentle throbbing of the centre strings. Only the natural rhythmic flow of the triplets could be said to move the tempo along imperceptibly, and within this context the gentle ripples of the harp and the near motivic downward phrases of the clarinets find their places with ease over the four bars in which Gerontius outlines his new-found lightness of spirit. Four bars before 6 the orchestra is quite suddenly expressive, in contrast to all the surrounding softness; but the tempo eases in the colla parte, and the clarinets may even need to allow extra time for the soloist's breath after 'myself'. The tenuto in the fourth beat has to be subdivided, but this is unnecessary in the poco più lento itself, where the *ppp* carries its own lilt anticipating similar passages in, for instance, *Dream Children* and the *Nursery Suite*.

The oboe does have a momentary subdivision as it leads into the fermata at 6 held only by the violas on a long pianissimo C (for Elgar the 'lunga' was particularly important). Their octave drop coincides with Gerontius's 'How still it is', after which the poco più mosso restores the strings' flow of the introduction, gaining even an extra degree of lightness since it now supports Gerontius's awareness that for him the clocks have all stopped, and even his heartbeat has been stilled. As at figs. 2 and 3 the conductor has the paradoxical assignment of having to preserve the gentle flow without appearing to control pulse in the slightest degree.

In the 5th of 7 there is a rit. and fermata for 'differ from the rest', during which the strings have a diminuendo hairpin down still further from *pp* to *ppp*. Here again a subdivision is a pre-essential as the voice drops to its own *pp* on the word 'from'; and in the next bar we are back to the original slower tempo as it was before 5.

Now there comes a change at the corner to 8. As at 5 the pulse is turned into a $\frac{12}{8}$ with 4 beats to the bar, the 2nd violins and violas resuming their throbbing; but this time it is preceded by a rit. in which the *fp* third beat is subdivided, so that the tempo relationship is disguised. A solo violin and cello take over the melodic line, but otherwise the passage is then handled just as the parallel one was between 5 and 6. Fig. 9 pulls the tempo back substantially in the approach to the Andantino $\frac{5}{8}$ which constitutes the next section, after two subdivided leads at 'and so sweet' in the bar before 9 and at 'and of pain' in the 2nd of 9, both of which need sensitive correspondence with the vocal line.

At the Andantino the strings divide at the desk into two groups. In the first bar the inner file are marked *ppp*, making a pronounced echo, and this effect recurs repeatedly, as at 4 before 11 and again after 11, 14, and 17. The fermatas are also worth examining: in the first $\frac{5}{8}$ bar the strings are cleared before Gerontius enters, and this is in fact again the case 4 before 11, but the full score wrongly shows the pause on his quaver instead of the previous rest.

The 5 in a bar is divided into 3 + 2 throughout, and since this occasionally conflicts with the voice, as in the 4th of 10, the accentuation needs careful watching, especially in the use of imitative entries across the divided string sections, which can give rise to confusion. At 10 and again four bars later extreme caution needs to be exercised, as the accompaniment dissolves into simple counts of five even *pp* quavers bearing little direct relationship to the voice line.

Gerontius is now about to meet with his guardian Angel, who is always masculine in Newman's poem, as indeed also in the present work (cf. the 3rd bar of 17), even though Elgar chose a mezzo-soprano soloist to personify him. This may have been in Elgar's mind when he scored the new motif, which dominates the syncopated background before 11, for clarinet and bassoon; for this will shortly reveal itself as the guardian Angel's 'Alleluia' refrain. Hence 3 bars before 11 is the point at which the Angel should stand, although it is still eight bars before the song actually begins.

These bars blend, by means of a change to $\frac{3}{8}$ and a slightly more moderate metronome mark, into the Angel's aria thanking God for an assignment successfully accomplished. This is a beautiful and serene passage requiring great sensitivity and flexibility from the conductor, who must allow for the element of rubato inherent in the character of the music. In particular, the 4th of 11 (and similarly 2 before 12) will be quite sustained to allow for phrasing; and the 2nd of 12 will also naturally subside into the 'Alleluia', which is a moment of sublime tranquillity. An a tempo is implied 1 before 13, and the music picks up considerably in the bars following 13 itself. Here again, however, the vocal line is usually taken somewhat freely, and it will be necessary to steer the divided strings in sympathy.

Four bars before 14 the expressive 2-note phrasings in the 1st violins will linger into the Alleluia in the same way as just after 12. The next five bars are also broadly parallel with the earlier passage, but this time the Angel's phrase makes a considerable climax 2 before 14, though the orchestra remains at various degrees of pianissimo. Once again, therefore, there is an implied a tempo at the 2nd of 14; but the allargando in the 5th bar is more pronounced than earlier, and the conductor must be prepared for a greater extent of subdivision.

The end of the aria comes at 16. The rit. three bars earlier is quite substantial (though only at the final quaver, as shown in the vocal score), and the horns, repeating in thirds their closing soli bar as at 13 and 14, start nearly at the original tempo before embarking on their own rit. into the fermata. The strings have become ever softer, making a final diminuendo from *pppp* to the long pause in which the horns are left alone from the second beat.

Gerontius reacts with wonder at the Angel's sublime address in a recitative marked at first merely by downbeats at the barlines, only needing to return to quavers one bar before 17.

At 17 the divisi echo phrases return as before; but this time, unlike at 11 and 14, the *pp* second bar notably has a swell marking the change of harmony. Gerontius takes the step (after a substantial cut in Newman's text) of addressing the Angel, and here the tremolo strings should not be too soft, so that when he sings 'My Guardian' they can back him up straightaway. In the Angel's reply the semiquavers should be controlled carefully at the end of the 2nd of 18 to allow her to take time on the stressed word 'brother'. The phrase dies away in the third bar to a silent fermata after 'what wouldst thou?'; these three syllables are marked staccato, giving emphasis to her query. (Again the full score shows an earlier, discarded version of the text here.)

Gerontius answers freely in his own time, but not too soon lest the fermata be swallowed. The following $\frac{4}{4}$ is in quasi-parlando style, marked ♩ = 72 at the second bar but so full of tempo variations that the stick needs a constant awareness to remain with the voices, for this is much closer to free recitative than any kind of straightforward 4 in a bar.

As Gerontius puts his question, however, the quasi in tempo of 20 is belied by the new ♩ = 54, which indicates a considerably steadier pulse, to be strictly maintained. The clarinets and bassoons enter *ppp* with the music from the very beginning of the Prelude, pizzicato basses marking the offbeats. Gerontius's own words make the meaning of the motif clear for the first time, as happens again with the Angel's answer and the rising theme at 24.

Meanwhile the shock of the *fpp* which initiates the violins' tremolo in the 2nd of 20, coming at the word 'moment', points the demarcation between life and death, one more dramatic than any Gerontius has experienced; for he had believed he would be precipitated into the awe-inspiring presence of God sitting in judgement. The 1st violin quavers into 21 need sensitive handling, after which attention turns to the melodic cellos, doubled by bass clarinet and bassoons, who, lacking any new *p* at 21, certainly need to be marked up. In the bar before 22 the flutes are cleared with the soloist, and only the horn sustains through the pause until after the gentle lead is given to the upper strings. The tempo changes to $\frac{3}{4}$ Allegretto, and very softly, in the quaver flow of the introductory music to the second part, the Angel assures him that he is under no illusion and that he is indeed being hurried along towards the presence of the Deity.

Clearly Elgar conceived this music as fitting a number of different tempos, of which 22 is the fastest. It flows along, if not 'with extremest speed', at least with a considerable feeling of agitato, until it comes to rest and Gerontius calmly poses his next question. This, however, soon works him up into a frenzy once more, and there is a dramatic animato to Allegro in a single bar, counteracted by an equally sharp pull-up in the colla parte. The subito *ppp* fermata to which this leads on the word 'terrible' is naturally somewhat delayed and produces an effect of extreme awe.

With fig. 24 the music returns to the Fear motif of the prelude, pared down by the use of only the inside players in the strings. The forte in the third bar is very much an accompanying one, within the context of the solo passage, and retreats immediately; similarly, the expansiveness of the largamente dissolves into an implied a tempo at the *pp*. At 25 the Angel's animato may happen somewhat later than printed; but in any case it should relax with the diminuendo, after which the whole of the third bar is occupied with the portentous crescendo in the violas and cellos, with its attendant subito *pp*. Now, to an emphatic statement of the theme from the original opening bars on the four horns, Gerontius is given to understand that his judgement has somehow already begun.

The Andante at 26 initiates the close of this whole first scene of Part II, and the Angel and Gerontius share a lyrical duet singing together against a richly embroidered tapestry on harp and strings. The expressive warmth of the cello line (as opposed to the 1st violins, who double the voice) may be encouraged, as again in the duet with the clarinet 2 before 27. Here the intricacy of the harp writing is particularly worth hearing, while at 27 the solo horn may be brought out a little. But generally the orchestra remains very subdued, only pointing the tenutos carefully, until 28, where, still more elaborated, it builds in what quickly grows to a forte coda before mysteriously subsiding into the next section, the approach to the Demons' Chorus.

Fig. 29 marks the beginning of the highly imaginative episode, and the chorus leaps up sharply even though its entry is not until 32. Gerontius comments at 55 that he 'sees not those false spirits'; but Elgar makes no attempt to hide them away by placing them off-stage.

For the Allegro at 29 the style changes diametrically from the peaceful lyricism of the preceding duet into a beat of nervous agitation as Gerontius describes the hubbub assailing his senses. The slurred quavers are marked with diminuendo hairpins, but in practice these will almost become accents if the passage is played with the necessary agitato character. An accelerando leads precipitantly to the fermata of the bar before 30, where the frenzy is replaced by a tam-tam stroke and a dramatic tremolo on cellos and basses, with a substantial crescendo across two full beats, for Gerontius's bar of demonstrative recitative.

The turmoil resumes as the Angel describes the scene close by the Judgement Seat, around which are assembled the demons hungrily pacing to and fro to collect their property in the form of souls destined for hell. Elgar depicts the pacing with staccato quavers in the deeper instruments, and in the general mêlée the irregularity of the dynamics repays careful study, with outbursts on different beats of the bar. This is equally true after 31, where the savage account proceeds; its brilliant colouring is exceptional for this composer, although a hint of it has been adumbrated in Part I at fig. 59.

The continual stringendo after 31 builds to the Allegro of the Demons proper; here the orchestration is lightened to allow for the tenors and basses, whose line is pitched low so that the intensity of the words needs to be especially emphasized. But the crescendos in the orchestra need to be encouraged too; these, and the dramatic bursts of sound that emanate from all directions, go to make up this highly colourful scene, which it is the conductor's job to bring to life.

At the 4th of 32 the full chorus enters with a shout to renewed and violent orchestral demonstrations. The succeeding piano is no less agitated, but the momentary lunge to forte 5 before 33 must drop very quickly so that the chorus entry is not obscured. Now there is an important crescendo in the chorus, which should grow steeply, with strong enunciation of all the words, while the orchestra remains piano until the last moment. At this point the repetitions of the crashes on the offbeats in the two bars before 33, the thud reinforced by heavy percussion, and the strepitoso syncopations at 33 itself all emphasize the savagery of the demons.

A feature of this chorus is the meticulous articulation markings in the voice parts, and all Elgar's contrasts should be observed and brought out: particularly, as they are more difficult to achieve, the staccatos on 'extra', 'stand' (at 33), and, above all, 'high' (in the following bar). It is worth recalling one similar effect in Part I which merits attention, on the word 'For' 2 before 39. These important details add greatly to the wealth of colour and expression in Elgar's choral writing.

The largamente 2 before 34 is perilous and almost never done, but if it can be achieved will give the chorus the opportunity to mark its entries even more clearly. However, the similar marking before the *ff* tam-tam stroke at the word 'light' is essential and holds up the impetus perceptibly. Then whereas 34 returns fully to tempo, the remainder of the 'light' bar, with its orchestral diminuendo, inevitably takes a little time in its preparation for the bar before 35, which dramatically recovers the intensity. Here Elgar is known to have always made an allargando at the end of the bar, beating out each of the last two quavers with maximum emphasis. The fiery syncopations of 33 are now passionately unleashed, at a tempo whose precision is crucial for the success of the notoriously tricky double fugue that ensues. If it is established at ♩ = 116 there will be just room for all the detail to be executed together with the appropriate frenzy of excitement and an illusion of considerable speed. Handled thus wisely and judiciously, this is by no means the most problematic area of the work, as will be seen in due course.

The fine and invigorating fugue subject is announced by the basses, and the other voices enter at two-bar intervals until the sopranos, coming last, are preceded by a great 4-bar build-up to 37, where they are greeted with a tumultuous percussion stroke. Throughout all this, the conductor must inspire enormous energy and drama, while providing clear leads for some tricky chorus entries, such as the altos in the 4th of 37 and the tenors two and three bars later. The addition of the trombones is also important in fuelling the flames of what is a colossal build-up to the high point of the whole scene; for this complicated passage bursts into explosion at the climax of 38, where the chorus, with terrifying emphasis, all comes together for the words 'who after expelling their hosts'. The chorus breaks off abruptly, and the orchestra initiates a series of bloodthirsty hammered quavers, after which all the chorus leads are important. At 39 these upbeat entries are followed immediately by the even more sharply accented brass outbursts.

This sinister tableau now gains momentum (from 40, despite the vocal score's 'stringendo' marking only in the following bar), and the semiquavers can be allowed to sound quite frenetic, though one must never quite forget that the 2nd of 41 has to be still (just) playable. Despite the marking in the 3rd of 41, once the Angel has entered little more stringendo can, in practice, be achieved, and even the new impetus at the 3rd of 42 is undermined by the more likely text in the vocal score, where the 'accel. molto' marking occurs only on the Angel's last note 1 before 43. Nevertheless, the tempos should merge at 43 so that crotchet equals crotchet.

At 40 the orchestra had dropped to piano (for the first time really since 33), but the demons continue unabated with their furious, untamed forte. Throughout the whole episode, the orchestra is primarily a backdrop to the infernal gestures of the chorus, and the conductor's attention will be focused virtually exclusively on the singers, for whom this is undeniably a taxing passage, even if not as supremely difficult as it may at first seem.

There could scarcely be a stronger contrast than with the textures of the next section. Elgar describes fig. 43 as 'Presto ♩ = 168', which evokes well the savagery of the music, strangely orchestrated with the bare trumpets in octaves answered by the frenzied descending fifths on the combined strings and the chromatic climbing crotchets on the horns and lower instruments. It is conducted in 3, but powerfully driven through the sardonic laughs which are the demons' best-known feature, while the starkness of its ferocity can at the same time be exaggerated. The chorus joins six bars later and is kept as a body, the sopranos being added after two bars for 'The purpose free'.

The trumpets return, and with a swoop on the wind the malicious interchange of question and answer beginning 'What's a saint?' comes to the fore, against a background of savage punctuation on wind and brass, the somewhat obscure words taking priority over the jagged interjections of the accompaniment. The laughter, in its irregular grouping, follows directly and throws up a problem as regards the articulation. The foreword to the new (1982) Complete Edition score quotes extensively from a useful letter written to Elgar in 1902 by the choral conductor Nicholas Kilburn, who at this point asked the pertinent question of how the slur (in the first three laughs) was to be interpreted, as opposed to the final staccato one. Elgar replied—fascinatingly, for one could hardly have guessed—that the slur indicated 'two distinct syllables', but without the aspirate to the second 'Ha'—i.e. 'Ha'a'—'throwing up the horrible "Ha!ha!" in the next bar'. The wild outbursts of the demons continue at 47 with the bitter lines 'A bundle of bones, which fools adore', which lie low in the voices and therefore need to be strongly marked with the stick, especially against the violence of the brass imitation.

After the laughs and the descending intervals the trumpets return yet again and the strings rush up and down, leading to the tenors' and basses' 'Virtue and vice, a knave's pretence', which does need to be brought through, doubled as it is by the four horns. The sopranos and altos hurl out ''Tis all the same', the cynicism of which knows no bounds.

Now, as again after 49, the 'Ha! Ha!'s are compressed from four bars to two, so that already the second one falls on the first beat, a change which has to be carefully registered. Spurred on by this added intensification, the whole ensemble boils over into a defiant unison refrain in all three upper voices, the basses interpolating an ironic snigger after each phrase; and here, prompted by the 'Animato' marking, the beat can at last go into 1. Nevertheless the Animato itself can be difficult to achieve, for there is an element of the frenetic about the whole of this Presto, and any further increase in speed can seem hardly in question. But once the trumpets start on their crescendo chromatic quavers, the tempo may be urged forward through the last two bars so that fig. 50 will travel at a genuinely quicker pace.

It is not obvious how the basses' 'Ha! Ha!' is to be executed, with three staccato quavers to one syllable, but in the same letter as that quoted above Elgar stipulates precisely that the vowel sound be repeated, but not the aspirate (i.e. 'ha-a-a'). This can be hard to synchronize with the trombones, who will need a sharply clicked beat in each alternate bar.

From here the episode winds down. The chorus sings ever more softly; but all its sharpness of invective must be retained in the articulation of the consonants, for in reality the demons have in no way calmed down. Like the anvils in Wagner's *Das Rheingold*, their chanting is eternal and incessant; it is we who are travelling away from them until they gradually become inaudible.

In particular, care should be exercised that the 't' of 'not' in the 7th of 51 is enunciated precisely and forcefully on the second crotchet. In the two bars before 52 some vocal slurs are missing in the full score; both places should sound 'ha-a', thus contrasting with the staccato four bars later. By 53 only isolated words can still be perceived, and these can be made quite sinister with a nasal, hissing quality, so that their essential character is never lost. As the basses fade away entirely, they must retain absolute unanimity in their final two consonants.

It is left to the orchestra to drop the curtain, starting with the violas, whose three-note arpeggio prefix to the Demons motif immediately recalls the scherzo of Beethoven's Fifth Symphony, a bizarre association in such a context. The last word is given to the contrabassoon, whose splendid solo descends to its very bottom B♭; the beat has been 1 in a bar throughout, without subdivision.

With the lowest note in the orchestra, the whole ghastly tableau disappears off the end of the audible spectrum, and we find ourselves once again in a more dreamlike continuum. At this point the chorus is sometimes directed to sit, but there is inevitably some sacrifice of atmosphere at such a magical moment of scene change, and the singers should if possible be enjoined to remain standing, despite the undeniable feeling of a lengthy sentence having reached its close.

The music returns to the timeless void of the beginning of Part II, and the 'Andantino' marking corresponds to the second of the earlier two tempos, the poco più mosso of fig. 6. Gerontius's misgivings are answered by an evocatively cavernous echo of the demons in the cellos and basses, but the phrase presses on to a colla parte which, though it starts with a rit., is then more inclined to flow towards the poco più mosso.

The Angel has the infinitely comforting, but also infinitely frightening, news to impart that the Soul will indeed, for one moment, see its Lord. Just as at 20 the word 'moment' is accompanied by a shock *fp*, so also here Elgar's musical resourcefulness is a match for the considerable demands of the imagery, and he succeeds in creating a truly magical effect out of no more than a simple major chord. C sharp major, in this context, scored with unerring instinct, pierces the air like a flash of far-away sunlight before it melts into F sharp for an evocation of the perfect bliss of being in the presence of Eternal Love. This needs gestures of rapt *Innigkeit* in which every quaver is caressed before a bar of recitative links into a description of some of the other effects of seeing the Most Fair.

Here Elgar produces something of a contradiction: an Allegro with a dotted minim metronome mark, but of such gorgeous, rich textures that 1-in-a-bar beating is unthinkable, as is any speed approaching the (in effect) printed $\downarrow$ = 144. Nevertheless it represents a considerable increase in speed, with even a touch of urgency, and almost a feeling, after all, of a slow underlying dotted-minim pulse. But the three solo cellos and solo violas can be encouraged to project their phrases with a warmth and breadth of expression normally associated with much slower tempos.

Fig. 58 forms a natural close to this part of the dialogue, and a moment of silence can elapse before the Angel embarks on the allegory of the stigmata of St Francis of Assisi. The violas and cellos then solemnly intone the Judgement theme, in a measured Moderato whose pulse should be unchanging and unaffected by any rubato, so that the whole section from 55 to 60 is a welcome episode of calm between the Demons and the Angelicals which follow.

Newman's poem includes, in all, five choirs of Angelicals, but Elgar cuts from the First choir's hymn to the last verse of the Third choir, and thence to the hymn of the Fifth, which is sung by the whole chorus in a great paean of praise between 74 and 101. From 60 to 74, however, the mood is much more intimate and ethereal, and the continuity is maintained by such fine threads that considerable confidence and expertise is required by the ladies of the chorus.

Fig. 60 marks a complete change of scene, as if the clouds are suddenly parted and the choirs of angels are revealed in all their glory. New colours are employed, with rippling harps and shimmering G sharp minor arpeggios on the upper strings, who are best divided by desks. The pizzicato 1st violins' higher notes, it will be observed, do not match the harmony, and some printings of both score and parts exist in which they are adjusted; but Elgar's autograph is apparently unequivocal, and the foreign notes intentional. The tempo is a reserved Andante, but this nevertheless represents a più mosso and should flow gently and easily.

The most important feature to bring out in the bars between 60 and 61 is the dynamics: the substantial swells first in semi-chorus altos answered by trumpets, then in both voices (this second diminuendo hairpin is missing in the full score), culminating in a quite specific effect 1 before 61 which, though repeated before 69, is often overlooked. In these bars the orchestra makes a rapid crescendo to the 2nd beat and immediately retreats to *p*, while the chorus, in an overlapping wave of sound, bring their swell to a peak at the 3rd beat. The rit. allows time for this to be achieved, but it is nevertheless advisable for the tutti chorus to start the crescendo later than printed, so heightening the effect. The cellos and basses are then addressed for their two important tenuto quavers leading into the Angelicals proper.

From here to 68 the music has the deceptive appearance of being almost childishly simple; in reality it is totally exposed, full of subtleties, and in performance the most perilous section of the work. Whatever plan is adopted for the seating of the chorus brings in its wake hazards of distance between one section and another—whether between sopranos and altos, 1st and 2nd altos (fig. 63), or 1st and 2nd semi-chorus sopranos (figs. 65 to 66)—inevitably causing difficulties of ensemble which may then also affect pitch retention. On the other hand, Elgar's own arrangement (see p. 226), while avoiding these drawbacks, can suffer from the problem of projection for the 2nd chorus, seated at the rear.

Fig. 61 is the first appearance of the hymn 'Praise to the Holiest', which in essence is always set to the same melody but with slight rhythmic variations, requiring careful study; for of the six statements of the first two bars (figs. **61, 69, 74, 88, 132**, and just before **137**) only two share the same rhythm. The scoring is so delicate that the chorus should have no trouble being clearly heard, and the enchanting new melodic figure in the violins at **62** may even be encouraged despite the importance of so many of the chorus leads. This is especially true of the divided violas 2 before **63**, who certainly need a more soloistic marking than their **ppp**.

The poco più animato of **63** comes subito, but can still feel very steady, care having to be taken that the **ppp** semi-chorus sopranos keep up with the gently swinging cantabile of all the altos together. A little time may then be allowed 3 before **64** for the detail in the alto parts before the real allargando, which gives space to the clarinet solo and the semi-chorus dynamics; the 2nd of **64** is then again subito a tempo from the barline, exactly like **63**, so that the altos' upbeat is always long in relation to the ensuing pulse. The significance of the words is thereby illuminated, reference to the Angels at **63** being followed by Mankind after **64**. This second phrase opens out into an expressive forte, which in practice comes virtually subito with the 1st sopranos' entry, and the bars after **65** are then handled exactly as at **64**. The delicate little duet between the 1st and 2nd sopranos of the semi-chorus is one of the very few places in the work where they divide at all and, with only three and two voices respectively, need hardly be kept down strictly to the marked **ppp**, though it is indeed a background to the primary strands of the altos.

The tutti sopranos answer with a forte hardly less sudden than that before **65** and even more forthright, followed by a subito **p** which seems to imply a separating breath but actually works exquisitely without one. The expressive harp arpeggios at **66** can then allow the diminuendo to spread a little before tempo is restored with the last of this series of alto phrases, uniquely marked **pp**. The contrast with the (again subito) **f** 3 before **67** is therefore all the more striking.

This time the allargando is preceded by an additional poco rit. so that the tempo continues to relax in the approach to **68**, rounding off the section. The solo horn continues the violins' 2-bar melody quite slowly, introducing the Angel's solemn words, and **68** is then treated exactly like **60**, though the tempo indication is a fraction slower than before.

It is all the more important, therefore, to remember that the Moderato of **69** is (on the contrary) quicker than **61**, and with its vehement 'Glory' in the altos and tenors (the male chorus voices being introduced at **68** for the first time since the Demons' Chorus), this Third choir of Angelicals represents a considerable intensification over the first verse of the hymn. Whereas at **61** the orchestra was primarily a very discreet background, here the many additional details can be allowed to contribute, such as the supporting horns at **69**, the independent and swelling violin syncopations in the fourth bar, and the turbulent arpeggios in the upper strings 3 before **70**.

The next two bars are far from simple to execute correctly. As the phrase reaches its peak, the downbeat 2 before **70** is again a tempo, and the tenors need to be urged forward onto their high G while everyone else makes a steep diminuendo. In the following bar the tenors join the decrescendo down to *p*, despite rising still further to A♭ and resisting all temptation to get slower. Nevertheless, with the semi-chorus entry and the weighty tones of the Angel, the tempo may broaden imperceptibly, while the 1st violins are encouraged to keep their tight tremolos extremely soft. The 2nd violins' entry 8 before **71**, on the other hand, constitutes the principal melodic interest, and their hairpins can be exaggerated, retreating as the tempo recovers.

In the bars before **71** attention naturally turns from the semi-chorus to the full chorus (where care needs to be taken over the sopranos' hairpins) and back again, but there is no doubt that this is the end of a sentence, and though there is no such marking, the tempo cannot quite plunge into the più mosso without a slight broadening across the last one or two bars. This should not, however, be so pronounced as to become static. Then 71 really can initiate an entirely new pulse, with already the feeling of 1 in a bar though it is at first conducted in 3.

Now the backdrop, as it were, flits from one scene to another as Gerontius continues his journey, and Elgar similarly requires the tempo to be constantly changing. The various relationships are spelt out precisely in all but the earliest printings of the full score as well as in the vocal score (where 2 before 72 ♩.= 84 is a misprint, however), though Elgar's instructions cannot quite be followed to the letter. At 71 ♩= 104 is just possible, but distinctly on the slow side if a mere 7-bar poco stringendo is really to arrive at ♩.= 72; and ♩= 126 is a better point from which to begin an accelerando that should, after all, not feel too precipitate, even if it can also start somewhat sooner than printed.

Since the beat at 72 is directed to equal the previous bar, it is a good plan to go into 1 two bars before 72, thus ensuring the exact relationship at 72 itself without ever having to beat absurdly fast crotchets. From here the accelerando continues, but instead of a further equation there is a cut-off, and 4 before 73 a new marking is provided which defines the tempo relationship at 73.

This all looks conveniently tidy on the page; but in practice it does not all work quite so well. The printed ♩= 42 is too slow for the music 4 before 73 (conducted in 2), and Elgar's own recording, in which his tempo is nearer ♩= 69, is a better guide despite the inevitable non-correspondence of the tempos at 73, where the beat goes into 4. Here the printed ♩= 84 is absolutely suitable, and only the 'l'istesso tempo' turns out to be unfortunately abortive.

The dynamics at 72, where the scene change to the last group of Angelicals is positively operatic, are stipulated but nevertheless hard to bring through. The intention is for each of the three pairs of bars to start subito *p*; but in the turmoil of the renewed accelerando the beginnings of the third and fifth bars are thickly scored, with added accents and 'sonore' markings, and the effect can easily be lost.

After a cut-off bar, in which Elgar liked to hear the full organ (he directed 'plenty of organ' already at 72), the violas need to be encouraged to project their melody, written in the most plaintive register of the instrument, before they are overtaken in the increasing wash of sound. Then at 73 the violins and harps need a very clear beat in this far-from-obvious tempo change, each barline being additionally pointed by a *fp* in the violins and first a solo horn, then trombones. The strings grow to *ff*, but one eye on the trumpets will ensure that they enter at no more than *p* before they too crescendo into the following bar.

Here the Angel usually takes her top A♭ as she hails the 'glad responsive chant', and this, together with the spectacular harps' glissando, warrants already some broadening of the tempo. The last two bars are in the nature of a massive *Ausholen* into 74, and blocks of root-position C major chords are built up, *Meistersinger*-like, and capped with a firm timpani stroke before the bass strides downwards into the most supremely glorious moment of the whole piece.

The blinding light of a thousand suns is suddenly revealed as the chorus, which has been on its feet all along, bursts forth in one mighty mass of sound for this final and most majestic Fifth choir of Angelicals. The whole section from here to 101 is one great outpouring, the last truly extrovert music in the work and an arch of sustained thought and power, a structure maintained in every bar at Elgar's highest level of invention and inspiration. It contains some of the most sheerly beautiful, most mysterious, and most dramatic writing, much of the most complex counterpoint, and the most exhilarating moments of all, and forms an overwhelmingly powerful climax to this whole portion of Part II from its beginning thus far.

Moreover, so strong is the feeling of finality as 101 is reached that it may not be too fanciful to extend the comparison with *Die Meistersinger* and view the whole work as one gigantic *Bar*, of which this great C major chorus naturally constitutes the culmination of the second *Stollen* (the first corresponding with Part I), and everything from 101 to the end as the *Abgesang*, a designation which indeed suits it perfectly.

Fig. 74's initial dotted minim might seem to presuppose a fairly flowing tempo, but on the contrary the upper strings' tenuto demisemiquavers in the second bar give a better clue to the degree of breadth required for this magnificent passage to make its impact. Elgar's own tempo was nearer $\downarrow$ = 56, which accords convincingly with his 'Maestoso' marking without ever seeming to drag. After the tenuto in the fifth bar, however, the song can briefly gain momentum before the further allargando and repeated heavy demisemiquavers in violins and violas.

The stringendo, linking the initial outburst to the main, extended, body of the movement, starts from the second beat and is then indeed molto, for 75 should work so that the final crotchet on 'His' equals the new dotted minim, marked at 72 and beaten, naturally, in 2. Elgar's only surviving recording of this passage is a good deal faster (about $\downarrow$. = 84), but it has to be said that it also feels more rushed than perhaps he would have always wanted.

The 'loving' melody in the sopranos and altos is first heard already at 75 in all four horns, whose syncopations can ring out cheerfully, even ebulliently. When the chorus enters, however, it is with a note of rather more tenderness, and the orchestral decoration should be kept discreet. For example, the violins may need to be kept down just before 78, using only little bows, and around 79 everything must be very subdued, even the woodwind, who may feel, with some justification, that their lines often seem soloistic in character.

In the 3rd of 79 the chorus unites as a body for the new sentence 'God's Presence and His very Self', and the previous bar needs a little time in order to introduce it. Despite the crotchet rest the chorus should be dissuaded from taking a breath in the middle of the phrase, but save it until the comma after 'Self', after which the 2nd violins and oboes may be brought through in a sweet cantabile *pp*.

Then at 80 all is calm, and even the tempo can be allowed to relax a little. The prevailing dynamic is a uniform *pp* with *ppp* backing, and despite the emergence from time to time of isolated fragments, the basic sound should never depart from this exceedingly hushed level. Indeed, Elgar himself had the greatest difficulty in achieving a degree of softness to satisfy him. But he made a particular feature of the difference between the espressivo crescendo in the sopranos and altos and the answering sempre *pp* in the tenors and basses; and other subtleties of dynamics are equally worthy of attention, such as the tenuto on 'smote' (which should nevertheless not sound actually louder) and the subito *pp* after 81.

The phrase comes to rest for the second time at 83, and there is a new feeling of lyricism, the tempo being pressed on a little towards the top note of each of the succeeding 4-bar figures before the whole sentence subsides finally into 85. The bassoons and bass clarinet now initiate a considerable build-up (ultimately aiming at 89, though 88 of course marks a high point where sheer dynamics are concerned), but they should not need to be marked up, though the trombones, at least, should come away after the accents to allow the melody through. Real urgency will be conveyed through the $\frac{9}{4}$ bars (where the altos need to start at least *mf* each time), even though this is only specified by the 'Animato' marking in the 3rd of 87. This is Elgar's version of Mahler's *steigernd*, and the voices pile on top of each other as the music drives towards the renewed outburst of 88.

At this point Elgar supplies the somewhat contradictory markings 'Molto maestoso' and ♩ = 96, an improbably fast tempo for what is a grand statement, though despite the added 'molto' it should not upstage the previous climactic outburst at 74. But for this, the score would seem to suggest that the Animato culminates at 88 in a ♩. = ♩ relationship; and only Elgar's recording enables us to reject this finally, so utterly does his performance avoid all semblance of such a scheme. More characteristically, perhaps, it shows us that 88 is, indeed, at a new and slower tempo (Elgar's own speed is as steady as ♩= 60), preceded not only by a slight *Ausholen*, but by a moment at the barline in which the assembled forces are cleared for a quick *Luftpause* before the *ff* attack. Indeed this, though found in neither full nor vocal scores, is in fact printed in all the orchestral parts.

But **88** must not be too slow, for the tension has to be maintained in the further largamente of the fourth bar, after which 2 before **89** recovers the tempo to that of **88**. The 2nd sopranos are particularly important 2 before **89**. This is the first of many such entries between here and **99** where Elgar's seating arrangement, with the 2nd chorus behind the 1st, can be found less than ideal; it naturally suffers most in this ensuing double chorus, with its antiphonal effects, and the question then to be addressed is whether it is worth enduring difficulties in the rest of the work for the sake of the ideal solution in just this one section.

Fig. **89** suddenly careers forward quite precipitantly, creating an immediate contrast, and now that the chorus is split into eight parts some of the individual lines can prove unexpectedly tricky. The steady increases in tempo are built up gradually; in the score the first increment is shown at **93**, but Elgar in his recording is already substantially faster at this point, having begun to press on at **92**. Indeed, from **93** there is a feeling of 1 in a bar, and the two choruses answer each other at 2-bar intervals in a way which definitely presupposes a quicker tempo. The textures, however, are as complex as before, and in many ways the section from **89** to **95** is the most technically demanding for the chorus, with some very quick word-patterns in the altos and tenors after **94**, where there is still no question of actually conducting in 1.

At **95**, however, the music opens out, emerging as if from the mouth of a tunnel, and the beat can finally break into 1— as, indeed, Elgar himself instructed in the letter to Kilburn quoted earlier. But it is important to remember that the Allegro molto of **96** has not yet been reached, and there are still eight bars of accel. molto in 1 remaining, so that the dotted minim beat at **95** should initially be very steady, corresponding exactly with the previous bar ($\musDottedMinim = \musMinim$), the necessary difference being made up over the succeeding bars.

Goaded by the horns' syncopations, the brakes are taken off once again at **98**, and maximum tempo is at last gained at **99**, where altos and sopranos repeatedly overlap with each other until, in a mighty swoop up to their top G, the tenors proclaim the approach to the final cadence of the Angelicals.

Such a massive gesture as this inevitably requires a degree of *Ausholen*, even from as soon as 4 before **100**; yet equally it can be overdone, and notwithstanding the paramount significance of this point in the structure, the illusion should be retained of unflagging momentum, only the crotchet in the 8th of **100** being slightly pointed within the dotted minim beat. The final rit. and crescendo, of course, spur the united forces to their ultimate efforts, the conductor creating maximum tension by delaying each successive barline.

Timpani, bass drum, and organ pedals are left holding, so that the take-off gesture has to be finely judged. The mood of total emptiness is by no means dissimilar to that after the opening fanfare of Strauss's *Also sprach Zarathustra*, composed only four years previously, and the atmosphere of mystery, as to what can possibly follow such extremes of blinding light, comparable.

But now begins the gradual build-up towards the Judgement itself, obviously a moment of supreme importance in the drama, so that the tension must not be lost, and the fermata accordingly not too long. Equilibrium and calm are restored, and the sombre Larghetto tempo set at the printed $\musMinim = 58$, which will feel disproportionately slow after all the preceding ebullience. By the third bar, with the continuity established, the chorus can be motioned to sit for the first time since **29**.

Even these dark, apprehensive tones sink still further, and flutes on their lowest notes are carefully guided so that their triplets arrive at a true Lento. The triplets themselves, like those at **103**, are not shown in the vocal score, so can come as a surprise to the soloists; the same is true of the little swell in the 2nd of 102, where the 1st violins should match the lower strings to peak at the 2nd beat, retreating for the clarinet solo. In measured tones, the Angel prepares Gerontius for his Judgement, and a touching episode follows, recalling the music of fig. 70 of Part I. It is given here with the same tempo marking, but the 2nd violin accents are new, adding a touch of poignancy.

The Angel of the Agony is introduced, his theme being given by the solo oboe with heavy, portentous falling fourths in the cellos. The woodwind are held on their fermata until the soloist is ready to continue, when the violins are coaxed in with a real quaver subdivision followed by clear beats for the cello pizzicatos. The accel. 3 before 105 is halted by the Angel's ad lib. phrase, 105 itself amounting to an a tempo, though somewhat slower than the previous passage.

Two bars before 106 there is a crescendo and a Mahlerian swoop up a minor seventh onto the 'appalling chord' (cf. 'Thine own agony' in Part I, just before 63) and this is the cue for the Angel of the Agony to stand. Both the rit. and the fermata are entirely controlled by the conductor, who in these three bars prepares the mood appropriately for the bass soloist's solemn declamation.

The trombones' 'sostenuto' marking will encourage an element of the soloistic in their playing, and they should be carefully guided to move in sympathy with the Angel of the Agony. However, the salient feature of the whole episode is the cellos' descending fourths, which should always be pressed out with heavy, long accents.

This whole section is full of rubato. Fig. 107 gains in urgency, but already the words 'pang of heart' curb the momentum, and by the printed largamente the tempo will be very slow indeed. Despite the darkness of the two bars before 108, movement is gradually restored so that the anguished, Franckian harmonies of 108 are intoned at the same stately Lento as 106.

The second pronouncement is similar, but **pp**, so less weighty; nevertheless the stresses in the cellos remain a paramount feature and can still be brought out. Fig. 109 is treated exactly as earlier, but in the fourth bar the soloist's rhythm is this time simpler, so that the tempo does not need to be brought back until the printed largamente.

The bars from the 3rd of 110 as far as 113 constitute a gentler middle section, where the sense of awe and dread gives way to the more tender tones of love and compassion. All the strings can play with warmth, and even the allargando is less severe than before. Then 112 moves on with very much the same feeling as after 56; both places, of course, are concerned with the presence of God, and the expressive rising sixth (whose first appearance was back in Part I, at the words 'Novissima hora est') will significantly recur after the Sight of the Lord at 120.

Similarly, the profound *Innigkeit* of 113 has much in common with the bar of 56, and there should be plenty of time on the fermata at the top. The 1st violins are taken off; then the upbeat has to be very clearly identifiable as such, and directed solely to the violins (with only half an eye on the woodwind), lest it be misconstrued.

The new fermata, like the other phrases prior to each pronouncement, is entirely the province of the conductor, who takes the responsibility of creating the right mood for the final and grandest of all the Angel of the Agony's three great utterances. Consequently it can be quite long, and the diminuendo gradual, so that the impact of the sudden *ff* comes as a real shock. As well as heightening the drama of the moment, this is a convenient opportunity for the chorus to rise prior to its next contribution at 115—unless this is sung seated, as will be discussed in due course.

These last commanding words subside quickly, and the Angel of the Agony's role is technically at an end. But he should remain standing a little while longer, for he is still involved with Gerontius's fate and thus part of the drama until the guardian Angel resumes this role at 116. The rit. continues through the harp arpeggios and settles on a long pause.

Now the atmosphere is one of total suspense, and the music seems hardly to move at all as Gerontius, awe-struck, faces in withdrawn tones the realization that the supreme moment of Judgement can no longer be delayed. This is the only place in the work where the organ, mostly an important background colour, needs a clear lead, being the single thread linking heaven with the voices on earth. The second beat extinguishes the clarinet; the third clears the strings; the two deep chords are spaced reverentially, addressing the bass drum (who has been long silent), and exquisitely gently the semi-chorus voices are given their entries, each in turn, in a tempo that does just travel, though the marked $\downarrow$ = 66 could be thought slightly on the fast side.

Whether or not the chorus sings the few bars at 115 seated may depend on a number of factors. To do so undoubtedly enhances the remote, other-worldly effect of the words coming as if from nowhere, and it is tempting thereby to seek an atmosphere of total stillness. Yet it is always harder to retain secure intonation while seated; and it also has to be borne in mind that any alternative, subsequent place to stand (124 is the usually favoured option) is less than ideal during such gentle, intimate music. It is, in fact, perfectly practicable for the chorus to remain on its feet from before 114 to the end of the work.

As the organ fades away the orchestral effects are fragmentary in the extreme, making each one an event, **pp** though they all are. If distinctly just audible, they may also be able to offer a tiny but welcome hint of assistance to the chorus, sinking gradually in carefully judged semitones.

In the same way as 3 before 60 but to a greater extent, the E minor leaps and bounds in the strings suggest a change of scene, and indeed the Angel takes centre stage once more. There is something of a problem here from the point of view of the sequence of action, for Newman's poem places the Angel's lines immediately *after* the Soul's momentary vision of God, which makes sense of the words in the four bars before 117, ending 'Consumed, yet quicken'd by the glance of God'. Yet this is, of course, entirely consistent with the work as it stood before Jaeger's intervention, the details of which are well documented elsewhere. Suffice it to say here that in the original version the bars before 118 led straight to what is now fig. 125; this was followed by 'Take me away' (after 120), joining up with the Angel's Farewell. The actual instant when the Soul sees its God was not depicted.

All this means that the music of 116 was written from the point of view of the Soul having already seen its Lord, perhaps during the preceding prayer, and now forms an almost light-hearted episode between the grave reverence of 115 and what is now the solemn path to Judgement at 118. Indeed, the tripping staccato string semiquavers before 117 recall the mood of a Mendelssohn quartet.

In the 3rd of 116 the downbeat simply stops short, and the second beat is carefully placed with the Angel. In the following bar the timpani's alternative low E is to be preferred to the upper octave, after which the strings swirl up to celebrate the saving of the Soul, the printed accelerando remaining valid even through the 2nd of 117, where the orchestra's diminuendo should not hold the Angel too long on her crescendo.

Two bars before 118 the molto crescendo can grow to f on what amounts to a pause, for any actual beats are quite superfluous, and the slightest gap is then necessary for the *subito p* accents at 118 to make their proper effect; this should not, however, amount to as much as a *Luftpause*.

Here is the episode Elgar inserted at Jaeger's repeated insistence. 'Of course it's biggety-big,' he replied, half apologetically, but the three extra trumpets and timpani he requests (ad lib.) solely for these bars are sadly never, in the event, drafted in. They are actually unnecessary, for the point of the passage is less the sheer panoply than the irresistible magnetic force driving single-mindedly towards the central point of focus that is the 'moment' of 120. The cumulative power of the cello/bass syncopations and the upward rushes in the violins are all directed forward and brought off together in a *Luftpause* which retains the urgency of the stringendo, so quickly must the downbeat follow.

The effect is of course shattering, and all intensity drains away as the Soul is left 'scorched, and shrivelled', or, in the line of the poem Elgar did set, 'consumed, yet quickened'. But Gerontius recovers immediately; as Jaeger wrote to the composer on 27 June 1900, 'the first sensations the soul would experience would be an *awful, overwhelming agitation*!; a whirlwind of sensations of the acutest kind coursing through it; a bewilderment of fear, excitation, crushing, overmastering hopelessness &c, &c, "Take me away!!"', and it is remarkable how precisely Elgar followed his friend's instructions. Gerontius cries out on a top A, and it is the conductor's responsibility to judge how long the tenor wishes to prolong this heart-rending moment, matching the poco accel. accordingly. After a final expressive swell in trombones and tuba, two rit. bars each punctuated by harps on the second beat, the episode is at an end, passing into Gerontius's last lyrical outpouring.

This is a considerable aria and needs sympathetic handling and accompanying. Yet in another sense its rapt but simple, almost light-headed beauty can be purely enjoyed, for his tribulations are over, and the expression is now without those undercurrents of anxiety which have obviously pervaded all Gerontius's music hitherto.

The corner into 121 wants to be steered sensitively, the upward figure in the clarinet handing over to the flutes while the horns are also spared a glance. The 'più tranquillo' marking gives time for every semiquaver in the serenity of Gerontius's 'sad perpetual strain', but the flow is essentially uninterrupted, and the 1st violin line, shadowing the clarinet solo, can keep a sense of forward movement through the long notes.

Strict tempo is maintained in the bars before 122, where the important 2nd violin phrase may be brought out. It is hard to resist giving the slightest pointing to the exquisite cadence into the 3rd of 122, placing the clarinets' **pp** chord with just an extra ounce of meaning, but the soloist's co-operation has to be enlisted in this effect beforehand, or, caught unprepared, he will inevitably continue 'my absent Lord' that fraction sooner than expected.

The cantabile of 123 broadens out, and though the tempo remains unaltered, a little time is necessary in the previous bar (without any need for subdivision) as the flutes, violas, and cellos softly effect the modulation into the sunny, comforting key of G major. The last phrase of the aria is then given to divided violas and upper cellos, who all merit at least a 'dolce' marking in addition to their *pp*.

Fig. 124 almost resumes tempo, albeit retaining an element of wistfulness that resists the earlier sense of onward flow, and then all is excessively hushed coda. The harp's deep octaves are clearly pointed, subsiding onto expressive high (but still very soft) cellos and passing to low violas for the D major cadence into 125. Gerontius sits, his role accomplished.

The Chorus of the Souls in Purgatory is so constantly, unremittingly subdued that it can easily be in danger of dragging. It should always be kept moving within the given Andante ($\flat$ = 72), the fugal entries and interplay between the voices taking place impassively, to a background of timpani, cellos, and basses, who are each quietly motioned in after 125. These will be entirely inaudible to the choir, so that the responsibility for the pitch rests to a large degree on the chorus basses, especially in the first three bars with their steps up to the A.

After ten long bars the dominant pedal descends to F$\sharp$ and the basses sing the opening bars in the new key. Elgar carefully ensures that this change in the orchestral basses is not highlighted by any increase in expression, and only one swell is allowed in the chorus before utter peace descends, the voices fading away *a niente*.

The infinitely moving Angel's Farewell is justifiably celebrated, both the sheer beauty of the song and the tender, soothing emotions it expresses making a sublime finale to this magical work. Elgar's 'andante tranquillo' is exactly the right indication of mood, but the metronome marking can create something of a problem. For whereas $\flat$ = 92 is by no means too slow—in fact it is, once again, exactly right—it suggests both a beat marking each quaver, which upsets the serenity implied by the 'tranquillo', and one as busy as 92 which inhibits the freedom demanded by the intricately weaving inner parts. As in other profound, rapt slow movements—the Adagio of Beethoven's Ninth Symphony is an obvious example—a crotchet beat is essential in order to portray the intimacy of this music, though there will of course always be the flexibility to go into 6 where the Angel takes time over particular phrases.

At the outset the duet between 1st violins and violas is brought to the fore, the 2nd violins remaining very subordinate. They too, with the solo oboe, have their moment of pre-eminence, and the horns should then be coaxed into a diminuendo of extreme sweetness.

Fig. 127 introduces the Angel's exquisite solo, the accompanying duet being shared between 1st violins and violas as before. In the fifth and sixth bars the beat subdivides for the colla parte, but it can remain in 3 with the simpler rhythmic figures after 128, despite the rall. These bars are, however, full of felicitous effects which mirror the Angel's words and should be featured: the harps and flutes, 'rolling' up the B major arpeggio; the 'poised' clarinet solo and pizzicato basses; and especially the 'held' *pp* oboe fermata, during which the other woodwind need to be taken off. The second beat is then gauged with the Angel's phrasing and given first to the oboe, then to the inner strings, the upbeat being directed to the chorus.

From the 3rd of 129 the beat once again goes into 6 so that all the semiquavers in 2nd violins and violas can match the rhythms in the voices calmly and without fuss. Three bars before 130 crotchet beating resumes, and a glowing horn solo leads into the serene repose of 130 with its caressing violin phrases at 'Sinking deep'. Again the semiquavers can spread slightly within the slow pulse, the pizzicato double basses' punctuations being carefully placed.

Every detail of the delicate scoring has a significance contributing to the beauty of this finale, and before the chorus's 'Come back' the harps, supported by woodwind, sound a G major arpeggio through three octaves, landing on a splendid low B sustained by a solo bassoon. The chorus now alternates between these two keys in a way which might seem to imply a swell both times; but instead, 'Come back' should be intoned in a pronounced diminuendo, to highlight the stress on 'Lord'.

The episode from 131 to 136 brings some contrast, including a memory of earlier themes and motifs. Fig. 131 recalls 11 with its attendant echo, and the colla parte bar is conducted in 6 much like the similar one after 14; the bassoons inevitably bring the tempo back, and the 6th of 131 is handled in the same way as 129. Quaver beats are given (for the last time) from the colla parte upbeat as far as 132, where, just before the chorus is addressed, the trumpets will appreciate a clear lead for their very exposed *ppp* octaves.

At 132 the Angelicals are marked 'distant', but there is no question of this being represented literally (any more than the 'very remote' of the semi-chorus 3 before 137), and they will merely make every effort to keep the sound as soft and veiled as practically possible. Despite their 'Praise to the Holiest' music, the tempo has returned to the original ♩= 46, but after the trumpet's leap up to the *ossia* high F♯, which is always taken, the fourth bar can be allowed to travel, giving a perceptibly more flowing movement until being reined in once more by the 'Sinking deep' motif 1 before 133.

Three bars before 134 the word 'Come' is actually marked with an accent, matching the same phrase before 131. In the poco più mosso the semi-chorus altos will need to be dissuaded from launching confidently into the tempo they know so well from 63, for as at 132, the distant memory is once again significantly slower than previously, corresponding with the Angel's noble 'Farewell'.

Instead of an echo, the bar of 135 is just this time followed by an intensification, and a 4-bar rit. leads back to the grand restatement of 126, conducted in 3 as always. It is combined with the tenors' and basses' 'Come back' music, and when the Angel joins as well for a few last words, there are some important chorus leads for 2nd altos, 1st altos, and 2nd sopranos in turn which must, however softly, be brought through the texture.

There is a final echo of the Angelicals—even now, in a new rhythm—round which the 1st violins need to be nursed, and the curtain gradually closes over nine bars of 'Amen'. Clear definition of the chorus staccatos will enable the pp chords to cut through distinctly, together with the decorated semiquaver run climbing delicately through the orchestra, and here the last two 1st violin notes inevitably require a fraction of time before melting into the top F♯. After a gentle crescendo and a gradual diminuendo in which the harps spread their chords ever slower, the sound expires.

This touching and valedictory conclusion to Elgar's most glorious work provides an appropriate culmination to this book, and hence to the series of 'Conducting' volumes.

Index

◀▶